Nancy Um

CW01498268

THE MERCHANT HOUSES OF *Mocha*

TRADE AND ARCHITECTURE IN AN INDIAN OCEAN PORT

UNIVERSITY OF WASHINGTON PRESS SEATTLE AND LONDON

PUBLICATION OF THIS BOOK WAS SUPPORTED IN PART BY A GRANT FROM BINGHAMTON UNIVERSITY, SUNY. PUBLICATION WAS ALSO SUPPORTED BY THE DONALD R. ELLEGOOD INTERNATIONAL PUBLICATIONS ENDOWMENT.

© 2009 by the University of Washington Press
Printed in the United States of America
Design by Pamela Canell
14 12 11 10 09 5 4 3 2 1

All rights reserved. No part of this publication may be reproduced or transmitted in any form or by any means, electronic or mechanical, including photocopy, recording, or any information storage or retrieval system, without permission in writing from the publisher.

University of Washington Press, P.O. Box 50096, Seattle, WA 98145 U.S.A.
www.washington.edu/uwpress

Library of Congress Cataloging-in-Publication Data
Um, Nancy.
The merchant houses of Mocha : trade and architecture
in an Indian Ocean port / Nancy Um. — 1st ed.
p. cm. — (Publications on the Near East)
Includes bibliographical references and index.
ISBN 978-0-295-98910-5 (hardback : alk. paper)
ISBN 978-0-295-98911-2 (pbk. : alk. paper)
1. Architecture and merchants—Yemen (Republic)—Mukha—History—17th century.
2. Architecture and merchants—Yemen (Republic)—Mukha—History—18th century.
3. Mukha (Yemen)—Commerce—History—17th century.
4. Mukha (Yemen)—Commerce—History—18th century.
5. Mukha (Yemen)—Buildings, structures, etc. I. Title.
NA2543.M47U4 2009 953.32—dc22 2008051590

The paper used in this publication is acid-free and 90 percent recycled from at least 50 percent post-consumer waste. It meets the minimum requirements of American National Standard for Information Sciences—Permanence of Paper for Printed Library Materials, ANSI Z39.48-1984. ∞ ♲

To R, E, and O

PUBLICATIONS ON THE NEAR EAST

PUBLICATIONS ON THE NEAR EAST

Poetry's Voice, Society's Song: Ottoman Lyric Poetry by Walter G. Andrews

The Remaking of Istanbul: Portrait of an Ottoman City in the Nineteenth Century by Zeynep Çelik

The Tragedy of Sohráb and Rostám from the Persian National Epic, the Shahname of Abol-Qasem Ferdowsi, translated by Jerome W. Clinton

The Jews in Modern Egypt, 1914-1952 by Gudrun Krämer

Izmir and the Levantine World, 1550-1650 by Daniel Goffman

Medieval Agriculture and Islamic Science: The Almanac of a Yemeni Sultan by Daniel Martin Varisco

Rethinking Modernity and National Identity in Turkey, edited by Sibel Bozdoğan and Reşat Kasaba

Slavery and Abolition in the Ottoman Middle East by Ehud R. Toledano

Britons in the Ottoman Empire, 1642-1660 by Daniel Goffman

Popular Preaching and Religious Authority in the Medieval Islamic Near East by Jonathan P. Berkey

The Transformation of Islamic Art during the Sunni Revival by Yasser Tabbaa

Shiraz in the Age of Hafez: The Glory of a Medieval Persian City by John Limbert

The Martyrs of Karbala: Shiʿi Symbols and Rituals in Modern Iran by Kamran Scot Aghaie

Ottoman Lyric Poetry: An Anthology, Expanded Edition, edited and translated by Walter G. Andrews, Najaat Black, and Mehmet Kalpaklı

Party Building in the Modern Middle East: The Origins of Competitive and Coercive Rule by Michele Penner Angrist

Everyday Life and Consumer Culture in Eighteenth-Century Damascus by James Grehan

The City's Pleasures: Istanbul in the Eighteenth Century by Shirine Hamadeh

Reading Orientalism: Said and the Unsaid by Daniel Martin Varisco

The Merchant Houses of Mocha: Trade and Architecture in an Indian Ocean Port by Nancy Um

CONTENTS

ACKNOWLEDGMENTS

My fascination and engagement with Mocha have endured for more than a decade. During that time, many people and institutions around the world helped me make sense of ruins, documents, stories, spaces, and images. Numerous granting organizations provided the financial support for travel, research, and writing. They included the Institute of International Education, with a Fulbright grant; the American Institute for Yemeni Studies, with a predoctoral and a postdoctoral research grant; the National Endowment for the Humanities, with a Summer Stipend; and the Getty Foundation, with a postdoctoral fellowship. At Binghamton University, Dean Jean-Pierre Mileur of Harpur College provided research funds as well as a generous subvention for the production of this book. I thank these organizations for their financial support. Of course, all the opinions and conclusions that follow are my own and do not reflect those of the institutions that funded my work.

In Yemen, three successive resident directors of the American Institute for Yemeni Studies in Sanaa facilitated my research—Noha Sadek, Marta Colburn, and Christopher Edens—along with the executive director, Maria Ellis. At the Centre Français d'Archéologie et des Sciences Sociales in Sanaa, François Burgat and Renaud Detalle were always helpful in every aspect of life in Yemen, both work and recreation. At the General Organization for Antiquities and Manuscripts, two successive presidents, Yūsuf ʿAbd Allāh and Muḥammad al-ʿArūsī, provided me with research permissions and lent their continuous support. GOAM staff members Aḥmad Shamsān, Mu'ammar al-'Amrī, and Aḥmad al-Sanḥānī helped obtain permissions, photographs, and access to sites. In Mocha, the gracious al-Maḥfadī family and 'Ādil 'Abd al-Wahhāb were the city's finest ambassadors.

In both Sanaa and The Hague, the Huh family of the Korean Embassy kept me alive with their friendship, food, and companionship. In the Netherlands, Judith Heijdra helped me make sense of eighteenth-century Dutch documents. Staff members at the National Archives in The Hague and the India Office Records of the British Library in London graciously made their documents available to me. The interlibrary loan staff at Bartle Library at Binghamton University procured more faraway sources for me than I can count.

The Ethnologisches Museum, Staatliche Museen zu Berlin, Stiftung Preußischer Kulturbesitz, the Bibliographisches Institut and F. A. Brockhaus AG, Mannheim, Germany, the Musée Bartholdi in Colmar, France, the Musée National de la Marine in Paris, the Peabody Essex Museum in Salem, Massachusetts, the Division of Rare and Manuscript Collections of the Cornell University Library, the New York Public Library, and the library at Leiden University graciously provided images and permission for their reproduction. Eric Franzon, Stan Kauffman, and Eugene Park helped produce the maps, which were then refined for publication by Barry Levely. Senem Zeybekoglu expertly drafted the final architectural plans, some of which were originally drawn by Mahā al-Ḥabshī. This project would have never come to fruition had it not been for the generous assistance of these people in far-flung parts of the globe.

My insightful mentor Renie Bierman oversaw this project from the very start. Without her encouragement and the model of her intellectual creativity, I would never have embarked on a project envisioning the architectural history of a city that lies in ruins today. The esteemed historian Cees Brouwer, drawing from his own experience, gave me confidence that the eighteenth-century Dutch sources could be culled for a history of Mocha. I thank him for his guidance and generosity during the conversations we shared in Amsterdam. Bernard Haykel offered valuable support at every stage, and his work provided the intellectual template for many ideas that appear here. Daniel Varisco read the whole manuscript and contributed constructive comments, particularly on chapter 2.

My colleagues in the art history department at Binghamton University have been overwhelmingly supportive intellectually, professionally, and personally, particularly by shouldering departmental responsibilities while I took much-needed time off to complete this book. In particular, Charles Burroughs, Karen-edis Barzman, and honorary art historian Rifa'at Abou-El-Haj trudged through parts of my writing and took time out of their busy schedules to comment. Jere Bacharach, Gary Okihiro, Nasser Rabbat, and Ned Alpers gave guidance and support at key stages. Fellow Red Sea scholars Li Guo, Roxani Margariti, and Jonathan Miran provided a community for me and contributed countless new sources for my work as I labored through the revisions. My friends and colleagues Ladan Akbarnia, Elisa Camiscioli, Anne Soon Choi, Santhi Kavuri-Bauer, Charles Perry, Wendy Shaw, and David Simonowitz offered their intellectual support, professional advice, and friendship throughout.

I benefited from valuable feedback from audience members who listened to me rehearse different parts of this book in public forums such as "VizCult: The Harpur College Dean's Workshop on Visual Culture" at Binghamton University; the Middle East Studies Association annual meeting; the Seminar for Arabian Studies at the British Museum; "Liquid Culture: Chocolate, Coffee, and Tea in Early Modern Europe," a conference held at the Bard Graduate Center for the Decorative Arts; "Cultural Exchange and Transformation in the Indian Ocean World," a conference held at the Fowler Museum of Cultural History at UCLA; and the Historians of Islamic Art annual *majlis*. An earlier version of chapter 6 was published as "Spatial Negotiations in a Commercial City: The Red Sea Port of Mocha, Yemen, during the First Half of the Eighteenth Century," *Journal of the Society of Architectural Historians* 62, no. 2 (June 2003): 178–93. I thank the Society of Architectural Historians for permission to reprint the article here in its revised and expanded form.

I also owe my sincere gratitude to Michael Duckworth, formerly at the University of Washington Press, who took on this project and sustained his confidence in it despite setbacks and delays. Marilyn Trueblood and Beth Fuget brought the book through the final stages of publication with uncommon patience and attentiveness. I am extremely fortunate for Jane Kepp's expert copyediting and valuable comments. During a particularly busy and eventful semester, Hala Auji took precious time and energy from her own project in order to prepare the index for this book.

Finally, I thank my family, who far too often watched me fly off to distant places but trusted that I would stay safe and productive. To them, this book seemed like a never-ending preoccupation. Most of all, Robert has always had confidence that I would someday be done with Mocha, even when I felt submerged in the waters of the Indian Ocean. His love, companionship, and humor have sustained me as I toiled in front of the computer and in the archives. This book would mean nothing to me if he were not there to share in the joy of its completion. I dedicate it to him and our two little ones, who waited patiently until I completed the manuscript before arriving on the scene.

NOTE ON TRANSLITERATION, DATES, AND ABBREVIATIONS

The sources consulted for this study use variable transliteration systems. Even the subject at hand, Mocha, goes by myriad spellings, including al-Mukhā, al-Mukhā', al-Makhā, Mocca, Moka, Mokha, and Mokka. I have chosen the most conventional and recognizable form in English, Mocha, and have not marked the alternative spellings that are used by other authors in quotations. For place names that have accepted spellings in English, such as Basra, Sanaa, Zabid, Massawa, Mecca, and Muscat, I use those spellings. Names of dynasties that have been Anglicized, such as the Rasulids, Tahirids, and Sulayhids, are not properly transliterated, whereas non-Anglicized names of dynasties, such as Qāsimī, are. The accepted forms of Arabic words that have common English usages, such as imam, riyal, sultan, wazir, and zakat, are not properly transliterated. For the ease of the reader, I do not use Arabic plural forms but add a final s to the singular form. In general, transliteration follows the format outlined in the *International Journal of Middle East Studies.*

When a date derives from a source that provides a *hijrī* date, I give the common era equivalent in the format *hijrī* date/common era date—for example, 1118/1706–7. When the source gives only a common era date, the *hijrī* date is not provided.

Throughout the book I use the following abbreviations:

b.	ibn, bin (son of)
VOC	Verenigde Oostindische Compagnie (Dutch East India Company)

THE MERCHANT HOUSES OF *Mocha*

Introduction

Bounded by water on its western and southern borders, Yemen has engaged in a vibrant, long-distance maritime commerce for more than two millenniums. Greek and Egyptian traders carried cargos of Arabian aromatics and African and Indian luxury goods from the now-lost Himyarite Red Sea emporium of Mouza to the Mediterranean lands of the Roman Empire, as described in the famous *Periplus of the Erythrean Sea*, written during the first century CE.[1] The Yemeni port of Aden ushered in the next era of Red Sea predominance as the key gateway to the Indian Ocean, thriving off the prosperity of Fatimid rule in Egypt (986–1171) and its economic dependence on Asian maritime trade. The continuing success of Aden's medieval trade is documented in the important fragments of the Cairo Geniza, a collection of medieval Jewish documents pertaining to trade and daily life that were discovered in an Egyptian synagogue, as well as in later local Yemeni histories of the Rasulids (1228–1454) and their successors the Tahirids (1454–1517).[2]

Although Aden dominated Yemen's trade through the early sixteenth century, Mocha—situated strategically inside the southern entry to the Red Sea, the strait known as Bāb al-Mandab—rose to assume the position of a major Ottoman harbor in 1538. As a global center where the vast reach of the Indian Ocean met the Arabian Peninsula and the periphery of the Mediterranean world, Mocha continued to thrive under the Qāsimī imams, who ousted the Ottomans from Yemen in 1635. Overseas merchants, Muslim pilgrims, peripatetic ship captains, and ambitious travelers from Asian,

African, and European shores flocked to the city to participate in the trade of Arabian coffee, Indian textiles, and South and Southeast Asian spices, aromatics, medicinal products, and precious and bulk metals. Maritime trade, primarily with Gujarat but also with Persian Gulf and Red Sea partners, constituted Mocha's economic lifeline. This traffic was intensified because of Mocha's strategic geographical position as a convenient stopping point for ships on the way to Jidda for the yearly pilgrimage. Additionally, Mocha was one of several lowland Arabian cities that facilitated the coffee trade when Yemen was virtually the only global exporter of the precious bean, a position it held until 1712, when coffee cultures in Southeast Asia began slowly to increase their output.[3] This commercial role earned Mocha an enduring association with the Arabian legacy of coffee, such that its name is attached to varieties of beans and drinks in coffee shops around the world today.

In this book I explore urban life, city space, and architecture in Mocha during its period of international renown, from 1650 through 1750, when the Qāsimī imams of Yemen's interior oversaw and benefited from the port's trade activity. During these decades, European merchants who frequented Mocha's harbor left enduring records of the city's trade, which add an important dimension to Yemen's scant and uneven historical record. The city of Mocha, which functioned as a significant transregional node, was no isolated entity defined by the limits of its walls. It was a product of the larger economic and political systems to which it belonged. Before arriving at Mocha's jetty or entering its fortified gates, I look to the larger history and trade of the region and the profiles of the administrators and merchants who animated the city's structures. Instead of rendering the buildings of Mocha as empty monuments in a bounded city, I highlight the city's tight and constitutive connections to Yemeni highland capitals of rule and to market towns in its inland network, as well as its major trading partners around the Red Sea and the Indian Ocean. Only by situating Mocha within the multiple and overlapping spheres of economy and culture that converged in and around it can one appreciate the textured and nuanced cultural character of this coastal society, its architecture, and its urban space.

The Story of Mocha

Mocha took a position of prominence in 1538 when the Portuguese defeated the Ottomans in a struggle for dominance on the west coast of India, obliging the Turks to strengthen their Red Sea territories. Turkish forces then successfully brought parts of lowland Yemen under Ottoman sovereignty and continued into the interior. During the century in which the Ottomans occupied Yemen, the port served as the primary Red Sea foothold and a key administrative, commercial, and communications hub for the Turks, as well as their main station for embarkation from and disembarkation to Yemeni posts. Two pieces of evidence confirm Mocha's status as a sixteenth-century Ottoman provincial outpost of considerable means, population, and facilities—a copper coin minted in the city in 970/1562–63 and an anonymous Arabic source from 1005/1597 that describes how Mocha ascended as Aden declined as the central port at the mouth of the Red Sea.[4]

Mocha's Ottoman administration witnessed the arrival of European merchants on Yemen's Red Sea coast, first the English in 1609 and then the Dutch in 1616. The European presence generated a large number of merchants' letters and travel accounts, a steep rise in Mocha's historical documentation. These early narratives reveal the great potential for a profitable European trade with Mocha, but they also attest to the obstacles that stood in the way of establishing a permanent trade presence in the Ottoman-controlled port. For instance, the merchants Sir Henry Middleton, in 1610, and Pieter van den Broecke, in 1616, had to travel the long journey to the court in Sanaa in order to make their commercial requests directly to the provincial Ottoman governor—and Middleton did so as a shackled prisoner rather than an esteemed envoy. In essence, it is in the first half of the seventeenth century that the city becomes accessible to the historian, as is demonstrated by the numerous studies published by the historian Cees Brouwer drawing on the records of the Dutch East India Company (Verenigde Oostindische Compagnie, or VOC).

Through fierce opposition from the local Qāsimī imams, the Ottomans were ousted from the Yemeni highlands and then the ports in 1635. Their departure ushered in the period known to historians of Yemen as the "first era of independence from the Ottomans." Eventually, under the leadership of the third Qāsimī imam, al-Mutawakkil Ismāʿīl (r. 1644–76), the entire southern Arabian Peninsula, including the Ḥaḍramawt, the southeastern region of Yemen that stretches along the Arabian Sea, was subsumed under Qāsimī dominance. This change of power did not alter the port's importance in Yemeni maritime life; Mocha continued to be used as the main port of the Red Sea. During these years, elite administrators, many of them from notable Zaydī Shīʿī families, were dispatched to govern the port and to assure the flow of revenue from Mocha to the inland mountain centers of the Qāsimī dynasty. Mocha's treasury provided the resources to maintain peaceful underpinnings throughout the Qāsimī dynasty, particularly through the financing of the imam's army to control tribal unrest and to curb any opposition to his rule. Although Mocha's trade was intermittently interrupted by piracy in the harbor and the adjacent seas, the post-Ottoman seventeenth century was a time of great economic gain for the port. Many notable figures, such as Bari Sahiba, the dowager queen of Bijapur, and an Uzbek sultan from Kashgar, appeared at Mocha's shore en route to Mecca and Madīna.[5]

In contrast to the seventeenth century, when the English and Dutch trading establishments were only partially operational, Mocha in the first half of the eighteenth century was marked by the presence of settled European companies at the port, including the English, Dutch, and French. The Ostend East India Company and the Swedish East India Company made sporadic appearances, and at the end of the century, American traders began to make their presence felt.[6] By that time Portuguese maritime dominance in the western Indian Ocean had waned. In May 1706 the appearance of a Portuguese ship requesting the privilege of trading in Mocha shocked the governor, who claimed it had been thirty-four years since the Portuguese had last called at the port.[7]

As settled residents who maintained permanent trading establishments and overwintered at the port, Europeans played a visible role in the city's trade, along with the core Arab and Indian merchant community. They also functioned as key recorders of events. Indeed, the story of the city is often told through their eyes as they raced to the emporium town of Bayt al-Faqīh to purchase bales of coffee that would be exported via Mocha for Europe. Through European documents we learn that the city's trade was greatly affected by highland conflicts, particularly those instigated by contenders to the imamate such as Muḥammad b. Isḥāq b. Imam al-Mahdī Aḥmad in the 1720s and by unruly highland tribal factions. Other threats to the city's stability came from the water. Three French Compagnie des Indes warships came to the port in 1737, seeking amends for violations of their initial trade treaty, established in 1709.[8] After bombarding the city and taking hostages, they gained the leverage to renegotiate their treaty and to receive restitution of tolls and taxes they had overpaid in previous trade seasons.

The beginning of the nineteenth century signals the end of Mocha's strategic hold over Yemen's Indian Ocean trade. The decline in the city's commerce may be attributed to problems at the Qāsimī court, particularly during the reign of Imam al-Manṣūr ʿAlī (r. 1775–1809), when local tribal uprisings and factionalism at court disrupted Qāsimī control over its territories. In the lowlands, local leaders such as Amīr Abū Nuqṭa al-Rufaydī and Sharīf Ḥamūd b. Muḥammad Abū Mismār allied themselves with the growing Wahhabi movement and established separate chiefdoms in the Tihāma region, the lowlands along Yemen's west coast. These provincial upsets provided the opening for Ottoman claims to reemerge after Egypt's Muḥammad ʿAlī began his anti-Wahhabi campaigns in the Ḥijāz region, along the Red Sea coast of modern Saudi Arabia, in 1811. In 1832 an Ottoman officer known as "Türkçe Bilmez" attacked Mocha and razed the southern part of the city.

Although his revolt was soon extinguished, Türkçe Bilmez's aggression marks the reentry of Turkish influence in the area. Mocha and the lowlands returned to Ottoman hands in 1849, followed by Sanaa in 1872. During this second occupation the Ottomans abandoned Mocha as their coastal base and opted to establish their presence in the port of al-Ḥudayda.[9] In 1839 the British occupied Aden under the premise of using the port as a coaling station between Bombay and Suez. They also saw in Aden a convenient halting point on the Indian Ocean mail route. This intervention resulted in a reinvigorated and restored Aden as a strategic British foothold on the Arabian Peninsula. While Aden was being built up and modernized, Mocha languished under the custodianship of temporary provincial Ottoman governors.[10]

By the middle of the nineteenth century, the repositioning of coastal sites under the British and the Ottomans led to the demise of Mocha's status from that of a preeminent international port to that of a harbor dependent on the fortunes of Aden to its south and al-Ḥudayda to its north. The scribe Aḥmad b. Muḥammad al-Jarādī, who traveled to Mocha with the German photographer Hermann Burchardt in 1909, chronicled the decrepit state of the port and its diminished population. The final stage in its structural decline came in 1911–12, with the Turkish-Italian War, when Italian forces bombed Mocha and destroyed the Great Mosque in its center. In 1950 Imam Aḥmad attempted to reinvigorate Mocha as a convenient coastal outlet to Taʿizz, his seat of power, by building a new, modern port to the south of the city. His attempts made little difference, however, because Mocha was no match for Aden's newly confirmed global prominence. The golden age of Mocha as a player in the Indian Ocean trade had faded into the shadow of the past.

On the Edge of Urban History

The past twenty-five years have witnessed a rise in studies examining the lived dimensions of early modern Arab city life—works such as Abraham Marcus's on Aleppo, James Grehan's on Damascus, and André Raymond's and Nelly Hanna's on Cairo.[11] These investigations have transformed Arab urban studies by relying on the wealth of available Ottoman legal documentation, which has allowed a retelling of facets of city life that are unattainable in the traditional Arabic topographic and historical records. My work was inspired by and is indebted to these studies of everyday life and urban order, but Mocha stands apart from those other Arab locations in important ways. Although Mocha was one among a number of Arab cities that attained global fame, hosted international residential communities, and is accessible through a combination of textual sources, it did not live under Ottoman rule in the late seventeenth and early eighteenth centuries. Indeed, Yemen freed itself from the yoke of the Ottomans for more than 200 years. It is a segment of this extended period of Qāsimī rule that is the primary focus of this book.

The authors of many laudable studies, such as those just mentioned, have sought to dispel oft-repeated notions of a homogenized or essentialized Arab Muslim city.[12] Aware of the limits of typologies, I position Mocha against the grain of general assumptions about the unchanging Islamic city with a strong, centralized religious core, a distinct separation between the public and private worlds, and spatially segregated ethnic quarters. In chapters 5, 6, and 7, I make the argument that in its urban form, built environment, and social fabric, Mocha must be understood as a singular case that responded to specific economic and social stimuli, rather than as a representational regional type that fulfills an anticipated model.

I locate Mocha within the vast rubric of the port city, a category that dissipates the uniformity of regional labels such as the Yemeni city, the Arab city, and the Islamic city by weaving together urban threads across national, linguistic, and religious boundaries. Indeed, comparative material from port cities around the Indian Ocean provides the most salient points of contrast and context for Mocha's urban shape and use of architectural space. Port city studies have emerged in recent years as an important subspecialty in urban history, as evidenced by substantial work on Mediterranean, Atlantic, and Indian Ocean sites such as Venice, Istanbul, Havana, Bombay, Colombo, and Batavia. The wealth of new research on these places highlights their cosmopolitanism and points to the rich interregional convergences that appeared at these coastal nodes. A single regional label is ill equipped to adequately define Mocha's urban life and built character. Its strategic shoreline location, at the junction of a number of land-based and maritime systems, must be taken into serious consideration.

Mocha stands apart from the majority of other early modern Indian Ocean ports, however, in not having been a European colonial city. Since Rhoads Murphey's influential article on Asian colonial urbanism, the Indian Ocean port city has received attention as a global pivot through which colonial powers extracted resources from occupied territories and transformed local systems of rule.[13] Although Murphey later revised his initial core ideas about the absence of a precolonial Asian port city system, the contours of his framework, which privileges colonial urbanism, continue to overshadow research on the noncolonial port city.[14] This imbalance in scholarly treatment has resulted largely from the limitations of source material for pre- or noncolonial sites, but regardless, the rubric of the colonial city has subsumed that of the port city, circumscribing the coastal urbanism of the southern hemisphere within the perspective of European power.[15] Following Murphey's early lead, historians have privileged the colonial site and examined port cities as "beachheads of an exogenous system," severed from the mainland.[16]

Mocha occupies a unique and important place in the larger urban history of the Indian Ocean as an early modern port city that was populated by significant European communities but was never colonized by a European power. As the architectural historian Deborah Howard remarked in regard to Venetian merchants living in Arab port cities during the Middle Ages, "inhabiting a foreign port by privilege . . . predicated a mentality that did not assume political superiority."[17] In the case of Mocha, the visible European trade presence cannot be conflated with local European authority or market primacy, although Europeans did receive certain trade advantages from Mocha's government. The city's unique story is that of a noncolonial port in the age when European economic and territorial domination was changing the face of trade and authority around the Indian Ocean.

Trade and the Built Environment

Although the maritime trade has long been considered an important aspect of Yemen's economy and history, art and architectural historians have touched only tangentially upon the effects of premodern maritime commerce. Prior studies laid the groundwork for understanding the tight material links between trading cultures mainly through the identification of objects of foreign manufacture, the work of migratory craftspeople, and the transmission of visual influence.[18] Yet it is the architectural record that holds the key to accounting for the cultural dimensions of commercial interaction during this moment of intense global contact on the Arabian Peninsula.

Ruth Barnes's examination of the use of Indian textile patterns in the decoration of the sixteenth-century ʿĀmiriyya *madrasa* and mosque in the Yemeni city of Radāʿ serves as an example of the primary ways in which art and architecture have been located alongside Yemen's trade history.[19] Barnes incisively demonstrated how the portable designs of everyday imported cloth from South Asia moved into the realm of monumental architectural painting in the Tahirid period. Her compelling pairing of textile fragments with similarly designed and colored patterns on the ornate mosque ceiling confirmed a relationship in which certain features of Indian trade objects that had been transferred to the Arabian Peninsula eventually made their way into the local lexicon of royal architectural motifs. The body of work on Yemeni trade of which her study is a part revolves around the notion that commercial cross-cultural exchange may be most effectively gauged by considering art and architecture at the point of its manufacture and by following relationships that are readily discernible to the eye.

Recently researchers have begun to expand the investigative scope by examining the ways in which visual objects and built spaces mediated the experience and practices of the trade.[20] Some of these scholars are intently concerned with the trading relationships maintained by Middle Eastern and Asian lands with Europe, so their works are relevant to mine in subject matter as well as approach. But even while trade is treated as a shaping force in visual culture and built environments, it must be read in terms of the reception of images and buildings, the cross-cultural production of economic and social meaning, and the ways in which objects and ideas about space circulated within the functional world of the traveling merchant. For instance, in his study of sixteenth-century European cartography, Jerry Brotton located maps within an elaborated context, not just as geographical tools in the age of exploration but also as "transactional images" that were suspended within matrices of desire for commercial expansion at a key moment of changing geographical awareness and diplomatic crisis over territorial borders.[21] According to Brotton, the significance of the map is only scarcely visible on its surface. Rather, maps must be understood as visual objects that guided the expansion that was associated with early modern trade and exploration but also emerged from the knowledge gained on such journeys. Furthermore, the map became a prized commodity that was then trafficked on its own terms because of the valuable information it yielded about lucrative southern hemisphere and New World geographies. Brotton suggested that visual objects such as maps could be read in a complex, multidimensional manner and that these objects might at once allow for, represent, and complicate the nature of trade interactions.

Deborah Howard's work on relations between the city of Venice and Egypt and the Levant is a sophisticated example of the ways in which architectural and urban historians may locate trade at a critical intersection with built culture.[22] Howard homed in on the encounters and experiences that shaped the consciousness of Italian merchants and seafarers who transmitted images of the Arab built environment back to Venice from their overseas journeys. Although she was concerned ultimately with visual confirmation of maritime relations, she proposed a complex mode of passage for the migration of forms, destabilizing the notion that architectural elements may travel efficiently from one place to another while maintaining the status of cultural icons without major shifts in meaning or modes of signification. As Oleg Grabar wrote, Howard's "vision goes beyond the common bag of influences, impacts, borrowings, or assorted hybridities in their intercultural settings. It argues rather that a visual idiom was created by a history of mercantile connections between two cultures."[23] Howard's study reveals a culture of trade in Venice that provided the framework for new building types, the city's specific urban organization, and the visual dimensions of its architecture.

Following these directions, I diverge from the productive context of buildings and notions of stylistic influence, cultural confluence, and visual similarity as the primary means of interpreting cross-cultural commercial relationships in architecture. Instead, I demonstrate that the culture of trade profoundly shaped the underlying structure of the port city, defining the principal orientation of its urban shape, the functional modes of its built elements, and the social hierarchies that dominated community life. Studies tracing the migration of motifs from the Indian subcontinent and East Africa to the Arabian coast, or tracking visual consistencies that cross national boundaries and tie maritime societies together, may be found elsewhere.[24] Here I explore the ways in which Mocha's buildings and city spaces facilitated the everyday conduct of the trade but also merged distant spatial paradigms with local architectural models, contributing to the foreign merchant's sense of belonging in a faraway city. Essentially, urban structures functioned as spatial tools of transition from one realm to another, allowing those who traveled to make sense of their long-distance journeys and to alleviate the alienation inherently involved in the interactions of cross-cultural trade.

Trade revenue from Mocha entered the hands of architectural patrons and eventually resulted in new constructions not only in Mocha itself but also in the Gujarati city of Surat and interior towns in Yemen far from the coasts. The built effects of Mocha's trade must therefore be traced within the larger sphere of a far-reaching trade network. The built environment of Mocha's coastal culture of trade becomes coherent through documentation of the city's layout, examination of the larger spatial processes of trade and migration, analysis of functional agendas in architecture, and reconstruction of the patronage programs of Mocha's related yet distant trading partners. The returns of Mocha's trade provided the stimulus as well as the funds for new construction throughout Yemen. It also motivated urban commercial activity in this maritime society of the Arabian Peninsula, which was in communication with the vibrant world of the Indian Ocean.

Sources

In many ways the parameters of this book have been dictated by the available sources that contributed to its production. I deal with a city in its trade network, but that city lies in ruins today. Mocha is still inhabited, but its historic quarters are almost entirely destroyed, and most residents live outside the former city walls. Few of the questions I pose could be answered by my many visits to Mocha and other key Yemeni sites. Thus I have relied on a combined reading of sources to understand and reconstruct city form, architecture, and urban life. These diverse sources consist of visual records and textual accounts, oral reports and archaeological remains, historical studies and modern investigations, in addition to my field visits.

The chief sources in Arabic from Yemen consist of two primary types, the historical chronicle and the biographical dictionary. Both genres follow formulaic outlines. The historical chronicles focus on major events such as battles, incursions, and natural disasters. Although they refer to the city of Mocha and its residents, they often do so briefly, in passing parenthetical comments. The biographical dictionaries explore the religious elites of Yemen, with a focus on highland Zaydī scholars and the families of the imams. These official histories and biographical texts were never written in Mocha or the lowland coastal region but rather from the distant vantage point of the highlands.[25] The distance between writer and subject is always evident. I have done my best to carefully incorporate into this study the partial and fleeting references gleaned from these sources, but they cannot stand alone as the foundation of the inquiry.

The European sources, which far outnumber the local Arabic sources for Mocha, include commercial documents left by merchants of the major European companies that maintained continuous trade establishments in the city, as well as the more fleeting travel narratives of transient visitors. Of the company documents, the diaries of the VOC, called Dag Registers (daily logbooks), constitute the backbone of this study. They are the most detailed and continuous of the sources, describing daily activity in the city for the first half of the eighteenth century from an eyewitness viewpoint.[26] I set the eighteenth-century Dutch trade documents apart from the other European company documents, as well as travelers' accounts, because the long-term residents of the VOC were keenly aware of local practices and customs of the trade and recorded daily events in minute detail. Some were even proficient in Arabic and other languages used by the major merchants in the city. A list of these archival sources is given in Appendix B. On the other hand, transitory visitors to the city were numerous throughout the eighteenth and nineteenth centuries, and their published travel narratives, often adorned with illustrations, circulated as popular accounts in Europe. The nineteenth century ushered in the era of photography, and every historical image of the now-ruined city serves as a valuable source about buildings and city vistas now destroyed.

Any study of Mocha requires a careful reading of these diverse texts and images, with an understanding of their orientation, in order to piece together the spatial organization of the city, its history, and its architecture from scattered accounts. Another source of immeasurable value is the contemporary local population. Although few of Mocha's inhabitants remember the city's past grandeur, some residents have taken an active interest in its history.[27] Most notable is the work of the local historian Muḥammad ʿAbd al-Wahhāb, who died in 2001. His grandson ʿĀdil gave me tours of the city's ruined landmarks by pointing to mounds of sand and rubble that remained monumental in his elderly grandfather's memory. This urban past is preserved in the historical work "Iklīl al-Mukhā'," by ʿAbd al-Wahhāb, which awaits editing and posthumous publication.[28] I refer to an unpublished copy of the Iklīl, as well as numerous personal communications with ʿĀdil b. Ḥusayn b. Muḥammad ʿAbd al-Wahhāb, who served as my intermediary to his late grandfather and other residents of the city. They often added personal insights absent from the Iklīl and the other documents I relied upon.[29]

Indian Ocean Currents

I have organized this book not as an architectural history told in chronological sequence but rather in chapters that funnel from the larger contours of the Mocha trade network toward the specificity of the urban sphere. My goal is not to offer complete coverage of Mocha's urban history between 1650 and 1750 but gradually to narrow my lens on the commercial space of the city from that of the entire maritime sphere down to the smallest units of study, the city's inhabitants and buildings.

I begin by locating Mocha within a large yet bounded space of travel, contact, and exchange surrounding the Red Sea, the western Indian Ocean, and Qāsimī Yemen. In chapter 1, I trace the changing dimensions of the Mocha trade network by looking at the overlapping histories of the Ottomans in the Red Sea, the Qāsimī imams of Yemen, and the western Indian Ocean trade. In chapter 2, I challenge the notion that Mocha played a singular role in the coffee trade by locating it within an interdependent matrix with other Yemeni and Red Sea ports and cities that administered the commerce in this precious commodity.

Next I turn to the peregrinations of the merchants, governors, brokers, and religious scholars who inhabited the city, albeit temporarily. In his wide-reaching maritime study *The Indian Ocean*, Kenneth McPherson wrote that although "it is relatively easy to sketch a general picture of Indian Ocean trade in the fifteenth century, it is much more difficult to give the story a human face."[30] The same holds true for the later Indian Ocean, so I try to recover the elusive persons who traveled the inland and maritime networks sketched in chapters 1 and 2 and who inhabited the buildings in the port. I introduce the imam's wazirs and Mocha's governors in chapter 3 and highlight high-profile sea captains and profit-seeking merchants in chapter 4.

Turning to the urban space of the city, I look at its built shape, major monuments, domestic architecture, and residential quarters. In chapter 5,

I reconstruct the layout of the historic city and show how it functioned as a scaled-down diagram of the networks it facilitated, responding to both the maritime world and the dynastic needs of the Yemeni imamate. In chapter 6, which is focused on the commercial practices of merchants in the city, I demonstrate that the merchants used their houses, rather than public structures, as the primary locations for their commercial interactions and that this pattern was tied closely to larger maritime practices. In the last chapter I highlight the tensions between the intramural and extramural city by showing how the social hierarchies of the maritime trade largely determined the residential patterns of the Baniyans, Hindu and Jain merchants from India.

Scholarship on the Indian Ocean tends toward the writing of broadly conceived studies such as those by Sugata Bose, K. N. Chaudhuri, and Kenneth McPherson, which oblige readers to traverse vast tracts of maritime space in the course of a single page.[31] Here I offer a more focused case of a port city within the worlds in which it functioned. Throughout the book I weigh comparative material from the Arab Mediterranean, the Red Sea, the Persian Gulf, and the Indian Ocean in order to highlight Mocha's relations with and comparability to other sites. I use comparison, however, only as a tool to underscore the specific aspects of built form and urban experience of the Mocha trade network and not to draw all-encompassing conclusions about the greater Indian Ocean region. The example of Mocha's architecture, urbanism, and society serves as a building block upon which future researchers may establish an understanding of the cultural dimensions of the Indian Ocean in a time of vibrant economic activity and momentous political change.

1 *The Mocha Trade Network*

In her broad study of the Muslim dimensions of the Indian Ocean trade, the historian Patricia Risso highlighted the scholarly disjuncture between the overwhelmingly land-based approach taken in Islamic historiography and the coastal focus of Indian Ocean historiographers.[1] Generally, Islamic historiography has been ordered by the logic of dynasties and their territories, which usually radiated from inland centers. Rather than overlapping with those narratives, Indian Ocean history reads like the portolan chart of a seafarer, oriented around sites on the coasts and their relationships to one another but painting the internal regions ambiguously, with broad, sweeping labels. This disjuncture was exacerbated in work treating the early modern period, when Asian littoral history found itself folded into the legacy of European trade and expansion.

Characteristic of this scholarly rift, Mocha's late-seventeenth- and early-eighteenth-century history, often drawn from European commercial documentation, stands starkly apart from that of the ruling Qāsimīs of Yemen, which is based on local textual sources in Arabic. The early modern period was a pivotal segment of Islamic history, when three major Muslim dynasties dominated—the Ottomans from Istanbul, the Safavids in Iran, and the Mughals in India. Among the familiar names of the gunpowder empires, the Qāsimīs of Yemen make hardly an appearance in the historical register. Even in the context of Arabian and Yemeni studies, interest in medieval, Ottoman, and contemporary peninsular history has occluded scholarly attention to the Qāsimī imams.[2] But whereas the Qāsimīs are often overshadowed, the port of Mocha has independently surpassed the reputation of its dynastic umbrella.[3] Mocha's name has long been established as that of a well-known port of the Red Sea, linked closely to the Persian Gulf, India, and Europe through the transit of ships carrying coveted goods during the yearly trade season.

In an effort to bridge the gap between land and sea historiographies, in this chapter I trace the processes by which control of Mocha moved from the maritime sphere of the Ottomans to the imamic territory of the Arabian Peninsula Qāsimīs. Mocha sat at the strategic hinge point where the peripheries of the Mediterranean and Indian Ocean worlds converged. Its relationship to both these systems shifted after the Qāsimī imams ousted the Turks from Yemen. Although the port city steadily maintained its key trade role under both sets of authorities, its place in the maritime trade was not static. Rather, its commercial profile was closely tied up with the larger political changes that took place around it. From the mid-seventeenth century, Mocha operated within a far-reaching yet delimited zone of commerce and exchange that stretched into the heart of inland Yemen and overseas toward western India.

The Ottoman Backdrop

Mocha's rise as a port must be attributed to the arrival of the Ottomans during the first decades of the sixteenth century as they expanded down the Red Sea coast in response to Portuguese commercial and naval control of the western Indian Ocean. As early as 1525 an oft-cited document attributed to the admiral Selman Reis identified Yemen as the key to the Indian trade and suggested that Yemen would be easy to conquer because of local political fragmentation and sectarian factionalism.[4] In 1538 the Ottoman naval officer Süleyman Pasha occupied Yemen and established himself in Mocha and Aden (map 1.1). By 1547 Özdemir Pasha had taken Sanaa. Initially the Ottomans believed they could control Yemen with relative ease, given the lack of an existing power structure and the fact that local Ismāʿīlī Shīʿī factions generally preferred Turkish rule to Zaydī intolerance. But they soon met with significant challenges to their governance throughout Yemen. The strongest resistance came from the Zaydī imam al-Muṭahhar b. Sharaf al-Dīn of Thulā, who wrested Sanaa from Ottoman control in 1567. Koca Sinān Pasha, who was sent from Egypt to put down this first major Zaydī revolt,

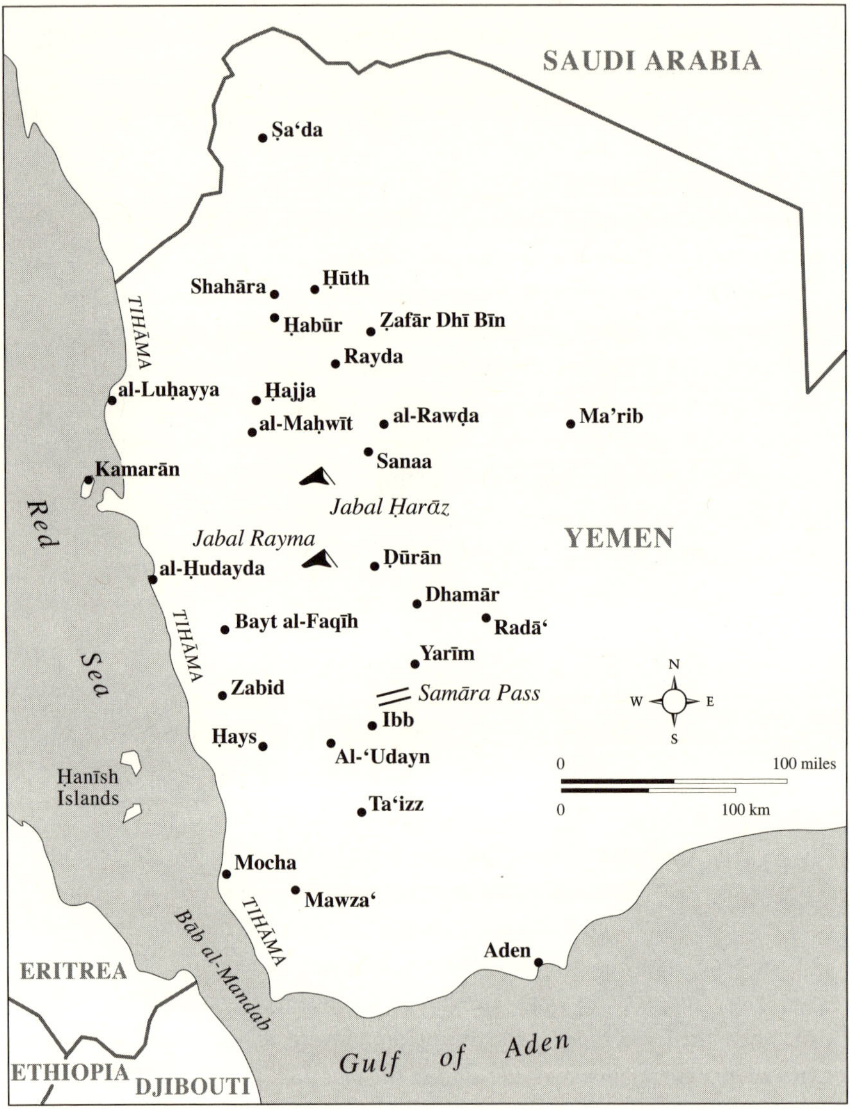

MAP 1.1 Western Yemen.

managed to regain Sanaa, but the final fierce battle with al-Muṭahhar in the mountain fortress of Kawkabān ended inconclusively in a truce.

After the death of al-Muṭahhar in 1572, the Ottoman governors Murād Pasha (r. 1576–80) and Ḥasan Pasha (r. 1580–1604) enjoyed relative stability in Yemen. Examples of monumental architecture in Yemeni cities reflect these peaceful decades, as well as the fact that many Ottoman governors gained great wealth that they dispensed on charitable contributions and public works. Ḥasan Pasha ordered that the mosque of al-Shādhilī be built in Mocha around the year 999/1590–91 and that the Bakīriyya mosque in Sanaa be built in 1005/1596–97 (fig. 1.1). The Bakīriyya is considered to be the largest and most visible mosque of Ottoman construction in Sanaa, surpassing even Ottoman additions during the second occupation in the nineteenth century. In 1598, however, the year after the Bakīriyya was constructed, a formidable enemy of the Ottomans, Imam al-Manṣūr al-Qāsim b. Muḥammad, proclaimed his *daʿwa*, or summons to the imamate, with the support of a number of powerful tribes. Sinān Pasha Kaykhiyā (not to be confused with Koca Sinān Pasha of Egypt) arrived in 1008/1599–1600 to respond to the threat of the new imam and his large following, particularly in the northern regions of Shahāra and Ḥajja. After fighting with Imam al-Manṣūr for more than seven years, Sinān Pasha could manage no more than a truce with him.

Under the next governorships, those of Jaʿfar Pasha (r. 1607–16) and Mehmed Pasha (r. 1616–21), Imam al-Manṣūr continued to be a significant threat, as is indicated by the fact that both governors preferred to make treaties with him than to wage war against him. After Imam al-Manṣūr died in 1620, his son Imam al-Muʾayyad billāh Muḥammad continued the tradition of the truce with the Ottoman governors Aḥmad Faḍlī Pasha (r. 1622–24) and Ḥaydar Pasha (r. 1624–29). This changed when, in 1626, he had garnered enough tribal support to counter the Ottoman presence. In 1629, after al-Muʾayyad had taken most of the northern regions and parts of the coastal Tihāma strip, the defeated Ḥaydar Pasha relinquished control of Sanaa to the imam. The last Ottoman successors, Aydin Pasha (r. 1628–30) and Qānṣūh Pasha (r. 1629–35), maintained the lowland coastal outposts of Yemen, such as Zabid and Mocha, but these were ceded by the end of 1635.

Although Sanaa was the administrative center of the province, Mocha was a key revenue-producing site for the Ottoman territory, as is clearly demonstrated by the resources that Ottoman governors devoted to building the port's commercial infrastructure (see chapter 5). The Tihāma region was

FIG. 1.1 Bakīriyya Mosque, Sanaa, viewed from the south, 2002.

the gateway to Yemen for the Ottomans, and Mocha was often the launching pad for Turkish activities in the greater maritime region. Additionally, the Tihāma lowland, which included the ports, was considered much tamer than the intractable and seditious mountain interior of Sanaa and its environs, and it functioned as a relatively safe haven during times of local instability. But the Ottoman occupation of Mocha must be seen not only in relationship to these internal territories but also in light of other acts of expansion along the Red Sea. After securing highland Yemen, Özdemir Pasha seized a number of Abyssinian cities, including Massawa, Arkiko, Tigre, and Deberva, in 1557–59.[5] Again the desire was to thwart the Portuguese from landing along the coast. Although the interior regions of Abyssinia proved just as untenable as their Arabian counterparts, an Ottoman garrison carefully oversaw and controlled the port of Massawa (map 1.2). Massawa functioned as the key Ottoman holding on the southwest coast of the Red Sea, even though it lay adjacent to less stable territory beyond.

The Jidda Gap

According to Michel Tuchscherer, from the mid-sixteenth century to 1635 the Red Sea functioned as an "Ottoman lake," with ships traveling freely along its length, calling at the Ottoman tollhouses on either coast.[6] The Cairo trade, reaching as far as India on the east, hinged upon Ottoman control of Yemeni and Abyssinian ports and a "delicate but durable balance" between the Portuguese and the Ottomans in the western Indian Ocean.[7] The legacy of the Egyptian merchant Ismāʿīl Abū Ṭāqiyya demonstrates the possibilities of commercial mobility available to people active in the Red Sea trade at the time. From the 1590s to 1624, when he died, Abū Ṭāqiyya's prosperous commercial empire stretched throughout North Africa, the Mediterranean, and the Indian Ocean, unencumbered by boundaries.[8]

Hence it was a momentous occasion when the Qāsimīs challenged the Ottomans and eventually ousted them from the Red Sea's eastern coast. This political upheaval transformed trade in the Red Sea in a way that ramified far beyond the Sinai Peninsula and Bāb al-Mandab. According to Tuchscherer, the Qāsimī period ushered in a new division of the Red Sea maritime zone that pivoted around the port city of Jidda as a global center and the place where two systems, those of the Indian Ocean and the Mediterranean Sea, intersected. After this watershed moment, the northern sector of the Red Sea was controlled by Ottoman administrators and dominated by Cairene merchants while the southern sector opened up to Yemeni governance and Gujarati commercial preeminence.[9] I refer to this invisible yet palpable late-seventeenth- and eighteenth-century split of the Red Sea commerce, detailed at length by André Raymond and Tuchscherer, as the Jidda gap.[10]

Dividing a vast, Ottomanized north and a largely post-Ottoman south, the Jidda gap was imprinted in the geographical consciousness of officials and merchants along the Red Sea coasts. Ports such as Quṣayr and Suez in Egypt functioned as major nodes for the northern half. In the southern half, the Yemeni ports of Aden, Mocha, al-Ḥudayda, and al-Luḥayya, along with East African Zaylaʿ, which was brought under the aegis of the Qāsimīs in

MAP 1.2 The Red Sea.

1695, were the principal ports. Both Massawa and Sawākin, in modern Sudan, remained under Ottoman control, constituting a liminal zone shared with Jidda. This zone was frequented by African, Arab, Turkish, and Indian merchants from both halves of the Red Sea. The invisible Jidda gap was effective as a barrier, limiting traffic and determining the nature of residence along the length of the Red Sea.[11] Although Cairene and Mediterranean goods entered Mocha's warehouses, it was not by direct contact but via the intermediation of Jidda's merchants.

Tuchscherer's and Raymond's findings are significant and allow for precise cultural characterization of Red Sea space in the late seventeenth and eighteenth centuries. While the world of the western Indian Ocean merchant in the eighteenth century was linked economically to the Mediterranean sphere, it was cut off from it socially. Such a split represents a marked distinction from earlier eras, such as the medieval times of the Cairo Geniza and the sixteenth-century high point of Ottoman maritime expansion, when the two spheres were fluidly interconnected. Raymond has shown that although many Cairene merchants of the first half of the eighteenth century, such as the al-Sharāʾibī family, worked in the coffee trade, none regularly traveled or lived below Jidda. Similarly, merchants from the south, and accordingly the east, maintained Jidda as a northern boundary. Merchants from India and the Persian Gulf seldom journeyed north of Jidda, even though they were active in and south of the city. Further, above Jidda one never found the Hindu and Jain Baniyan communities that were ubiquitous and central to the trade in all the southern ports of the Red Sea, in major cities in inland Yemen, and on the coasts of the Persian Gulf. As both Tuchscherer and Raymond noted, when the Gujarati merchant ʿAbd al-Ghafūr's ship transgressed the Jidda gap in 1698 and sailed all the way to Suez, observers were shocked by his unusual contravention of standard practices in the Red Sea. ʿAbd al-Ghafūr was duly penalized in Jidda the next year and never attempted such a venture again.

It is also worth noting that King Fasiladas of Ethiopia was aware of the new opportunities that arose after the expulsion of the Ottomans from the southern half of the Red Sea.[12] He sent diplomatic envoys to the Qāsimīs in the 1640s in the hope of establishing a trade alliance between the African port Baylūl and Mocha, which would have bypassed Turkish-held Massawa and confirmed joint local control of the lower Red Sea. Although Imam al-Mutawakkil reciprocated by sending his emissary Aḥmad al-Ḥaymī to Abyssinia, trade agreements never materialized. Regardless, it is clear that the authorities on both sides of the southern Red Sea understood the potential advantages of the post-Ottoman power vacuum.

The Space of Qāsimī Yemen

The post-Ottoman period brought about a clear split in Red Sea commerce while ushering in a time of great unity for the southern Arabian Peninsula. Historically, Yemeni geography has been defined by two topographically distinct regions, the mountainous highlands of the interior and the north and the coastal lowlands along the Red Sea and the Arabian Sea in the west and the south. Throughout much of Yemen's Islamic history, these two regions have been divided from each other politically and along sectarian lines. Major medieval dynasties such as those of the Sulayhids, Ayyubids, Rasulids, and Tahirids ruled from points in southern Yemen such as Ibb, Zabid, and Taʿizz. While maintaining ties with the outside world, these dynastic powers were often in conflict over territory with the less-centralized Zaydī north. For instance, the Rasulids maintained strong diplomatic relations with Mamluk Egypt in the thirteenth through fifteenth centuries, and their successors, the Tahirids, used Aden for royal trade with India. The cosmopolitan south has always provided contact with the external world via maritime travel and trade as well as international diplomacy.

In sharp contrast, successive imams in northern Yemeni villages such as Ṣaʿda and Ẓafār Dhī Bīn sustained the continuing existence of the southern Arabian Zaydī imamate from the late ninth century. Zaydism, one of three major subsects of Shīʿī Islam, has been historically represented by only two major communities, one in Yemen and the other in Tabaristan on the Caspian Sea. When the Caspian Zaydī community declined in the twelfth century, the Yemenis became the dominant representatives of Zaydism into the modern era. The Yemeni Zaydīs, however, maintained their power and preeminence only through the careful garnering of local tribal support in the northern region. Alternatively, Sunnī dynasties that followed the Shāfiʿī school of law ruled the area south of the Samāra Pass, with the exception of the Ismāʿīlī Sulayhids, who were Shīʿī but also at odds with the Zaydīs. An oppositional contrast between the interior north and the coastal south has thus been maintained, characterized by the archetypal dichotomy between an isolated and untouchable Shīʿī backwater and a region defined by Sunnī cosmopolitanism.

The Qāsimī dynasty therefore represents a unique and noteworthy turn in Yemeni history. Founded by Imam al-Manṣūr Qāsim b. Muḥammad (r. 1598–1620), the Qāsimīs constituted a significant anti-occupation force, ruling for two and a half centuries between two eras of Ottoman rule. Although Imam al-Manṣūr Qāsim died before he could complete his mission to expel the Ottomans, his son, Imam al-Mu'ayyad billāh Muḥammad (r. 1620–44), continued his legacy by devoting most of his lifetime to ousting the Turks from Yemen. After finally succeeding and establishing Qāsimī control over all the Ottoman-held areas, al-Mu'ayyad consolidated Zaydī power from the northern mountain fortress of Shahāra.

Without the opposition of the Turks, al-Mu'ayyad Muḥammad's brother, the subsequent Imam al-Mutawakkil Ismāʿīl (r. 1644–76), established the foundations of the Qāsimī empire from his new capital farther south, in Ḍūrān, by instituting administrative and economic reforms and seeking territorial expansion. Imam al-Mutawakkil's long reign is considered the high point of Qāsimī rule and was marked by the greatest extension of the Qāsimī dominion, into the eastern stretch of Ḥaḍramawt. Never before had one titular head unified all of Yemen, nor had a Zaydī imam controlled so much territory outside the traditional isolated strongholds in the north. Al-Mutawakkil Ismāʿīl initiated new taxation policies that allowed the imamate to benefit from the profits of all of Yemen, particularly the lush and lucrative lowlands, which had never before been under Zaydī control. As the leader of an expanded territory, al-Mutawakkil also formalized many aspects of Qāsimī external relations by appointing an official to oversee the Yemeni pilgrimage caravan and establishing diplomatic dialogue with other major powers, such as the Ottomans, the emperor of Ethiopia, and the Mughal ruler Aurangzeb.[13]

Al-Mutawakkil's reign, however, was plagued by episodes of internal discord as Yemen's Jewish community witnessed the rise of a number of messianic movements, some of which were locally cultivated while others, such as Sabbatai Sevi's movement, were imported from outside. The fervor that emerged around these movements heightened the visibility and vulnerability of this long-settled minority community, eventually leading al-Mutawakkil to command from his deathbed that the Jews be expelled from Yemen.[14] Al-Mutawakkil's nephew and successor, al-Mahdī Aḥmad b. al-Ḥasan (r. 1676–81) attempted to execute this dying wish. During his short rule he expelled the Jews of Sanaa and other cities and sent them to a temporary exile in the Tihāmī city of Mawzaʿ. Although they were eventually allowed to return to Sanaa, the Mawzaʿ exile stands as the most devastating and cataclysmic event in Yemenite history.

The Zaydī system of leadership was characterized by inherent political instability, because anyone who fulfilled the necessary qualifications and received the support of the community could rise up at any time to contest a seated imam. Qāsimī history and larger Zaydī history appear as a string of overlapping battles between reigning imams and those who challenged them, resulting in repeated periods of unrest and political contestation. When Imam al-Mahdī Muḥammad (also known as Ṣāḥib al-Mawāhib, r. 1686–1718) declared himself imam in the mountain fortress of al-Manṣūra in the region of al-Ḥujariyya, he had to mobilize his troops in order to force the allegiance of the notables. Throughout his long rule he was known as a fickle and arbitrary imam who was not bolstered by the claims of erudition and community approval of his predecessors. Strong contenders such as Ḥusayn b. ʿAlī b. Aḥmad and al-Manṣūr Ḥusayn b. al-Qāsim b. al-Muʾayyad Muḥammad, both from the line of al-Manṣūr Qāsim, declared themselves imams during his rule. Each achieved a great measure of support in his region—respectively, Ṣaʿda, the northern birthplace of Yemeni Zaydism, and Shahāra.

Furthermore, al-Mahdī Muḥammad had lost control of many of the southern and eastern regions that al-Mutawakkil Ismāʿīl had taken under the fold of the Qāsimīs, such as Yāfiʿ and Ḥaḍramawt. Hence the geographic sweep of Qāsimī influence on the Arabian Peninsula was largely compromised by the early eighteenth century, despite the fact that Ṣāḥib al-Mawāhib succeeded in taking the island of Zaylaʿ in 1695. Al-Mahdī Muḥammad's nephew, Qāsim, was known for his military prowess and engaged in many campaigns on behalf of his uncle, who eventually resorted to jailing him for fear of his popularity and charisma. The pressure of contenders for his rule compelled him eventually to release Qāsim. Soon after regaining his freedom, Qāsim rescinded his allegiance to al-Mahdī and declared himself Imam al-Mutawakkil (r. 1718–27). Al-Mahdī died during the siege of Qāsim in 1718.

In the seventeenth century, after the Ottomans were removed from power, each Qāsimī imam chose his own capital, according to his local ties and power base. Generally the capitals were located near the major city of Sanaa—for example, al-Ghirās, northeast of Sanaa—or Dhamār, which included the mountain fortress of Ḍūrān, Hijrat Maʿbar, and the hilltop village of al-Mawāhib. During this early period Sanaa remained an important religious and administrative center regardless of the imams' changes of capitals. From 1718, when al-Mutawakkil Qāsim declared himself imam, the imamate took a permanent place in Sanaa, which was to remain the single site of consolidated highland power until the second Ottoman occupation. Even more significantly, Imam al-Mutawakkil Qāsim's reign marked a distinct break with tradition, for he was the first of seven generations of hereditary imams who passed on the imamate as a family right for more than 150 years.

His son, Imam al-Manṣūr Ḥusayn (r. 1727–48), succeeded him but was also plagued by challenges to his rule, particularly by Imam al-Nāṣir Muḥammad b. Isḥāq, who was believed to be better suited for the imamate than al-Manṣūr because of his scholarship and erudition. After engaging in military conflict with al-Manṣūr for two years, Muḥammad b. Isḥāq eventually submitted to him. Additionally, al-Manṣūr Ḥusayn's brother, Amīr Aḥmad, established a semi-independent princedom in and around the city of Taʿizz, thereby circumscribing al-Manṣūr's political orbit and diverting the profits of the outlying agricultural regions to his own coffers. Al-Manṣūr was succeeded by his son, Imam al-Mahdī ʿAbbās (r. 1748–75). Like the reign of al-Mutawakkil Ismāʿīl, al-Mahdī ʿAbbās's rule, which witnessed relative stability, is considered to be a high point of the Qāsimī era, a time when beneficial economic reforms were put in place and official abuses that had become commonplace before him were abolished.[15] Furthermore, al-Mahdī ʿAbbās's *daʿwa* went unchallenged, which was a rarity by this point.

Before the Qāsimī period, the Zaydī imamates of Yemen had always been limited in scope and defined oppositionally against other power holders in Yemen, either the Sunnī dynasties in the south, the Ismāʿīlīs, or the Ottomans. With such a small sphere of influence, the Zaydī imams ruled with little administrative infrastructure, no standing army, and no need for established policies of governance or procedures for handling any revenue that was generated. The inception of the expanded Qāsimī dynasty necessitated the innovation of a structure of administrative policies and the kind of governing apparatus appropriate to any large territorial power, as described by the historian and scholar of Islamic law Bernard Haykel. He highlighted the internal transformations that the Qāsimī imamate experienced from its beginning, with the expulsion of the Ottomans, through the Turkish return in the nineteenth century. Haykel emphasized the imamate's newly arisen need to develop systems of taxation, to muster armed forces, and to administer large tracts of territory, thereby taking on "state-like qualities it had never before developed fully."[16] By the mid-eighteenth century, Qāsimī Yemen had been transformed from a localized Shīʿī imamate led by an imam who was invested with community support into a territorial dynasty ruled by an imam who had inherited his title from his father and maintained control over his realm by managing a large and powerful army.

Most studies of Zaydī Yemen have been focused on the imams' reliance for political stability upon the northern tribes, who served as their military base. This focus has led to an assumption that the maritime world and commercial affairs were irrelevant to the highland Zaydīs, including the Qāsimīs. R. B. Serjeant, for example, wrote that "the Zaydī Imāms derived their authority and support from their influence with the war-like tribes of the northern mountains—landsmen without a seacoast. In this respect they differed from the Rasūlid Sulṭāns of Taʿizz of the 13th to mid-15th centuries who were able, through control of the sea, to exert their influence along the southern coast of Arabia."[17] As Haykel demonstrated, however, the Qāsimī era ushered in an unprecedented administrative structure uniting northern and southern Yemen under a Zaydī head, which led to a new level of political saturation, religious exchange, and cultural diffusion between the two regions.[18] Indeed, beginning in the seventeenth century the two realms—the highland Zaydī north and the largely Sunnī coastal lowland with its maritime ties to the Red Sea and Indian Ocean—became tightly intertwined and economically dependent on each other. The strong economic relationship between coast and interior contributed to a new, heightened maritime sensibility in Qāsimī Yemen, and Mocha served as the primary gateway for its maritime connections. This often overlooked facet of the geographical consciousness that defined the period must be added to the more conventional and narrower perspective emphasizing the highlands and its tribes.

The Trade of Mocha

In the late seventeenth and early eighteenth centuries, Mocha's port welcomed a wide range of ships from trade routes originating below the Jidda gap. Every year the first ship from India was awaited with great anticipation, because it marked the beginning of the trade season. Long-distance vessels such as large dhows with two or three masts, called *ghurābs*, along with galleys, brigantines, and barks from the Indian subcontinent constituted the most significant portion of the international trade of Mocha.[19] A veritable pipeline of maritime traffic ran from the Red Sea to Gujarat, particularly between Mocha and Surat (map 1.3). Together these cities functioned as twin ports along a maritime highway. Although vessels arrived from other Indian ports, such as Cambay in Gujarat, Diu and Porbandar on the Kathiawar Peninsula, Karwar in Karnataka, Kannur, Kozhikode, and Kochi on the Malabar coast, Pondicherry on the Coromandel coast, and Hugli in Bengal, Mocha's trade depended on the constant flow of goods and merchants along the Mocha-Surat route.

Some vessels that traveled this route may be defined as official or royal ships. The Mughal emperors and other members of the royal family sent ships from Surat to the Red Sea laden with cargo and carrying pilgrims destined for Mecca via Jidda.[20] These ships stopped at Mocha to replenish supplies and unload goods before continuing to the Ḥijāz. Trade activity overlapped with pilgrimage activity, particularly during seasons when the pilgrimage month, Dhū al-Ḥijja, coincided comfortably with the timetable dictated by the sailing winds. Furthermore, the imam of Yemen sent two ships from Mocha to Surat yearly. Private trade was also conducted by merchants who hailed from Surat, such as the well-known members of the Gujarati ship-owning family ʿAbd al-Ghafūr and its Turkish rival, the family headed by Muḥammad Ṣāliḥ Chalabī.

Following the natural calendar of the monsoon winds, ships from India began to arrive as early as January and continued to appear throughout the spring. They sailed eastward in August, leaving Mocha's harbor relatively empty by October. Textiles constituted the key Indian manufactured commodity of the port. Made in the production centers of Gujarat, the Coromandel coast, and Bengal, the textiles represented a multitude of varieties, styles, and qualities, a range reflecting the huge market for Indian cloth in Yemen and other parts of the Middle East.[21] The vast majority consisted of cotton calicoes and chintzes that were block-printed or resist-dyed and intended for everyday garments and uses. More lavish printed cottons and silks were also shipped, traded, and given as gifts. Varieties included salampore, a kind of chintz, usually white, that was originally made in the Coromandel region; *betelles*, a light muslin cloth made in Bengal that had great appeal throughout the Middle East; and canvas for sails and other utility purposes. An Indian textile known as Guinea cloth, made for the

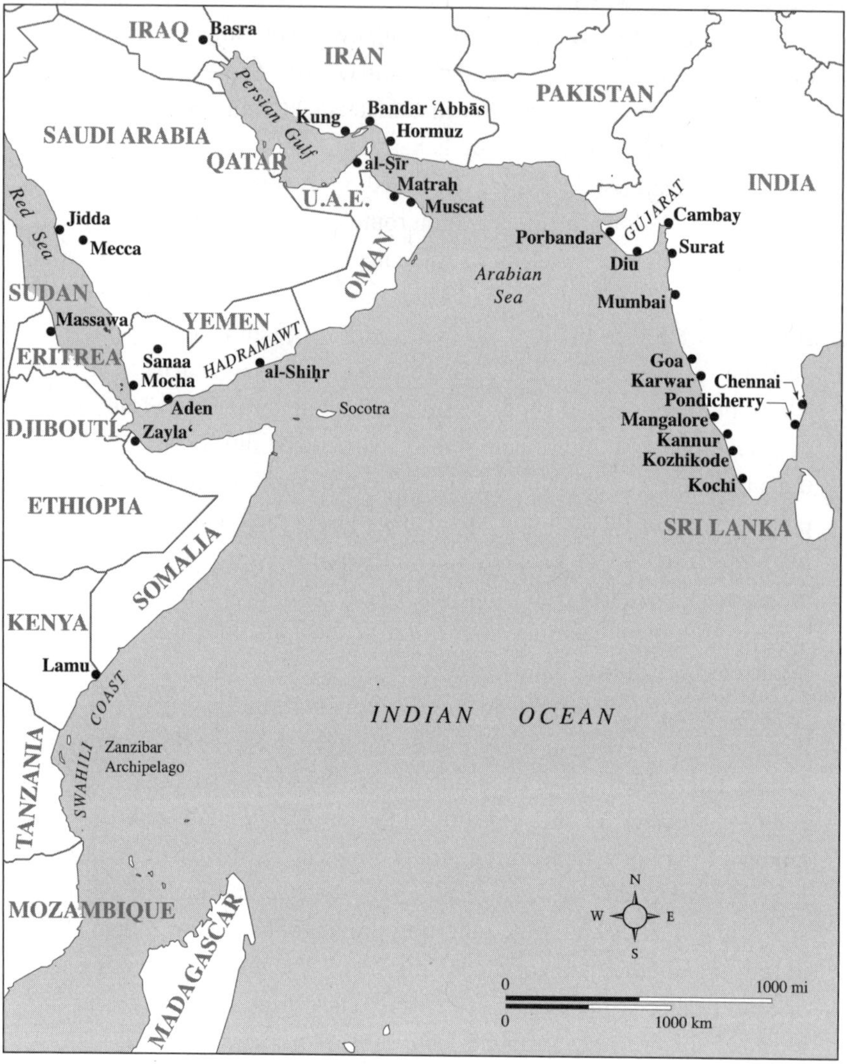

MAP 1.3 Mocha in the early modern western Indian Ocean.

African market, traveled through Mocha, eventually ending up as far away as the West Indies to clothe slaves on Caribbean plantations.

Spices from India and Southeast Asia included cloves, pepper, cardamom, mace, turmeric, cinnamon, dried ginger, and nutmeg. Various bulk metals arrived in Mocha, many of which, such as tin, copper, steel, lead, and iron, were transshipped from East and Southeast Asia. Chinese silks and damasks added to the textiles from India, and porcelains arrived in the port in all shapes and sizes, from small coffee cups to large kitchen wares.[22] Both powdered sugar and loaf sugar were available, along with rice, oil, and ghee from India. Dyestuffs such as sapanwood and aromatics such as gum benjamin also passed through the port from Asia. The vessels that carried these eastern goods to Mocha returned to the Indian coast carrying loads of bullion and cases of specie shipped from the Mediterranean for reminting into Mughal coins in India. Other items that returned to India were ivory from the African coast, medicinal products such as aloe, local aromatics, and dye materials such as *wars*, a Yemeni plant that produced a yellow pigment. During the seventeenth and eighteenth centuries, coffee was shipped from Mocha to Surat mainly on European boats.

Persian Gulf shipping, from Basra in Iraq, al-Ṣīr province on the Musandam Peninsula, Muscat and Maṭraḥ in Oman, and Kung in Persia, also served both the commercial market and the pilgrimage. The vessels, which included *ghurābs* and trankes, arrived in the city during the high season as well as the off season, between September and January.[23] These smaller Gulf vessels usually outnumbered those coming from India into Mocha's harbor, sometimes equaling up to forty per trade season.[24] The chief export product of the Persian Gulf was dates, and in the months after the autumn harvest, many Persian Gulf ships loaded entirely with dates entered the Red Sea. Although dates spoiled if they were stored for too long, they were convenient as maritime products because they served as ballast for ocean-going ships.[25] Additionally, raw copper, worked copper vessels, tobacco, ginger, and rosewater were sent to Mocha, as were clothing and textiles such as black Arab or Persian "over robes" and rough silks transshipped from India.[26] Ships returned to the Persian Gulf filled with Yemeni coffee as well as local aromatics, medicinal products, and dyes.

In contrast to the Indian Ocean and Persian Gulf vessels, the rest of Mocha's ships can be characterized broadly as local Red Sea traffic that traveled up, down, and across the waterway. The longitudinal traffic consisted mainly of small Red Sea *jalbas* that traveled between Jidda and the Yemeni ports al-Luḥayya, al-Ḥudayda, and Mocha.[27] As discussed in the next chapter, this transregional traffic was dominated by coffee, which was directed north toward Cairo via Jidda from all three Yemeni ports. There was also a good deal of traffic between Mocha and Massawa and Zaylaʿ on the western shores of the Red Sea and Gulf of Aden, routes by which products from the African interior entered the Indian Ocean. For instance, gold, ivory, amber, and civet exited via Massawa, in addition to large numbers of African slaves destined for Yemen, Egypt, the Ḥijāz, and India. After the island of Zaylaʿ, in modern-day Somalia, was taken by Imam al-Mahdī Muḥammad, that port also provided African slaves for the Yemeni market.[28]

Jalbas from Aden, Zaylaʿ, and other small ports on the African side arrived in Mocha in large numbers throughout the year to provide the city with mundane but necessary items such as butter, sheep, firewood, mats, and even drinking water. Rather than carrying high-volume trade items, these smaller Red Sea vessels left Mocha with retail quantities of goods that had been shipped originally from other Indian Ocean sites. Their cargos included spices and textiles as well as local products obtained from the interior, such as Yemeni sorghum, accommodating the everyday, practical needs of the inhabitants of port communities. The records mention Zaylaʿ as the main port of origin for such traffic, but other small, unnamed ports on the Abyssinian coast served the same purpose.

Land-based traffic was also crucial to Mocha's livelihood. Camel caravans trekked to the highlands daily, filtering the goods of the Indian Ocean trade into the interior of Yemen. The most frequent route led out of the city to the east via Taʿizz and then north through Dhamār to Sanaa (map 1.1). The other option left Mocha via Mawzaʿ, veered north along the Tihāma road to Bayt al-Faqīh, Yemen's major coffee emporium, and then entered the highlands through the Ḥarāz Mountains. Agricultural products such as sorghum and fresh fruits came from the interior to supply the Mocha market. Messengers and visitors from the Yemeni court frequented this imperial highway as well, arriving in Mocha with letters from the imam and valuable news regarding the political situation in the interior.

Overlapping Systems of Exchange

The world of Indian Ocean trade overlapped with the realm of Qāsimī governance in Mocha in the late seventeenth and early eighteenth centuries.

Both systems informed city life and commercial activity, although in different and uneven ways. Two good examples of this social, cultural, and economic overlay may be seen in Mocha's systems of accounting, both its calendar for payment and its currencies. The dominant calendar in Mocha was the local lunar hijrī one, which determined the major dates for feast days and the yearly pilgrimage to Mecca. Even the non-Muslim inhabitants of the city acknowledged the landmark dates and temporal rhythm of the Muslim calendar. For instance, the customs house closed during the religious festivals of ʿĪd al-Fiṭr and ʿĪd al-Aḍḥā, and trade came to a standstill for all merchants in the city on those days. Fasting during the month of Ramaḍān slowed many of the functions of the trade, even for those who did not participate.

In Mocha, however, another maritime system of accounting for time, called the Nayrūz calendar, coexisted with the local Islamic one for the purposes of trade transactions. All wholesale goods in Mocha except for coffee were sold on credit, as they were in port cities throughout the western Indian Ocean. This pervasive system of credit and account debits required a rigid and binding schedule for payment. Originally devised and used in Sasanian Persia, the solar Nayrūz calendar was not widely diffused in the early modern Arab world, but it maintained resilience in the maritime realm as the primary calendar by which Indian Ocean sailors and navigators planned sailing schedules and anticipated shifts in weather patterns.[29] In Mocha, merchants paid for their goods at intervals based on this Nayrūz calendar that were reckoned in relation to the seasonal arrival and departure of ships.[30] The Nayrūz year began after the ships left for India in October, a date that also corresponded to the Gujarati New Year. The 365-day year was then split into segments of 100 days, with 100 Nayrūz falling in January, 200 Nayrūz in April, and 300 Nayrūz in July, dates that corresponded to key moments in the annual sailing and trading season.[31] In Mocha, accounts for goods sold after the departure of the ships in the fall were not settled until 200 Nayrūz in April, a date that allowed the overseas ships to return with new goods before payment was made. All other accounts were settled on 300 Nayrūz in July, thus assuring that all debts were settled before the ships began to leave the harbor for the season.[32] All merchants in the city followed this calendar for accounting and paid debts according to its landmark dates.

The situation surrounding Mocha's coinage was even more complex. Yemeni numismatics is a perplexing field of study, and the few textual records, from both Arabic and European sources, do not correlate with the scant existing numismatic evidence. The early Qāsimīs issued coins from a number of highland mints. Imam al-Mahdī Muḥammad, for instance, had coins minted in at least three cities, Dhamār, Radāʿ, and al-Khuḍrāʾ. By the mid-eighteenth century the mint was centralized in Sanaa and placed under the control of a Jewish chief treasurer named Salīm al-ʿIrāqī.[33] In general, Qāsimī coins were minted in gold, silver, and copper, although the scarce gold examples extant today were used not as actual coins of exchange but as commemorative pieces.[34] The silver coins from the time vary in size and weight, from 6.35 grams to 19.6 grams. Unfortunately, these silver coins cannot be matched with the many names used in the texts, such as *ḥarf*, *qirsh*, and riyal. One cannot be sure how much the most frequently mentioned silver coin of this era, the *ḥarf*, weighed, although we know that it was subdivided into smaller units called *buqshahs*. Silver and copper coins minted in Sanaa under the imam's authority were in use in Mocha, and it appears that the silver *ḥarf*, as it was known in Sanaa, was called a *komassi* in Mocha and other lowland cities. The *komassi*, most likely from the Arabic *al-khumsiyya*, or a fifth, was used for everyday purchases from Mocha's bazaar and all types of small local exchanges.

As Raymond described for early modern Cairo, Mocha had in place a double system of currency in which international wholesale currencies coexisted with local denominations.[35] In the first half of the eighteenth century the Spanish riyal, also known as the Spanish *real* of eight, the Spanish dollar, and the Spanish peso, was a veritable global currency, made of silver mined in Central America, minted on the authority of the Iberian king, and transferable in the Americas, the Middle East, and Asia. In the eighteenth century the Spanish riyal was the dominant silver currency of the Arabian Peninsula, used for all wholesale trade transactions in Mocha.[36] The Maria Theresa silver thaler, known as *al-riyāl al-faransī* in Yemen, eventually replaced the Spanish riyal's prime status later in the century.

Another international unit of exchange, called the Mocha dollar, was also used by wholesale traders in the city. According to Carsten Niebuhr, a German traveler who visited Yemen in the mid-eighteenth century, the Spanish riyal, locally called *qirsh ḥajar*, was differentiated from the Mocha dollar, which went by the name *qirsh dhahab*.[37] The Mocha dollar was an accounting currency devised by the city's Baniyan brokers, but although its values were calculated, they were never tendered. The Mocha dollar, used widely in this port city but unknown in any other city, was always valued

21.5 percent lower than the Spanish riyal. All major transactions except for the purchase of coffee were conducted using values calculated in Mocha dollars. When the deferred payment was due on 100, 200, or 300 Nayrūz, it was converted from the original value in Mocha dollars to an amount tendered in Spanish riyals.

With its two calendars and multiple currencies, Mocha maintained a unique culture of trade and accounting that integrated inland and overseas systems. Through this integrated method of payment and exchange, merchants from both Gujarat and Sanaa approached Mocha's accounting system with at least a modicum of familiarity.

Mocha, then, might be said to have begun its international history as the southernmost Turkish holding in the Red Sea. From 1538 to 1635 it was overseen from Istanbul and administered by Ottoman officials sent from Egypt. During this period it was linked tightly to both the Mediterranean and the Indian Ocean, its trade extending to Cairo in the north and India in the east. By challenging Turkish preeminence along the length of the Red Sea, the Qāsimīs catapulted Mocha into a different realm of trade and exchange that terminated abruptly at Jidda and was cut off completely from direct relations with Cairo. Connections to the western Indian world, the Persian Gulf, and other lower Red Sea ports were correspondingly intensified, leading to a situation in which two distinct poles—Qāsimī Sanaa to the north and Mughal Surat to the east—defined Mocha's livelihood, trade, and governance. At the port city of Mocha the Qāsimī sphere of administration and authority converged with the commercial maritime world below the Jidda gap, which stretched toward India and away from Cairo and the Mediterranean.

2 The Yemeni Coffee Network

In the sixteenth century the Red Sea spice trade experienced an economic downfall caused by Portuguese disruption of the traditional Asian conduits to Europe. A new product, coffee, emerged fortuitously to fill the trade gap. After the Ottoman state fully harnessed coffee cultivation in Yemen in the second half of the sixteenth century, it became an important item exported to other areas under Ottoman control, including the Ḥijāz, Cairo, the Levant, and Istanbul. Under the succeeding Qāsimī imams, coffee became the most important revenue-producing crop in all of Yemen. For that reason the Qāsimī state has been dubbed "the coffee imamate," its yearly exports of the bean estimated at 12,000 to 15,000 tons during the eighteenth century.[1] Carsten Niebuhr, who claimed that Yemen's imam received one quarter of the price at which coffee was sold, attests to the imam's having profited directly from the popularity of the beverage.[2] The Qāsimīs also witnessed the expansion of the coffee market, which in the second half of the seventeenth century grew to include European consumers who had picked up the habit from their Turkish counterparts. The demand for coffee brought much New World silver to Yemen's coast, which in turn lured Asian traders to its ports. Although European exports from colonial coffee plantations on the islands of Java and Réunion in the eighteenth century had a mounting negative effect on Yemen's coffee trade, the local market remained hearty through the nineteenth century.[3] Today Yemeni production has dwindled to a minimal presence in global markets.

Regarding the first half of the seventeenth century, the Dutch historian C. G. Brouwer asked, "Is coffee to be considered synonymous with al-Mukhā? Can the city simply be described as a coffee port?"[4] Challenging the ways in which Mocha had been popularly identified as a unique emporium for coffee trade or shipment, Brouwer contended that although coffee was a major early modern Yemeni export item, it was a minor object of trade and shipping in the port of Mocha during the last years of the Ottoman occupation and the beginnings of the Qāsimī state.[5] Rather, the port's maritime centrality derived from its role in the exchange of precious metals from the Mediterranean to India. Coffee was sold and transshipped through a number of other ports, not just Mocha, as well as along land-based routes. Brouwer aptly responded to the many historians, not to mention popular writers, who inaccurately situated all early modern trade with Mocha in the realm of coffee commerce, even though the port dealt in a variety of goods and Europeans first arrived on the Yemeni Red Sea coast in search of a stake in the strategic western terminus of the Indian Ocean trade, not because of the coffee bean.

Brouwer was right to challenge the long-standing popular myths about Mocha's singular place as Yemen's coffee capital during the time when the name Mocha became associated with the coffee bean in European circles. The port was only one point in a matrix of trading sites that included inland places of coffee cultivation, the emporium Bayt al-Faqīh, established under the Qāsimī imamate, and other regional ports to the north of Mocha. Tracing coffee's itineraries into and out of Yemen reveals how the local system of coffee exchange was imbedded in a larger network of trade encompassing a rich diversity of products, merchants of many nationalities, and the whole of the western Indian Ocean.

Bean and Beverage

In his book on the origins of coffee drinking, its spread, and its prohibition in the Middle East, Ralph Hattox concluded that Yemen was the first place in which coffee was consumed as a beverage—namely, in Sufi circles in the fifteenth century.[6] Other widespread myths locate the birth of the habit in Ethiopia, home of the coffee plant, or cite earlier, fleeting references to coffee in Arabic literature.[7] Many of these popular stories include dancing goats that led curious goatherds to discover the caffeinated beans or imaginative images of the Prophet Muḥammad as the first coffee aficionado. The bulk of textual evidence, however, points to fifteenth-century Yemen as the site where and the time when coffee entered the realm of visible consumption as a drink, as well as its birthplace as a global commodity.

The Arabic language distinguishes coffee beans before they are ground and brewed as *bunn*. The prepared drink is called *qahwa*. Economically, but imprecisely, most other languages use the single nebulous term *coffee*, derived from the Arabic *qahwa* and its Turkish derivative *kahve*, to refer to the bean, the commodity, and the beverage.[8] The conflation of beverage and commodity bears upon the history of coffee and its spread. Although Yemen played a unique and pivotal role in the trade of *bunn*, or the coffee bean, its role in shaping the global culture of *qahwa* and coffee consumption was minimal outside of its early beginnings. In fact the social and ceremonial context of coffee consumption became ritually codified at the Ottoman court at Istanbul, passed in some cases through neighboring Ottoman territories, and eventually reached western Europe. The Arabian consumption tradition, in contrast, made no lasting imprint beyond the peninsula.

Qishr, for instance, is a notable coffee beverage that was consumed in early modern Yemen, is still popular there, but is unknown elsewhere. *Qishr* refers to the husk of the coffee bean, which is often simply discarded. The hot beverage is made from dried husks that are steeped in hot water for the effect of a mild tea with a light honey color, spiced with finely ground ginger and sugar. Initially *qishr* was exported to and consumed in the Ḥijāz and Egypt through the sixteenth century, along with *bunn*. After 1600 it disappeared from the trade registers and accounts of consumption outside of Yemen, having been replaced by more common coffee beans.[9] In the eighteenth century, local administrators and merchants served the drink exclusively to welcome and formally receive guests in Mocha.[10] European travelers called it "the sultan's coffee" or "the sultana's coffee" to differentiate it from black brewed coffee roasted from the bean, which was largely absent from Yemeni ceremonies at the time.[11] Despite the global prevalence of brews from roasted coffee beans today, the less flavorful, less caffeinated, and less expensive *qishr*, derived from a usual coffee waste product, still prevails in Yemen, but not outside its borders.

In contrast to the limited scope of influence of Yemeni coffee consumption, habits of coffee drinking from the northern Ottoman world served as the model for the coffee culture of cities around the Mediterranean and western Europe during the late sixteenth and the seventeenth centuries.

For example, Venetian travelers and merchants who visited Anatolia and Ottoman cities in the Levant wrote extensively about the habit in their travelogues, bringing vivid images of the beverage to audiences at home. Coffee's potential as a social lubricant was demonstrated on European terrain by Süleyman Agha, the Turkish ambassador of Sultan Mehmed IV, who served coffee to Louis XIV and other visitors at lavish parties. Public awareness of the beverage in mid-seventeenth-century France was tied largely to a surge in interest in Turkish cultural fashions. Similarly, the 1683 Ottoman siege of Vienna marked a turning point in the Austrian Hapsburg awareness of the enticement of coffee. By the end of the seventeenth century, coffeehouses existed in all the largest European cities.

One must credit both Yemen and the Mediterranean Ottoman world for shaping European and further global traditions, although their roles were distinct. Although the Ottoman world, stemming from cosmopolitan Istanbul, initiated and transmitted the social customs that have become associated with global coffee consumption today, Yemen provided the early roots of the consumption of coffee as a beverage. Throughout the seventeenth and early eighteenth centuries, Yemen also served as the sole provider of the beans to the international market. Thus, in order to understand Yemen's role in the global legacy of coffee, one must isolate the history of the bean, which has become entangled with the story of the beverage.

Growing Coffee

Much has been written about coffee consumption and prohibition in the Middle East and about European stakes in the dissemination of coffee. Less is known about the dimensions of the coffee trade in Yemen at the stage before the beans left the imam's territory. According to Michel Tuchscherer, the Ottomans encouraged the development of this cash crop by harnessing the cultivation of coffee plants for export in Yemen after 1571, when they instilled temporary peace after Imam al-Muṭahhar's rebellion.[12] Before then, limited amounts of Ethiopian and Yemeni wild crop supplied the market.[13] Coffee was never grown in or around Mocha itself, which sits on a barren, sandy spot on the coastal strip that stretches from Bāb al-Mandab, the southern entry to the Red Sea, northward up the Arabian Peninsula. This lowland strip, known as the Tihāma, is hot all year, and rainfall is scant. The land is workable in only small areas, mainly the *wādis*, or valleys where freshwater flows down from the mountains and allows for irrigation.

In the interior of Yemen, mountain formations come together to border the coast, stretching from north to south and setting the Tihāma plain apart from the interior heartland. Yemen's historic coffee cultivation sites are located in the heights that stretch along the Tihāma and benefit from adequate rainfall at elevations of 1,000 to 2,000 meters above sea level. In the north, around the larger perimeter of Sanaa, the main coffee growing areas included Ḥajja, al-Maḥwīt, Ḥarāz, Ḥayma, and Banī Maṭar. These areas lay at least a week's travel from Mocha, but mountain passes linked them to the lowland network of northern Yemeni market and port cities such as Bayt al-Faqīh, al-Ḥudayda, and al-Luḥayya. The coffee growing areas of the south, situated around Jabal Rayma and the cities of al-ʿUdayn, Ibb, and Taʿizz, were closer to Mocha and accessible by a well-traveled road.

Steven Topik, a Latin American historian, has written about the problems surrounding the use of certain labels for coffee types, which may be abbreviated, homogenized, and inaccurate. For instance, today the qualifying term *mocha* is used liberally to refer to any coffee bean of Ethiopian or Yemeni provenance. In the eighteenth century, coffee sellers often used the names Mocha and Java to identify Latin American beans by the original provenance of the plants, thereby lending the beans an aura of authenticity and raising the value of a bale of coffee.[14] Another problem with the identifying label Mocha is that all the beans that left Yemeni shores on European boats were called Mocha coffee indiscriminately, despite the fact that the beans had been grown in various areas of the Yemeni highlands. Although European coffee merchants were aware of the diversity of regional varieties and often knew the original provenance of the beans they purchased, they used Mocha as a generic label for all Yemeni beans.[15] Hence the famed historic label "Mocha coffee" is an abbreviated and often arbitrarily applied title for a range of coffee beans grown in many different highland sites but never in the city of Mocha.

Buying Coffee

Under the Ottomans there was little regulation of wholesale coffee sales. According to Brouwer, until 1640 merchants entered Yemen through the ports or by overland caravan and proceeded to the highland cultivation areas to purchase coffee beans.[16] Tuchscherer suggested that these transactions took place in weekly markets near the cultivation areas through the commercial intercession of Indian Baniyan brokers.[17] Coffee middlemen and even some farmers brought beans to the coasts as well, but any merchant who desired a large quantity at a wholesale price would profit from a trip to the interior.[18]

After the Ottomans were expelled in 1635, Yemeni coffee wholesaling began to shift administratively. The historical texts are silent about the details of this shift, but it is clear that a significant change was in place by the end of the seventeenth century, most likely instituted under Imam al-Mutawakkil Ismāʿīl, who innovated in other economic sectors such as local tax collection and the administration of the Sanaa market.[19] Rather than selling beans to individual purchasers close to the sites of cultivation, growers (or their intermediaries) brought the beans to the wholesale market in the lowland city of Bayt al-Faqīh. Bayt al-Faqīh, which still holds a large weekly regional market today, became the single global entrepôt to which all purchasers went to procure bales of Yemeni coffee.

That this central coffee emporium was instituted so that the Qāsimī imam and his officials could maintain firm control and surveillance over the coffee trade is clear. It was described as the central place for all major coffee transactions, with "two great courts, having covered piazzas," where "the Arabians of the country round about bring their coffee in sacks made of matts."[20] The governor of Bayt al-Faqīh or one of his representatives sat on a raised platform in the center of the bazaar to observe transactions. There he would "take an account of the weight and price of all the coffee sold in their presence, for the payment of the King's duties."[21] This centralized and panoptic caravanserai at Bayt al-Faqīh allowed for increased Qāsimī surveillance and gain from the coffee trade. Furthermore, the rise in regional shipping associated with coffee gave the imam the opportunity to levy tolls and duties on the merchants at Bayt al-Faqīh and then again at the port of embarkation.[22] The Tihāma, with its Red Sea ports and the inland market town of Bayt al-Faqīh, was one of the most important revenue-producing provinces for the imam at the time.

The advantages of buying at Bayt al-Faqīh were enormous, particularly because merchants could avoid the significant surcharges that were added to retail coffee in Mocha and other secondary purchase points. The traders who bought in Bayt al-Faqīh with the intention of selling wholesale quantities at the ports charged the purchaser exorbitantly for the basic costs of renting pack animals, paying the governor's duties at Bayt al-Faqīh, buying packaging materials, and paying tolls at the gates at each point.[23] Also, the coffee bales for purchase at the port and other secondary sites were limited, delivered in inconsistent quantities, and often of inferior quality. Many bales were too green and too wet to export, or they were adulterated with small rocks and other debris. In 1704 the Dutch claimed that no coffee came to Mocha except for impure quantities left over from previous years.[24]

Most merchants, consequently, bought coffee for themselves in Bayt al-Faqīh or sent a Baniyan representative to purchase coffee for them.[25] But buying coffee at Bayt al-Faqīh was no easy task. It was sold only on cash exchange, so purchasers were responsible for carrying large quantities of silver on roads that were easy targets for plundering marauders. Timing was the most important aspect of a successful sale. The European merchants at Mocha often waited until the Jidda merchants came and left before they proceeded to the coffee market. Regardless, even the mention of a new ship in any of the major harbors sent prices skyrocketing in the inland coffee market. After purchases were completed, the precious cargo needed to be well guarded. European merchants complained that camel drivers from Bayt al-Faqīh and crewmen from the lighter ships of Mocha stole small quantities of beans from their bales while transporting them.[26]

Despite the clear centrality of Bayt al-Faqīh and its market in the Yemeni coffee trade, attractive legends of Mocha as an emporium for the sale of coffee beans mislead historians. In his introductory description of Mocha in the eighteenth-century, Pierre François Guyot Desfontaines wrote in 1739 about "a beautiful bazaar or market for coffee" that was made up of two large courts with covered galleries where coffee was sold by local Arab merchants with the help of Baniyan brokers.[27] He drew freely from the descriptive account of early coffee transactions in Yemen compiled by Jean de la Roque in 1716.[28] Without direct citation, Desfontaines pulled this image of the coffee market from La Roque's text but mistakenly located it in Mocha, not Bayt al-Faqīh. Curiously, Desfontaines' misreading has been repeated in subsequent sources.[29] By situating such a wholesale trade structure in Mocha, this account and others that followed it provided a strong visual image that contributed to the erroneous yet popular notion of Mocha as a coffee emporium rather than a site for transshipment.

Shipping Coffee

In the late seventeenth and early eighteenth centuries, merchants flocked to Bayt al-Faqīh to purchase coffee beans in large quantities and ship them through three Yemeni ports on the Red Sea: Mocha, al-Ḥudayda, and al-

Luḥayya (map 1.1).[30] Of the three, al-Ḥudayda, which was established during the Rasulid period, lay within a journey of a day and a half from Bayt al-Faqīh.[31] Al-Luḥayya, founded in the early fifteenth century, was situated to the north. Mocha was the southernmost Red Sea port, below al-Ḥudayda. Both of the last two ports were four or five days from the inland market of Bayt al-Faqīh. Although the three ports shared coffee shipment activity, Mocha is often singled out as its hub, an imbalance due largely to the fact that European traders primarily used Mocha while non-European merchants used the other two ports.[32] European merchants were not the most significant merchants of Mocha or of the Yemeni coffee trade, but their copious record keeping and the accessibility of their documentation has allowed their experience in Arabian commerce to greatly inform coffee trade history today. Regardless, it is clear that European purchases constituted only one sector of Yemen's coffee trade.[33] Although Mocha played a role as one site for global coffee exports, it was not the single or the major Yemeni port for coffee exports during the period under consideration. In fact the records reveal a fluid coffee trade in which information, coffee beans, silver coins, and merchants moved between the three ports and Bayt al-Faqīh over land and sea routes.[34]

Indeed, al-Ḥudayda and al-Luḥayya were closer and more convenient for seafarers from the upper Red Sea. Turkish and Arab merchants who shipped coffee beans to Jidda frequented these two northern ports. From Jidda, most of the beans were destined for the lucrative market in Cairo, from where they would be shipped throughout the Mediterranean. André Raymond estimated that the economy of coffee imports and exports constituted one-third of Egypt's foreign commerce in the seventeenth and eighteenth centuries.[35] He stressed, however, that Egyptian merchants rarely dealt directly with their Yemeni counterparts. Instead, transactions were made through Jidda, the pivotal crux of the Red Sea. Those Jidda beans came from al-Ḥudayda and al-Luḥayya but rarely from Mocha.[36]

Historians such as Peter Boxhall, John Baldry, and Patricia Risso have provided quantitative evidence supporting the notion that the northern Yemeni coffee export market was more vibrant than that of Mocha. While conceding that Mocha was generally larger and more active as a port than al-Ḥudayda, Baldry demonstrated that al-Ḥudayda dealt in greater volumes of coffee than Mocha because of its relationship to the northern points of the Red Sea, particularly in the eighteenth century.[37] Risso hinted at the size of the coffee trade in the two northern ports by describing the Jidda market as ten times larger in volume than the Persian Gulf market, which was often served by Mocha.[38]

The Dutch merchants in Mocha, too, indicated that the trade of coffee from the northern ports was substantial throughout the later seventeenth and early eighteenth centuries. Although the Dutch merchants resided solely in Mocha, they were keenly aware of any trade activity that affected the price of coffee at Bayt al-Faqīh, so they eagerly tracked all available information regarding the arrival of merchant vessels in other port cities. In what follows I offer some excerpts from the records of the 1719–20 trade season in order to illustrate the geographic fluidity of the coffee trade and to highlight Mocha's connections to other sites of exchange in the Yemeni coffee trade network.[39]

On August 1, 1719, the English supercargo, a Mr. Albert, returned to Mocha from Jidda, where he had met with no success selling his textiles. He informed the merchants, however, that coffee was selling for a lower price in Jidda than in Bayt al-Faqīh. Two days later the Dutch resident in Mocha, Joan van Leeuwen, wrote to Daniel Hurgronje, the VOC director in Surat, confirming that he had shipped a total of 1,686,321 pounds of coffee, along with aloe, lead, and sapanwood, to India and Batavia on two VOC ships.[40] On August 23 word came from Bayt al-Faqīh that coffee could be obtained for 130 to 136 Spanish riyals per Bayt al-Faqīh *bahar* of 735 pounds. On the same day an English ship left the port for Karwar, Bombay, and Surat with 208,800 pounds of coffee. The day after that an Ostend ship left with 366,966 pounds of coffee.

About a month later, on September 21, 1719, samples of coffee were sent from Bayt al-Faqīh to Mocha for the Dutch to inspect. The Dutch traders, however, heard that the Turks had already bought up all of this more expensive and drier fruit. Further, 600,000 Spanish riyals had arrived in Bayt al-Faqīh from Jidda so that the Turkish merchants could buy new fruit when it became available in December. This large sum would allow the Jidda merchants to purchase more than 3 million pounds of coffee at the highest bracket of the current price. These Turkish shipments of coffee and cash were taking place through the northern ports, not Mocha, where the Dutch merchants were hearing such news secondhand. On November 22 the Dutch heard that 200,000 more Spanish riyals had come to Bayt al-Faqīh from al-Luḥayya to buy coffee for the Turks, but because of the small number of purchasers at the market, coffee was still selling for the low price of

130 Spanish riyals per *bahar* of 735 pounds. At that time the Dutch made a contract with Baniyan merchants to procure 405,000 pounds of coffee.

January of each year heralded the coming of ships from India and the beginning of the new trade season. On January 13, 1720, two VOC ships came into the harbor. Because of their arrival, the price of coffee rose at Bayt al-Faqīh two weeks later. On February 9, the Dutch closed another deal to buy 405,000 pounds of coffee at a higher price than they had paid the previous November. On February 13, a *ghurāb* arrived at Mocha from Kung, on the Persian coast, to buy coffee. Four days later another Persian *ghurāb* arrived for coffee, carrying some dates and silver coins. On February 26, three trankes, presumably from the Persian Gulf, left Mocha to go to al-Ḥudayda to load coffee. On March 11, letters from Bayt al-Faqīh informed the Dutch merchants that coffee was selling for 145 to 150 Spanish riyals per *bahar* of 735 pounds and that Turkish merchants had arrived with another 200,000 Spanish riyals. This sum brought the total Turkish capital amassed at Bayt al-Faqīh to 1 million Spanish riyals over seven months. On May 11, two large trankes, believed to be from Muscat, came in sight of Mocha but sailed past to load coffee in al-Ḥudayda. On June 1, three *ghurābs* arrived from al-Ḥudayda, al-Luḥayya, and Jidda, all carrying coffee beans and heading to Muscat. Two days later another ship came into Mocha from al-Ḥudayda filled with 156,600 pounds of coffee, heading for Muscat. On June 6, a French ship arrived in Mocha with some goods and a large but unspecified quantity of Spanish riyals to buy coffee. On July 11, the Dutch completed the loading of their coffee bales, which amounted to 1,847,880 pounds.

Although the preceding excerpts focus disproportionately on the trade activity of European merchants, they were not the most numerous or most active at the port. In fact only eight European ships called at Mocha in 1720, among seventeen ships from India, four Yemeni-owned vessels that also came from India, numerous ships from the Persian Gulf, and one from Massawa, as well as many smaller, local vessels that went unrecorded. Unfortunately, precise information on the trade figures of the merchants from India, the Persian Gulf, and the African coast are unavailable. Although Mocha was not a unique coffee transshipment point for all merchants, it was the main coffee port for European merchants, as the trade logs demonstrate. The English and French experimented with loading coffee at al-Ḥudayda but maintained their consistent trade establishments in Mocha.[41]

The Jidda merchants would arrive in al-Ḥudayda or al-Luḥayya in fleets and then proceed to the inland market at Bayt al-Faqīh to buy large quantities of coffee with bulk sums of Spanish silver. After their purchases were completed, the bales were brought overland back to al-Ḥudayda or al-Luḥayya, where they were loaded on Red Sea *jalbas* for Jidda. After being unloaded at Jidda, the majority of the bales were redistributed on the northern fleet destined for Suez and eventually Cairo.[42] Raymond noted that this disjunctured system of localized transshipment around the Jidda gap was "illogical . . . and led to serious inconvenience" for the merchants, because commodities were on- and off-loaded multiple times within the space of the Red Sea, requiring considerable labor and associated expenditures.[43] Yet irrespective of these practical inconveniences, the Jidda gap segmented the Red Sea and interrupted the smooth flow of coffee from Yemeni ports to Suez.

The other major purchasers of coffee in the Red Sea, the Persian Gulf merchants, arrived in *ghurābs* and trankes from Muscat, Kung, and Basra and shipped from all three Yemeni ports.[44] Unfortunately, it is impossible to gauge the exact shipping figures for Persian Gulf coffee exports, because documentation is scant for the northern ports. But it is clear that unlike the Europeans, who had to negotiate cautiously for each contract to trade or set up an establishment, the Persian Gulf merchants were flexible in their shipping agendas. For instance, on December 13 and 14, 1727, several trankes from Basra and Muscat called at Mocha's harbor. It took the traders only a couple of days to recognize that their dates were not fetching the highest price, so they quickly left and headed north toward al-Ḥudayda and al-Luḥayya.[45] On other occasions the Dutch remarked on how the oppressive policies of Mocha's governors drove merchants from the Gulf and India away from the port to the two northern alternatives.[46] It appears that Persian Gulf and Indian merchants determined where they would ground their shipping activity among the three Red Sea ports on the basis of local and temporal factors.[47]

Mocha Coffee Myths

Because of its widespread popular association with coffee, many believe that Mocha relied on the trade of coffee for its survival as a port, such that the historian Ashin Das Gupta claimed, "The sole export of Mocha was coffee."[48] In his popular compendium on the global beverage, Alain Stella reiterated, "The temporary fame and fortune of this Yemeni port . . . rested solely on coffee."[49] But in the late seventeenth and early eighteenth centuries coffee was not the major commodity of Mocha, as Brouwer attested to for the earlier Ottoman era. Precious metals, textiles, spices, bulk metals, medicinal products, aromatics, dyestuffs, and resins were also bought and sold at the port. Other bulk items such as dates, sugar, rice, and wax candles were mainstays of the city's economy. Coffee was only one cargo item that left Mocha, most often on European and Persian Gulf ships.

Although popular legends extol Mocha as a global coffee capital, this exaggerated association overshadows the major roles played by the other important yet less famous cities in the Yemeni coffee trade network. The Qāsimīs' establishment of Bayt al-Faqīh as the key coffee emporium of Yemen allowed for the centralization of a littoral commercial zone that included Mocha but also al-Ḥudayda and al-Luḥayya as its major ports. And the coffee networks that extended from Bayt al-Faqīh originated in the highland agricultural areas. A geographic web of coffee movements, migrations, and transactions tied the interior mountain coffee cultivation sites to the cosmopolitan cities of the Yemeni coast as well as to the key ports of the Red Sea and Persian Gulf. Mocha was indeed the preeminent port of the Qāsimī dynasty, but not because of the coffee trade alone.

3 *A Littoral Society in Yemen*

Maritime historians have long struggled over the question of which direction port cities face. In many studies the maritime world is sacrificed for the interior hinterland; in others the prospects of the sea far outweigh the significance of the isolated inland. In light of this conflict, the Indian Ocean historian M. N. Pearson urged that maritime scholars use the notion of a "littoral society," which inherently "includes both land and sea."[1] A littoral society is one that is linked to the maritime world through key ports but extends into the interior territories that are also affected by the shaping forces of the sea, its travelers, and its cargos. The Ḥaḍramawt region in eastern Yemen is a prime example of an extended littoral society. The effects of Indian Ocean trade and travel have tangibly penetrated into its heartland, not simply stopping at coastal nodes. As the anthropologist Engseng Ho described, generations of Ḥaḍramī diasporic families have retained vital connections with relatives in East Africa, India, and Southeast Asia, thereby functioning as "local cosmopolitan" residents of the key inland cities of Tarīm and Say'ūn, far from the open sea.[2] Whereas Ho and other scholars have cast the Ḥaḍramawt in this interregional Indian Ocean framework, the broad influence of maritime economies and cultures in the landed Red Sea region has not received the same attention.

In the case of western Yemen, certainly all of the lowland Tihāma coast, which includes Mocha and stretches along the Red Sea, may be considered a littoral society tied closely to the fortunes of the Red Sea basin. Yet Pearson's concept may be extended even further to trace the influence of this littoral society as it stretched into the core of Qāsimī Yemen, radiating away from Mocha's port. Although the seat of the ruling imam was located in the interior highlands, a journey of at least ten days from the southern Red Sea coast, historians of early modern Yemen agree that the profits of the Mocha trade had a major economic effect on the entire southwestern Arabian Peninsula.[3] Goods, capital, and ideas entered by sea through the port of Mocha and were brought into the interior by the traveling merchants and Qāsimī administrators who frequently traversed the roads linking Mocha to the centers of activity in the Yemeni highlands. Indeed, these paths between coast and capital represent the channels of elite mobility that were central to the functional integrity of the Qāsimī domain. Ashin Das Gupta stressed that the nexus of power in eighteenth-century Yemen "stretched from the quays at Mocha to the palace at Sana."[4]

In this chapter I look at the administrative structure of Qāsimī Yemen as that of an extended littoral society, with a focus on the governance of its major port, Mocha. The biographies and patronage histories of three of Mocha's long-seated governors reveal the tight social and economic fabric that linked the central highlands to the coastal port society and allowed for the relative internationalization of the Qāsimī dynasty, which is often cast as an inaccessible and isolated Shīʿī imamate, far from contact in the mountains of Yemen. The port's significant profits stimulated the construction and renovation of buildings, an effect that penetrated throughout Yemen, bringing the maritime sphere into the most inaccessible mountain enclaves. Together, the administrative structure, flows of revenue, and the tangible products of architectural and cultural sponsorship provide a clear understanding of the ways in which agendas of Yemeni authority and Indian Ocean profit intersected during the era of Qāsimī rule.

The Imam

Zaydism differs from Imāmī Shīʿī Islam in its concepts of leadership and authority. Zaydīs, unlike Ismāʿīlīs and Twelvers—the largest Shīʿī subdivision—do not believe their imams are infallible, nor do they insist on an uninterrupted succession of hereditary imams. Rather, their focus is directed to the preeminence of a righteous imam. In principle, anyone may become imam who is of age, is male, is pious, and has moral and physical integrity and courage. He must also be a member of the family of the Prophet (a *sayyid*), descended through Fāṭima and ʿAlī, have knowledge in religious matters, be a *mujtahid* (someone who is capable of independent legal reasoning), and have the military prowess to defend the territory of Islam. The community of scholars and notables must accept the imam's *daʿwa*, or summons to the imamate.

The image of the ideal Zaydī imam, then, encompasses scholarship, might, erudition, lineage, and community approval. As Bernard Haykel outlined, however, Qāsimī Yemen witnessed a growing departure from this standard in the late seventeenth century. Whereas the first century of Qāsimī imams upheld the model, with upstanding scholarly and pious figures such as al-Muʾayyad Muḥammad b. al-Qāsim and al-Mutawakkil Ismāʿīl b. al-Qāsim, the late-seventeenth-century Ṣāḥib al-Mawāhib, who gained his position through military might, was less suited for the role, behaving more like a king than an ideal imam.[5] Indeed, from the rule of Ṣāḥib al-Mawāhib's successor, al-Mutawakkil Qāsim, in 1718, the imamate became a dynastic state in which the strongest son of the imam inherited the right to rule from his father regardless of qualification.

The Wazir

By the mid-seventeenth century a rigid bureaucratic structure was instituted in Yemen, with a complex hierarchy of administrators to oversee the expanded Qāsimī territory.[6] The wazirs, or ministers, stood at the top of this chain of command, directly under the imam. Unsurprisingly, the Qāsimī structure of governance echoed the Ottoman model, with a chief wazir at the head, under whom served several lower ministers who were in charge of particular sectors. Individual provinces were ceded to capable wazirs, who were responsible for collecting taxes. The allocation of territory was not fixed but rather was determined for each wazir as he was assigned. Some wazirs were given large areas, such as the lowland Tihāma stretch and the entirety of the verdant agricultural region of Rayma. Others might be given the lesser responsibility of a single port or a smaller province. Tribal affairs, *waqfs* (pious endowments), and public works were also parceled out to selected wazirs.[7] A study of the wazirs who served under Imam al-Manṣūr ʿAlī in the second half of the eighteenth century by the historian of Yemen Husayn al-ʿAmri revealed a cross section of men that included several *sayyids*, *faqīhs* (learned persons), a *qāḍī* (Muslim judge), and a Hamdānī shaykh. The appointment of *sayyid* elites and learned religious figures is unsurprising, but few tribal leaders were selected to serve in these high ministerial positions.[8]

The wazir served at the will of the imam, so the position was tenuous. Any misstep could lead to direct dismissal and even the confiscation of personal property, so it was important always to maintain the imam's favor. Similarly, the governor of Mocha, far from the capital, needed to maintain strong ties with the wazir at court, in order to stay on good terms with the imam. This was particularly important considering that the imam's principal wazir, rather than the imam himself, usually oversaw affairs at Mocha.[9] Some administrators of Mocha were elevated to the post of wazir after their tenure at the port. The governorship of Mocha served as a professional stepping stone for those with larger administrative aspirations.

Maritime Administration

The imam directly assigned a number of important posts within the city, such as Mocha's governor, whom I discuss at length later, and the *amīr al-baḥr*, the overseer of the port. The *amīr al-baḥr* played a major role as the keeper of maritime activities, executing the governor's commands regarding the embarkation and disembarkation of goods and crew members.[10] As new ships arrived in the harbor, he greeted the *nākhūdha*, the ship's captain and highest-ranking person on the vessel, who held responsibility for all ship functions at sea and in port. The *amīr al-baḥr* cleared each ship for departure after assuring that the appropriate tolls and duties had been paid and all accounts were settled.

As the harbor master, the *amīr al-baḥr* participated in all activities related to the trade, outside the port as well as inside, and was often called upon to mediate commercial disputes in the city.[11] That he played a key role in urban affairs is demonstrated by the events of December 1727, when Muḥammad b. Isḥāq, who had declared himself imam, countering the *daʿwa* of Imam al-Manṣūr Ḥusayn, gained control of Mocha. One of his first acts was to appoint a trusted official, Sayyid Qāsim Amīr al-Dīn, as governor of Mocha on December 9, 1727. As another matter of immediate importance, he followed up three days later with the appointment of a new *amīr al-baḥr*, who immediately took his post. The swiftness of his appointments underlines their importance, particularly considering that Muḥammad b. Isḥāq was orchestrating these administrative changes far from the coast, in the mountain fortress of Ẓafār Dhī Bīn, where he was based at the time.[12]

The scribes, inspectors, and weighers at the customs house of the port, whose positions were directly linked to the collection of customs duties, were also assigned from the highland capital. These junior positions held potential for further promotion, as is evidenced by ʿAlī b. Yaḥyā al-Shāmī al-Ḥasanī al-Ṣanʿānī, who spent twelve years as a scribe at the port of al-Luḥayya in the mid-eighteenth century and was then promoted to the post of scribe at Mocha.[13] After four years of service to Imam al-Mahdī ʿAbbās in this post, he was again promoted, this time to a position of greater importance, as wazir overseeing Wuṣāb, Ḥays, and al-Rūs. Being a scribe in the customs house could also have negative ramifications, as the situation of ʿAbd Allāh Ḥajjāj shows.[14] During the early eighteenth century the European merchants at Mocha often called upon Ḥajjāj to draft letters in Arabic to the imam, usually expressing complaints about the misconduct of local officials. In 1731 the governor of Mocha, Aḥmad Khazindār, imprisoned and then temporarily banned Ḥajjāj from the city in order to stop the steady stream of incriminating letters from reaching Sanaa.

The imam chose men for other administrative and military positions in Mocha, such as the *naqīb*, captain of the al-Shādhilī gate, who monitored the major eastern entrance to the city.[15] This strategic post was important because all caravans coming from the highlands and Bayt al-Faqīh were levied tolls there, and all outgoing merchandise was checked as it headed toward Sanaa. The head *ṣarrāf*, or money exchanger, tended to all the major financial transactions in the city and was often a favored official who held close ties to the imam's court. An example is Ḥasan Ḥasūsā in the mid-eighteenth century, who was later appointed governor of Zabid in 1738 and then served as chamberlain under Imam al-Mahdī ʿAbbās.[16] Commercial roles and individual merchants are discussed fully in the next chapter, but it is important to note that the imam's commercial transactions in Mocha were conducted by his *wakīl*, who oversaw royal activity while carrying on his own trade.[17] Although they were not associated with the long-distance wholesale trade, the captain of the soldiers, who was the highest-ranked military official, and the *muḥtasib*, the inspector of the bazaar, also received their appointments directly from the imam's court.[18]

The Qāḍī and the Religious Scholars of Mocha

The imam appointed the chief *qāḍī*, or judge, of Mocha, who attended to all legal disputes among Muslims in the city.[19] Like the other appointees, many judges were highlanders, such as ʿAlī ʿAbd Allāh al-Tihāmī al-Ḥabūrī, whom Imam al-Mutawakkil Qāsim appointed to Mocha as *qāḍī* from Ḥabūr, the mountain enclave of Zaydī teaching.[20] He died in Mocha in 1137/1725. The *qāḍī*, however, rarely played a role in the trade and only occasionally intervened in issues concerning the merchant community, sometimes serving as a witness in the negotiation of written contracts. In 1737, when the French sailed into the port in three warships to demand retribution for the governor and *ṣarrāf*'s misappropriation of duties on their goods, they specifically requested that the *qāḍī* participate in settling the treaty with the Mocha government, a testament to his impartiality.

Although they were not chosen by the highland administration, a number of religious scholars relocated to Mocha to participate in its religious life and education. In particular, scholars from the Mizjājī family of Zabid, who were well known for their instruction of *ḥadīth* and their affiliation with the Naqshbandi Sufi order, came to teach in the city.[21] Shaykh ʿAbd Allāh b. ʿAbd al-Bāqī al-Mizjājī, for instance, taught in Mocha in the late seventeenth century. Sayyid Ḥusayn b. Zayd Jaḥḥāf (b. 1054/1644–45) was one of his students in 1078/1667–68, during the period when his father was governor of the city.[22] After studying with al-Mizjājī in Mocha, Ḥusayn Jaḥḥāf went to Zabid to continue his religious training, a choice that represented a stark break from his Zaydī roots. Although he traveled briefly to Sanaa, Ḥusayn Jaḥḥāf eventually returned to Zabid, where he stayed until his death in 1137/1724–25. The younger Jaḥḥāf's tutelage is a classic example of the way in which commercial and administrative ties with the south allowed for the Sunnification of the Zaydī elite, which Haykel described as an important transformative attribute of the period.[23] Although the teachers of the Mizjājī family were of the Ḥanafī order rather than the more common Shāfiʿī tradition, in Mocha they served as the catalysts by which some Yemeni highlander administrators and their families became conversant in Sunnī texts and teachings in the years after the first Ottoman occupation. Another prominent figure, Ṣadīq b. ʿAlī al-Mizjājī, became well known outside the Tihāma after having lived and taught in Mocha in the 1780s. In 1203/1787–88 he moved to Sanaa, where he granted the famous jurist Muḥammad al-Shawkānī an *ijāza*, or license.[24] He lived out the last years of his life in both Zabid and Sanaa and died in 1209/1794–95.

The Favored Post

Al-ʿAmri remarked that the governor of Mocha "was always a prominent and capable person" who filled the important role of furnishing the customs duties and tolls from the trade for the imam's treasury.[25] Historically, the importance of port revenue in Yemen cannot be underestimated. Particularly during the Qāsimī imamate, revenue from the ports supported much of the imam's military activity in the highlands and contributed to the maintenance of political stability over the entire region. The twentieth-century historian and biographer Muḥammad Zabāra called the region of Mocha in the late seventeenth century "absolutely the greatest district of all of Yemen," and so it remained for many decades to follow.[26] The post of governor—*wāli* or *ʿāmil*—was the highest appointment in the city and one of the most important posts that the imam could offer to a distinguished and accomplished official.[27]

Mocha's governor held a cherished position not only because of its high status but also because of the profits gained from direct involvement with the trade. Writing in the early nineteenth century, Viscount George Valentia colorfully described the perquisites of the governor's position: "The government of Mocha is the best in the gift of the Imaum. . . . They say, that when a Dola [governor] is appointed, he weighs nothing; that on going out of the gates of Sana he weighs a frasel; that on arriving at his government, he weighs two and goes on growing heavier and heavier during his stay."[28]

This official participation in the trade, with the governor acting as the city's head merchant, is documented from the late seventeenth century and continued throughout Mocha's trading history. Although the financial benefits of the governorship made the post that much more desirable, it caused the merchants in the city to complain of wayward and unjust official trade policies.[29] That the conflicting responsibilities of the position could compromise the integrity of its holder is clear. Regardless, in Mocha, as in other Indian Ocean port cities such as Surat, commercial involvement and official concessions came to define the role of the coastal governor.[30] Any instability in the highlands, however, rippled down to the lowlands, and the holders of these official posts enjoyed little job security. Mocha's governor could be summoned at a moment's notice by a messenger from the highlands and replaced according to the imam's whim. In these cases, the second in charge, who aided the governor, took the reins of power.[31] The records show that governors' appointments, removals, and reappointments to the position were dynamic and unstable during the period of Qāsimī rule.

The biographies of three of the city's major powerbrokers—all governors of Mocha from the mid-seventeenth through the mid-eighteenth century—represent the political and geographic mobility of the elites in this century and exemplify the possibilities of promotion and demotion in the Qāsimī administration. The remains of their architectural and cultural patronage, although difficult to reconstruct, serve as the permanent imprints of their commercial and personal commitments throughout Qāsimī Yemen. The products of their patronage mark the flow of revenue from the port throughout the Qāsimī realm in a tangible fashion. Interest in reconstructing the agendas of architectural, artistic, and cultural patronage of local officials stems from a growing body of work on sub-imperial patronage as a rich area of research that reveals the interconnected dynamics of regional politics and imperial order, as well as the texture of the personal relationships between emperors and their agents.[32]

In art and architectural history, other formats have superseded biography as instrumental types of narratives, but here I use the biographical structure in order to reveal a transparent relationship with the sources. Islamic historiography privileges the lives of significant pious and erudite men (and occasionally women), rather than events per se, as a fundamental way to record history. I draw primarily on this biographical tradition, although a complete examination of sub-dynastic movement and the life histories of these officials would have been impossible without the details of everyday life provided by the European merchants of Mocha. Their records add depth and character to the information available in the Arabic biographical accounts and chronicles, which often focus on central dynastic figures from the formal perspective of highland official history.

Sayyid Zayd b. ʿAlī Jaḥḥāf

At the height of Qāsimī expansion, Imam al-Mutawakkil Ismāʿīl bestowed the great honor of the Mocha governorship upon his favored advisor, Sayyid Zayd b. ʿAlī Jaḥḥāf, who was born in the highland town of Ḥabūr, in the vicinity of Jabal Shahāra. Members of the Jaḥḥāf family were famous religious scholars and the most notable residents of the *hijra*, or protected enclave, of Ḥabūr. They were descended from a tenth-century imam named al-Manṣūr billāh Qāsim b. ʿAlī al-ʿIyānī. Imam al-Mutawakkil Ismāʿīl's mother was from the Jaḥḥāf line, so al-Mutawakkil's ties to the Jaḥḥāf clan were closely maintained through family relations.[33] Sayyid Zayd Jaḥḥāf's reputation was widespread outside Yemen during his time, as is indicated by the fact that the Damascene scholar Muḥammad Amīn al-Muḥibbī mentioned him in his extensive seventeenth-century compendium *Khulāṣat al-athar* and included his verses in the anthology of poetry *Nafḥāt Rayḥāna*.[34]

Jaḥḥāf was one of the elites of the age, and his position in Mocha increased not only his status and fame but also his riches. He was assigned to Mocha in 1066/1655–56 and officially discharged from the port in 1080/1669–70 or 1081/1670–71, when Sayyid Ḥasan b. al-Muṭahhar al-Jurmūzī, a notable from another important *sayyid* family, replaced him.[35] Jaḥḥāf is an important figure whose biography and architectural patronage exemplify the mobility and resources provided by the Mocha governorship.

Aside from Jaḥḥāf's firsthand role in observing and monitoring the trade, he served as the imam's representative to greet and welcome passing notables, many of whom stopped at Mocha on their way to perform the pilgrimage. For instance, in 1661 Bari Sahiba, the dowager queen of Bijapur, arrived at the port on a Dutch ship accompanied by an impressive retinue.[36] According to the historian ʿAbd Allāh al-Wazīr, she presented the governor with a great gift.[37] Other notable visitors came from more distant and less predictable places. The Uzbek sultan from Kashgar, on the Silk Road, for example, arrived in Mocha en route to the Holy Cities in 1079/1668–69 with an imposing number of retainers and an army of 500 soldiers.[38] As governor of Mocha, Jaḥḥāf had to deal with the military and defensive aspects of port life, a difficult task for this land-based overlord who possessed no naval fleet. In the 1660s a pirate named Hubert Hugo, who may have been French but often flew English colors, engaged in exploits in the Red Sea that were recorded as part of maritime folklore around the Indian Ocean, in both European and Arabic accounts.[39] Jaḥḥāf was unsuccessful in containing Hugo and suffered great losses at his hands. In the years 1079/1668–69 and 1080/1669–70, Omani pirates who were plundering the Red Sea and Arabian Sea coastlines arrived in Mocha's harbor, but Jaḥḥāf lacked the sea power to fight these rovers as well.[40]

Jaḥḥāf used the riches from his post to contribute to the sweep of al-Mutawakkil's empire, not just through his participation and encouragement of the trade but also by restoring pious structures, contributing to public works, and marking the landscape with luxurious residences. His public projects, which included the digging of new wells and the paving of steps on footpaths, were scattered throughout the Qāsimī highlands, in Ḥabūr, Rayma, Ḍūrān (the seat of the imamate at the time), and the Tihāma.[41] These sites were places where Jaḥḥāf himself lived and was posted as an official, along the coast as well as in the highlands. His extensive program of patronage must be situated within his personal administrative trajectory, because his good fortune and economic success enabled his capacity to build. His sites of patronage represent the extent to which the Indian Ocean trade and its bounty penetrated the interior of Yemen, from the coastal realm to the most far-flung mountain towns of the southern Arabian Peninsula.

While serving as governor of Mocha, Jaḥḥāf also maintained intermittent residence in Sanaa and the nearby garden suburb of al-Rawḍa in order to sustain strong connections with the imam and other notables in the highlands. The direct correlation between his building in the center of the imamate and his financial opportunities in Mocha was noted vividly by the early eighteenth-century historian Abū Ṭālib:

> In the year 1068/1657–58, Sayyid Zayd Jaḥḥāf, governor of Mocha, moved to Sanaa. He liked settling there and brought his family. Aḥmad b. Ḥasan [the imam's nephew, later to become Imam al-Mahdī] was there and treated him with great hospitality and he bestowed his favor upon him. The above-mentioned *sayyid* prospered there and in al-Rawḍa. He [Jaḥḥāf] had property in Wādi Ẓahr, which had a value of 50,000 that he obtained from the customs house at Mocha. He built a house in al-Rawḍa that was known for its perfect construction. Jealousy took hold of some of the men of letters and they wrote a poem that deeply affected him and led him to give the house to the imam.[42]

Jaḥḥāf's great house in al-Rawḍa was described hyperbolically as reaching a width and height of a *farsakh*—several kilometers. The poem written by his fellow notables scorned its size and opulence, saying:

> It was built by the money of Muslims.
> Bestowed by those who donated.
> Don't you see its history?
> It is the house of Mocha's returns.[43]

The onlookers criticized Jaḥḥāf for building the house in al-Rawḍa using the customs duty and toll revenue he had obtained from the port. As a *sayyid*, he was especially blameworthy for misappropriating these funds and using them in such a blatantly extravagant and self-serving fashion. The structure, which no longer stands, met an unfortunate fate. Abū Ṭālib continued: "It was the strangest of coincidences and omens that the house was destroyed because of this [controversy], and its foundations collapsed. Five years passed before anyone lived there. It had no inhabitants and no household."[44]

Clearly, the chronicler Abū Ṭālib and the angry notables perceived a direct relationship between this building in the highlands and the owner's profits in faraway Mocha. The extravagant house may be seen as a transactional monument marked by the source of its owner's riches, Mocha's treasury.[45] Generally, prominent houses in Yemen may be easily identified by the names of their inhabitants, and monumental buildings may be known through their patrons' legacies, often immortalized in prominently placed inscriptions. In this case the source of the funds for the house's construction was also conspicuous on its façade. There is no evidence that the building bore any tangible visual connection to Mocha, such as the distinctive woodwork or plaster ornamentation of Red Sea–style buildings. It appears that the house conformed to the conventions of domestic architecture in highland al-Rawḍa, resembling the other mud-brick tower houses that surrounded it except in its size and grandeur. Regardless, contemporary onlookers acknowledged it as a product of the Mocha trade and associated it with the governor's maritime profits.

As the account tells, Jaḥḥāf never lived in this luxurious house in al-Rawḍa, nor was he ever to return to reside in Ḥabūr, the remote mountaintop village of his birth. But although he continued to live in Mocha, in the heartland of the empire at Sanaa and another house in al-Rawḍa, and at Ḍūrān, the seat of the imamate, he funded a substantial program of building in his hometown, which was accessible from Sanaa only by a long journey through tortuous mountain passes. There he built another great house and ordered the excavation of a massive public *birka*, or cistern, in front, which was large enough to serve the whole community after the other cisterns in the city dried up.[46] Jaḥḥāf also engaged in a major patronage project, the rebuilding and expansion of the Great Mosque of Ḥabūr, an undertaking completed in 1072/1661–62, during his tenure as governor of Mocha and following the scandal over the house in al-Rawḍa. Although this project was not distinctly noted as related to his Mocha riches, only great wealth would have afforded him the 33,000 riyals reputedly spent on the project. Perhaps the previous scandal prompted him to use his new wealth for a pious purpose rather than to expand his private holdings.

Unfortunately, a contemporary study of the mosque reveals only fragments of Jaḥḥāf's patronage. Egyptian antiroyalist forces bombed the mosque from the air in 1385/1965–66, almost completely destroying it in the mistaken belief that Imam Badr was hiding there. A decade later, in 1394/1974–75, the Saudi king Fayṣal supported its rebuilding to attain its present shape, so a late-twentieth-century mosque (fig. 3.1) stands in place of Jaḥḥāf's seventeenth-century pious contribution.[47] The general layout of the contemporary mosque complex, however, faithfully matches the detailed description of Jaḥḥāf's restoration provided in his biographical entry. A few surviving features of the older building also demonstrate that the original plan of the northeastern part of the mosque was maintained during the twentieth-century restoration. A partial segment of the exterior corner displays seventeenth-century plaster relief carving and a small part of the sawtooth band that encircled the original mosque. Furthermore, the size restrictions of the site would have limited any major variations on the original plan.

As it stands today, the prayer hall of the mosque is a large, flat-roofed, hypostyle hall. The biographer and historian Zabāra recalled that Jaḥḥāf was responsible for the expansion of this hall by sixty columns, so his contribution was a great enlargement of the original space.[48] He also doubled the number of carpets and other interior necessities. But the present external accessory facilities located to the east of the mosque complex represent Jaḥḥāf's main contribution. His biographical entry says, "He built the eastern and western courtyards, the great *birka*, about twenty-two ablution stations, and multiple residences for the students."[49] Today, two broad lateral courtyards still flank the building. Entry to the mosque can be made only from those two sides, because the closed *qibla* façade, which marks the direction toward Mecca, faces the village, and the other side of the mosque abuts a sharp cliff. The cistern, the ablution booths, and the residences of the *madrasa* (fig. 3.2) stand in the eastern area.

The most striking feature of the eastern part of the complex is the large rectangular cistern, or *birka* (fig. 3.3), with its balanced, sloped staircase descending from the western side. A smaller flight of stairs descends from the northwestern corner. The cistern is majestically placed at the edge of a cliff, with dramatic views that plunge hundreds of meters down to the bottom of Ḥabūr's slope. Large cisterns are not unique in Yemen, particularly at such high altitudes, where rainwater and runoff are vital resources to be collected and preserved. But many mountain cisterns are amorphous in form, following the natural topography of the site, rather than strictly rectilinear like this one. And few mosque cisterns are as large in relation to

FIG. 3.1 Eastern façade of the Great Mosque, Ḥabūr, 2002.

FIG. 3.2 Ablution stations at the Great Mosque, Ḥabūr, 2002.

their entire built complexes. The irregular semicircular cistern at the nearby Great Mosque of Shahāra (fig. 3.4) is a good example of the free-form shape and more modest scale one might expect.

The Ḥabūr cistern, added by Jaḥḥāf, makes clear visual reference to the most significant Qāsimī structure of the time, the mosque complex of Ḥasan in Ḍūrān. The Mosque of Ḥasan was begun by Ḥasan b. Imam al-Manṣūr Qāsim in 1048/1638, and most of its structural elements were completed before he died the next year.[50] Although Ḥasan never became imam, he gained fame for his successes in the battle to oust the Ottomans. It was not Ḥasan who made the mosque famous, however, but his brother Imam al-Mutawakkil Ismāʿīl, who took over the fortress of Ḍūrān as the seat of his rule when he ascended to the imamate in 1644. It was al-Mutawakkil who appointed Jaḥḥāf governor of Mocha and later elevated him to the rank of wazir.

The mosque complex in Ḍūrān (fig. 3.5) stands in ruins today on a deserted mountaintop that was abandoned after an earthquake razed the entire village in 1982. The outlines of the foundation as well as historical photographs provide evidence for the previous shape of the mosque and its extensive facilities. In plan the mosque was almost an exact replica of the Great Mosque at Ṣaʿda, the quintessential architectural emblem of Zaydī preeminence in Yemen, with a wide, shallow prayer hall to the south and a U-shaped northern extension around the open-air courtyard. The *madrasa* and the freestanding tomb chamber of Ḥasan stood to the west of the mosque.[51] To the south of the mosque one finds an elaborate system of water collection and distribution for ablutions. Two *birkas* sit at the centerpiece of this complex arrangement of open-air elements. The western *birka* is the smaller of the two and is surrounded by ablution stations with high walls. A wide slope of stairs approaches the large, rectilinear eastern *birka* (fig. 3.6)—which resembles Jaḥḥāf's cistern at Ḥabūr—on its northern side. The size of the eastern *birka* is impressive, 24 by 18 meters and 6 meters deep, larger than its counterpart in Ḥabūr but sharing the latter's prominent relationship to the larger complex.

Although the two mosque complexes differ in dimensions and layout, the two large *birkas* clearly link them by the distinctiveness of their shapes, their visual and spatial distinction within their respective complexes, and their broad, sweeping flights of steps. By building a monumental cistern adjacent to his mosque in Ḥabūr, Jaḥḥāf made a direct architectural statement that solidly located his interests within the realm of the empire. Using

FIG. 3.3 The *birka*, or cistern, at the Great Mosque, Ḥabūr, 2002.

FIG. 3.4 The *birka*, or cistern, at the Great Mosque, Shahāra, 2002.

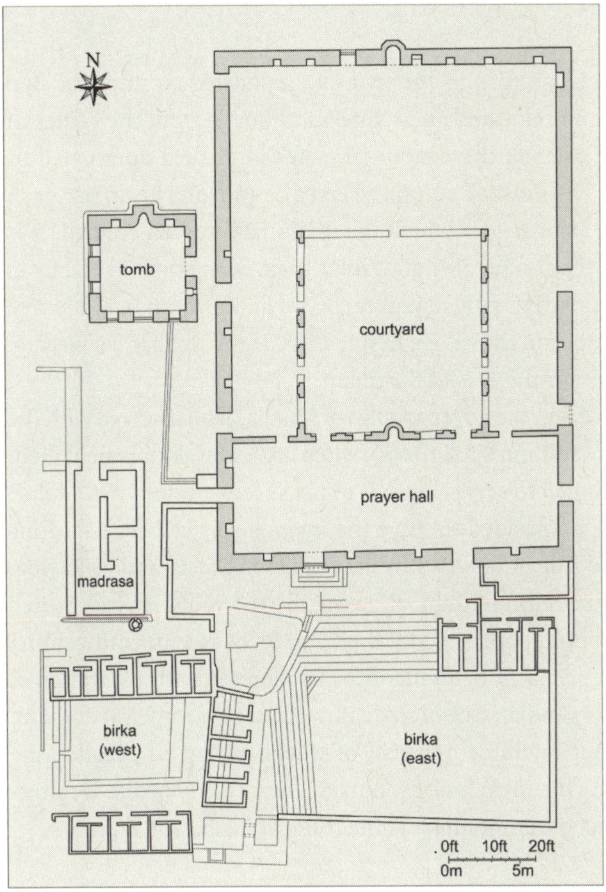

FIG. 3.5 Reconstructed plan of the Mosque of Ḥasan, Ḍūrān.

FIG. 3.6 Ruins of the eastern *birka*, or cistern, Mosque of Ḥasan, Ḍūrān, 2000.

the imam's mosque complex as the icon, he replicated an imperial sign in his hometown and relocated an architectural image from the center of the empire to one of its farthest mountain sites in an area dominated by the Ḥāshid tribes. The mosque complex served to consolidate an image of territorial unity in an area over which the imam had uneven control. It is important to note that Imam al-Mutawakkil spent some time in Ḥabūr in 1059/1649–50 after marrying the daughter of Sayyid al-Ḥasan b. al-Ḥusayn Jaḥḥāf, and he returned to the village frequently.[52] Hence Jaḥḥāf's construction was also meant for the eyes of the imam.

After formally leaving the governorship of Mocha, Jaḥḥāf stayed with the imam in Ḍūrān as wazir until 1087/1676, when al-Mutawakkil Ismāʿīl died. Afterward he continued to serve as wazir to his successor, Imam al-Mahdī Aḥmad. Eventually he decided to leave the imam's service because of his age.[53] He spent the rest of his days in his homes in Sanaa and al-Rawḍa, where he died on the tenth of Rabīʿ al-awwal in 1108/1696. He was buried in Sanaa.[54] His building patronage in diverse parts of seventeenth-century Qāsimī Yemen, but primarily in highland areas, represents the saturation of wealth from Mocha's Indian Ocean trade throughout the imperial domain. Yet Jaḥḥāf never built anything in the city of Mocha during his decade-long tenure as governor. One must look far outside the city to view the architectural products of his governorship and the fruits of his personal profits.

Shaykh Ṣāliḥ b. ʿAlī al-Ḥuraybī

Shaykh Ṣāliḥ b. ʿAlī al-Ḥuraybī (d. 1135/1723) played a major role in Yemeni administration as a wazir and as governor of Mocha in the early eighteenth century.[55] Unlike Jaḥḥāf, who came from a notable family of Zaydī *sayyids*, religious scholars, and imams, al-Ḥuraybī, who was from the region of al-Ḥujariyya, south of Taʿizz, boasted no erudition, scholarship, or elite pedigree. He forged ties with al-Mahdī Muḥammad in the early years when he declared himself imam in the fortress of al-Manṣūra in al-Ḥujariyya after the death of Imam al-Muʾayyad Muḥammad b. al-Mutawakkil.[56] In 1097/1686 he helped al-Mahdī successfully defend the fortress from the forces of his enemies and thus earned al-Mahdī's high regard.[57] Al-Ḥuraybī held his position as wazir over the Tihāma and the ports from 1109/1697–98 until the imam's death in 1130/1718.[58] He continued as a wazir under the next imam, al-Mutawakkil Qāsim. From as early as 1702 until around 1712 he held his advisory position from the lucrative seat of Mocha, where he served as both wazir and governor and resided with his family.[59] Later, in 1719, he used the inland Tihāmī entrepôt of Bayt al-Faqīh as his base.

Both Yemeni chronicles and European trade records from Mocha detail al-Ḥuraybī's career vividly, particularly for the years he was in residence in Mocha, from 1702 to 1712, during the rule of Imam al-Mahdī.[60] That the scope of al-Ḥuraybī's influence as a wazir was bolstered by his Mocha governorship is indicated by the French captain La Merveille, who in 1709 noted, "This governor hath under him seven other governors or lieutenants in several parts of the country: he is absolute, extremely rich, and trafficks much himself: he pays to the King of Yemen thirty thousand piasters, which he levies on the people."[61] The Indian Ocean historian Ashin Das Gupta believed that al-Ḥuraybī was the first of Mocha's governors to become actively involved in the trade, a pattern that continued after his departure.[62] For example, in the trade season of 1705–6 al-Ḥuraybī was an avid purchaser of Dutch goods. Through his dispenser, Shaykh Sālim, he made bids on Dutch iron, steel, cinnamon, and textiles such as chintz, cotton, and canvas.[63]

It appears that he was purchasing these goods to be resold and shipped within the Red Sea on his *ghurāb*. Although many *ghurābs* had the capacity to travel across the open sea to the Persian Gulf and India, al-Ḥuraybī used his to transport Indian Ocean goods to other Red Sea ports.[64] He usually sent Indian textiles to Jidda on this ship, but in 1708 he loaded it with tin, pepper, steel, copper, zinc, gum benjamin, sandalwood, and turmeric and sent it to Massawa on the African coast of the Red Sea, in modern Eritrea. In the spring of the next year his *ghurāb* (perhaps the same one that had left for Massawa) returned from Jidda.[65] At that time he was also in a position to increase his shipping activity. When French traders tried to sell *Le Vainceur*, a Dutch ship they had captured on their journey to the Arabian Peninsula, al-Ḥuraybī came in with a bid, much to the anger of the resident Dutch merchants in Mocha, who demanded that the ship be returned to their ownership.[66]

Like Jaḥḥāf's, al-Ḥuraybī's job involved public relations and diplomacy. In June 1701 he greeted an ambassador from Persia, called by the Dutch Mirza Chalardin, who docked in Mocha to visit Ṣāḥib al-Mawāhib's court.[67] In 1704 Aurangzeb's formal pilgrimage ship stopped by the port with an elite religious scholar named Nūr al-Ḥaqq, and in 1709 the new Ottoman pasha of Jidda traveled through the port.[68] An unnamed *sharīf* from Mecca stayed in Mocha for three months in 1708–9 with a retinue of twenty horsemen and a healthy stipend paid by the imam.[69] European merchants were in constant communication with al-Ḥuraybī, although they were not treated with the same regard as the Muslim notables. The Dutch, English, and French chief factors visited the governor every few days, sometimes simply to converse and socialize and at other times to voice complaints, problems, and requests. In 1706 the governor even invited the Dutch VOC residents to celebrate ʿĪd al-Fiṭr at his palace.[70] As a merchant and port administrator, al-Ḥuraybī was clearly conversant with maritime practices and could communicate in Persian, a lingua franca of the Indian Ocean.[71]

All accounts of al-Ḥuraybī, both Arab and European, highlight his greed and his unscrupulous actions as governor of Mocha. Without the praises of piety and erudition that usually accompany biographical accounts, Zabāra wrote that al-Ḥuraybī was "skillful, clever, and changing of heart" and that he attained "a leading position and great worldly fortune."[72] La Merveille wrote that he was "very fond of a gainful trade."[73] The Dutch added harsher words, calling him "a second Caligula" and highlighting his miserliness.[74] Many incidents incited the imam's suspicion of al-Ḥuraybī's opportunism, and most of them involved his closest associate, Muḥsin b. ʿAlī al-Ḥubayshī (d. 1737), who also served as a wazir to Imam Ṣāḥib al-Mawāhib and his successor, al-Mutawakkil.[75] While al-Ḥuraybī spent a great deal of time in Mocha and other cities in the Tihāma, al-Ḥubayshī resided in Ibb, his hometown, at the imam's court, and in the nearby city of Dhamār, where he had a house. Al-Ḥubayshī served as a highland intermediary to the imam and court politics while al-Ḥuraybī managed the dynamics of the trade from the lucrative post at Mocha.

Their joint exploits during the early years of the eighteenth century were numerous, and the historians did not shy away from blaming the illustrious pair for profit-making schemes and political machinations. In 1112/1700–1701, for instance, the chronicler Abū Ṭālib, one of al-Ḥuraybī's most prominent detractors, scorned him for convincing the imam to banish the innocent Niʿamat Allāh al-Lāhūrī from Yemen to India and later destroying the exile's house in Taʿizz.[76] When the poet Aḥmad b. Aḥmad al-Ānisī died imprisoned in Zaylaʿ in 1115/1703–4, Abū Ṭālib again blamed his fate on al-Ḥuraybī, claiming that the governor had caused him great harm. He vividly described how the poet was found dead with his lips and ears eaten away by a mouse.[77] Al-Ḥubayshī schemed to turn the imam against his own son Muḥsin, leading to his imprisonment in 1116/1704–5.[78] Muḥsin b. al-Mahdī died in prison in Dhamār the next year.[79]

Imam al-Mahdī became aware of al-Ḥuraybī and al-Ḥubayshī's dealings around 1709.[80] He had al-Ḥubayshī's houses in Ibb searched, and valuable textiles, costly weapons, precious gems, secret letters, presents meant for the imam from abroad, and a great deal of money were found hoarded within.[81] Clearly, the foreign gifts that bore imperial stamps had been intercepted by al-Ḥuraybī in Mocha and then directed for safekeeping to al-Ḥubayshī, rather than to the intended recipient, the imam. As a result of these incriminating findings, al-Ḥubayshī was sent to al-Mawāhib, to be kept under the imam's watchful eye.

Al-Ḥubayshī's betrayal sparked the imam's concerns regarding al-Ḥuraybī as well.[82] Soon after al-Ḥubayshī's house was searched, the imam sent a servant named Salmān to investigate al-Ḥuraybī's dealings in Mocha firsthand.[83] Salmān arrived in Mocha on July 24, 1709, and ordered that al-Ḥuraybī return to the court to report to the imam. Al-Ḥuraybī stalled Salmān with the excuse that there were too many boats in the harbor and he could not leave until they all departed, but he invited Salmān to stay at the port for as long as he wished. Two days later al-Ḥuraybī sent the imam a letter coyly apologizing for his delay, along with an escort of thirty camels carrying gifts worth 40,000 Spanish riyals, gold and silver textiles, and silks from Persia and India. A week later the imam sent 200 more soldiers to Mocha to escort the governor and some of his cohorts to the court. Again al-Ḥuraybī used the ships in the harbor as an excuse and prepared gifts for the messengers to try to win them over. A month later, when the Dutch merchants left the port, al-Ḥuraybī still had not budged from Mocha.[84] He did go up to the court eventually, bringing with him copious treasures and an ample amount of money. When he got there he gave a long explanation regarding his actions and apparently doled out enough gifts for the commotion to die down.

In the fall of 1711, when the French docked at Mocha, al-Ḥuraybī was absent but was represented by his brother ʿAmr at the port. The doctor of the French company found the former governor at the imam's court in al-Mawāhib when he went up to cure the imam of an ear infection. The Dutch suggested that the imam had brought al-Ḥuraybī back to the highlands to curtail his power and keep him under close supervision, rather than as a boost to offer him more responsibility. But al-Ḥuraybī was able to rebound into a position of power when he ingratiated himself with the imam's nephew, Qāsim b. Ḥusayn, who would eventually challenge the imamate of al-Mahdī and assume the title Imam al-Mutawakkil. Al-Ḥuraybī was one of al-Mutawakkil's early supporters, a distinction that earned him the position of wazir with jurisdiction over Bayt al-Faqīh and the Tihāma after the accession of the new imam in 1130/1718. Al-Ḥuraybī died in 1135/1723 and was buried in al-Rawḍa.[85] Al-Mutawakkil and other notables attended his funeral.[86]

Although al-Ḥuraybī was not an active architectural patron like Jaḥḥāf, some of his building activity and patronage can be gleaned from the available sources. Al-Ḥuraybī used some of his profits from the trade for charitable contributions, although his pious building activities were not extensive. Early in his career, in 1112/1700–1701, he restored and enlarged a mosque in Bayt al-Faqīh, for which he was praised.[87] The name of the mosque is not given, but it likely was either the Great Mosque or Masjid al-Mashraʿ, both of which predate the eighteenth century and stand as locally significant structures.[88] His geographic choice was strategic, because Bayt al-Faqīh was a key commercial city in the Tihāma and Yemen's global coffee emporium.

While al-Ḥuraybī was in Mocha, his building additions were mostly practical and related to the defenses of the city. The Ottomans, in their last efforts to hold onto Yemeni territory before their imminent expulsion, had built the walls of Mocha in the early seventeenth century. During the eighteenth century the walls and fortifications required constant upkeep to defend the city from both land and seaside attacks. In 1114/1702–3 or 1117/1705–6, al-Ḥuraybī extended the walls by twenty *dhirāʿ*, or cubits. He also added the Mālṭa Fort (see map 5.1) to the southern part of the wall, providing a major lookout station for that sector of the city.[89] Although these contributions were largely practical, they were attributed to him more than thirty years later by the Meccan traveler and short-term transplant to Mocha Sayyid ʿAbbās b. ʿAlī al-Mūsawī al-Makkī, so apparently his imprint on the city's fortifications remained strong long after his tenure as governor.

Faqīh Aḥmad b. Yaḥyā Khazindār al-Ṣanʿānī

Faqīh Aḥmad b. Yaḥyā Khazindār (d. 1157/1744–45) was named governor of Mocha in 1133/1721, when the previous governor, Amīr Rizq Allāh, died suddenly.[90] Khazindār had served as Amīr Rizq's second in charge, so he had experience with the port and general knowledge of its trade. Khazindār's family roots were Turkish, as is indicated by his name, which refers to the title of treasurer, the Ottoman post of his ancestor. It was said that he was part of the faction of Ottomans who remained in Yemen after the Turks were expelled in the early seventeenth century.[91] His personal roots, however, were firmly grounded in Sanaa, as the suffix al-Ṣanʿānī confirms.[92] Like al-Ḥuraybī, Khazindār was not a *sayyid* or a religious scholar; he entered the circle of notables of al-Mutawakkil's time by being a skilled and loyal administrator. Although Khazindār never attained the position of wazir, he held the governorship of Mocha twice, first in 1721–24 and again in 1730–37.[93]

Khazindār spent a great deal of time in Sanaa, the seat of the imamate under al-Mutawakkil Qāsim and his successors, because he was not always able to stay in the imam's favor while he served in his post in faraway Mocha.[94] He often left a deputy at Mocha to serve in his place during these extended visits. The following example illustrates the instability of his position. In January 1724, rumors circulated that the imam was going to call Khazindār up to the court. When a rider appeared to escort him to Sanaa three days later, he hurriedly prepared a rumored sum of 140,000 Spanish riyals, 80,000 for the imam and 60,000 for his own use. With his wife and children he left Mocha on January 20, 1724, entrusting the deputy governorship to his nephew Muḥsin Khazindār.[95] On February 4, Muḥsin, too, was called to Sanaa. He departed quickly and silently in the middle of the night, without the customary ceremony and pomp dedicated to an official leaving for the court. According to the letters of the English factor, the imam, who was dissatisfied with Khazindār's remittance, decided to replace him.[96] On February 13, the imam sent a message informing that ʿAlī b. Amīr Rizq, the son of the previous governor, was to be named the new governor of Mocha. Rumors circulated for weeks that Khazindār was being forced to pay penalties that equaled an additional 55,000 Spanish riyals to the imam.

Like al-Ḥuraybī, Khazindār was able to regain the imam's favor. Although he was removed from the governorship of Mocha early in 1724, in August 1725 he was elevated to the even more coveted position of governor of Sanaa, a post usually entrusted to one of the imam's sons. Khazindār's case exemplifies the ability of a Mocha governor to move fluidly into an elevated position in the highlands, even after slighting the imam with insufficient remittances. In regard to his governorship in Sanaa, the eighteenth-century historian Luṭf Allāh Jaḥḥāf praised his actions, remarking that he "fixed the weights and measures and whatever embellishes it. He managed affairs and finances, put down evil-doers in it, and took vigorous measures to deal with and punish a group of evil-doers."[97] Khazindār, then, held two of the most important positions in all of Qāsimī Yemen, the governorships of Mocha and Sanaa, within a decade's time.

The most lasting record of Khazindār's governorship in Sanaa is an eighteenth-century manuscript copy of the *Qānūn Ṣanʿāʾ*, the Statute of Sanaa, an ordinance that dictated policies of trade and fixed prices for commodities, brokerage, and services in the market of Sanaa. It includes prices for the full range of commodities available in Sanaa's *sūq*, such as textiles, spices, agricultural products, and locally made crafts. An important early modern copy of the ordinance was drafted in Sanaa under Imam al-Mutawakkil Qāsim, during the governorship of Khazindār, whose name is noted prominently in the document's heading. It then was copied again by al-Mutawakkil's successor, al-Manṣūr Ḥusayn, in 1161/1748.[98] Imam al-Mahdī ʿAbd Allāh added his seal to it in the nineteenth century. It is fitting that as governor of Sanaa, Khazindār was writing and enforcing policies to control the Sanaa market, one of the endpoints of Mocha's wholesale trade, thereby determining prices and trade regulations that affected the commerce of the port even from his position in the highlands. Notably, the first item on the list of the *Qānūn*'s regulations addresses the price of Indian cloth from Mocha.[99]

Khazindār's biographers, Zabāra and al-Mūsawī, praise him to the highest degree, but the European documents present an entirely different story. Khazindār developed a bad reputation among the European merchants because of his wayward policies for demanding customs duties above the accepted limits and purging money from the brokers and merchants when he felt the need of it. The Dutch gave him nicknames such as "Mocha's Nero" and "the Tyrant."[100] As an example of Khazindār's treatment of the merchants, in 1722 he tried to procure yearly gifts from the European merchants with force and coercion.[101] On August 13, the Dutch sent a small lighter boat full of coffee to load one of their ships in the harbor. Without reason the boat was called back. The next day the VOC merchants learned that the governor wanted 500 Spanish riyals for the release of the commodity. Anxious about completing their shipment, they sent the money, which was promptly returned to them. Additionally, the governor sent four soldiers to stand at the door of their broker's house. Brokers were often implicated in disputes between merchants and the port administration, because the temporary loss of a broker brought any merchant's trade to a standstill, and the Baniyan brokers were often helpless to retaliate against such sentences. In this case the imprisoned broker was even forced to pay his guardians six Spanish riyals a day for their captive watch. When the Dutch brought their departing gifts to the governor on August 17, 1722, he sent them back, too, claiming that they were not nearly as much as those of the French or the English, and the Dutch would have to send a gift for the illustrious wazir Faqīh Muḥsin al-Ḥubayshī as well. Once they had done that, Khazindār at last allowed them to load their coffee beans on board.

Khazindār directed such demands not only toward the European merchant community. On September 9, 1723, for example, he sent soldiers to the house of Muḥammad Yāsīn, a merchant from Basra, demanding 2,000 Spanish riyals.[102] The next day he followed up by forcing Muḥammad Ḥajj, some Gujarati merchants, and some Baniyans also to contribute to the royal treasury.[103] Khazindār levied some of the costs of keeping the urban order on Mocha's residents. On October 17, 1722, a fire broke out in the city.[104] As usual, many residents rushed to the site to aid in extinguishing the fire, lest it spread throughout the town. Three days later the governor sought out everyone involved and rewarded those who had helped put out the fire with two *komassis* each. He fined those who had not helped six to seven *komassis*, and he made the Baniyans whose houses were in the vicinity of the fire give five *komassis* apiece.

Khazindār had a formidable enemy in the highlands, wazir Muḥsin al-Ḥubayshī. Although al-Ḥubayshī had aided al-Ḥuraybī from the center of the imamate, he intervened at al-Mutawakkil's court to harm Khazindār. Upon hearing of al-Ḥubayshī's promotion to a higher rank as wazir after the death of al-Ḥuraybī, the Dutch highlighted the animosity between the two, remarking that the newly elevated wazir was "not a friend of this governor [Khazindār]."[105] Thus it is no surprise that Khazindār's first governorship in Mocha was short-lived; al-Ḥubayshī had a hand in removing him from the position in 1724. Khazindār took the job of governor of Sanaa only after smoothing out his relationship with al-Ḥubayshī in 1725.[106]

After Imam al-Mutawakkil died and his son Imam al-Manṣūr Ḥusayn replaced him, Khazindār returned to serve as Mocha's governor from 1730 to 1737. His injustices in Mocha during this second term merited extensive documentation in all the European sources. Ultimately, the French bombardment of the port in 1737 brought about the governor's downfall. The French East India Company blamed Khazindār and Mocha's head *ṣarrāf*,

Ḥasan Ḥasūsā, for violating the conditions regarding customs duties that were laid out in their initial trade treaty, established under al-Ḥuraybī in 1709.[107] When the French arrived at the port in three warships, they took hostages and bombed the city. Then they occupied Mocha's southern fort, which allowed them complete access to the city and the upper hand in settling their demands. The final, renegotiated treaty included twenty-four articles addressing the restitution of the money that was overpaid in customs and seized from the French unjustly, a number of conditions regarding their trade procedures and personal freedoms within the city, and a clarification of the original trade treaty items. The 1737 French bombing marked the end of Khazindār's last prominent role in Qāsimī administration. Imam al-Manṣūr Ḥusayn stripped him of his position, and he disappeared from public life. He died in Sanaa in the month of Rabīʿ al-awwal 1157/1744.

Like al-Ḥuraybī, Khazindār contributed to the defenses and public works of Mocha, but he built no religious or private structures in the city. His main building effort in Mocha focused on the digging of wells and the erection of protective structures around them in an area just outside Bāb al-Shādhilī, the gate to the east of the city (see map 5.1). There Khazindār ordered that one large well be excavated in addition to the group of existing reservoirs known as the al-Shādhilī wells.[108] In 1730 he built two forts to protect these water supplies.[109] The forts, which were described as more strongly built than any others in Mocha, were also meant to provide a convenient spot for inland surveillance of the east. One of the forts, called Qalʿat al-Qāḍī (fig. 3.7), still stands.[110] It was named for Qāḍī Muḥammad Ṣāliḥ, who lived outside the walls and was buried in this area in 1140/1728.[111] Potable water was a constant source of concern in the city, and Khazindār's contribution was intended to make a great improvement in everyday life in Mocha.[112]

Again one must look to the highlands to find further evidence of the patronage of Khazindār. Although the acts I mention were not ascribed directly to Aḥmad Khazindār but rather to his whole family, including another relation named Ḥusayn Khazindār, it is clear that the governor was a key member who participated in building and pious endowments, supported by his Mocha riches. The Khazindār family built great houses in the area of Sanḥān, near Sanaa, and in many other places in the eighteenth century.[113] Their pious generosity, however, was focused not on buildings but on the production of books. They sponsored the copying of Qurʾān manuscripts for study in the mosques of Mūsā and al-Abraz in Sanaa and in the Great Mosque of Ibb, as well as other, unnamed places.[114]

One can refer to the fragmented eighteenth-century Qur'ān pages found in Ḍūrān after the 1982 earthquake and published by the Leiden codicologist Jan Just Witkam in order to get a sense of the artistic conventions these Qur'ān manuscripts may have adhered to.[115] The few pages that remain of the fifteen-volume Qur'ān sponsored by Shaykh Aḥmad b. ʿAbd al-Raḥmān al-Qarābī (fig. 3.8) and dated 1151/1738–39 represent the most closely contemporaneous known manuscript. Together these fragments suggest that no tradition of elaborate Qur'ān manuscript illumination existed in Qāsimī Yemen. Using these pages as a reference, one can imagine that Khazindār's Qur'ān manuscripts were multivolume sets, each volume small like the al-Qarābī example, which measures 200 by 145 mm.[116] The al-Qarābī example features simple frames of thin, double, black ruled lines, filled in with ochre, surrounding the text and rings of alternating dots in red and ochre as verse dividers. Each page includes seven lines rendered in large script. This multivolume manuscript would have constituted an appropriate pious contribution for a local shaykh such as al-Qarābī, for whom no biographical record remains aside from these fragments. A well-endowed official such as Khazindār might have sponsored more costly examples than this, perhaps slightly larger in format and with more ornamentation.

Aside from the patronage of Qur'ān manuscripts dedicated for use in urban mosques in the Yemeni highlands, Khazindār sponsored the writing of a historic text—perhaps his greatest act of cultural patronage. Under his sponsorship and support, Sayyid ʿAbbās b. ʿAlī al-Mūsawī al-Makkī wrote *Nuzhat al-jalīs wa munyat al-adīb al-anīs*, which merged the genre of autobiography with that of travel narrative.[117] Al-Mūsawī was born in Mecca in 1110/1698–99 and grew up there under the tutelage of the local *ʿulamā'*.[118] He began his travels with his teacher, Sayyid Naṣr Allāh al-Ḥā'irī, who left Mecca with the Iraqi pilgrimage caravan to Karbalā' in 1131/1718–19. Once in Iraq, al-Mūsawī traveled to the Shīʿī shrines of Najaf and Karbalā' and then headed to Isfahan. From Isfahan his journey was transformed from a Shīʿī pilgrim's path into an Indian Ocean excursion as he spent most of the year 1132/1719–20 around the Persian Gulf, in Basra and Kung.

From there he embarked on his first extended sea journey, to Surat in India in 1133/1720–21. After six years in India, studying with notable religious scholars and traveling throughout the region, he left for the Arabian Peninsula, docking in Mocha in 1139/1727. His first stay in Mocha lasted for less than a year, after which he returned to the Ḥijāz. Clearly he was not inclined to stay home, because he left for Yemen again in 1141/1728.

FIG. 3.7 The eighteenth-century fort known as Qalʿat al-Qāḍī, Mocha, 2000.

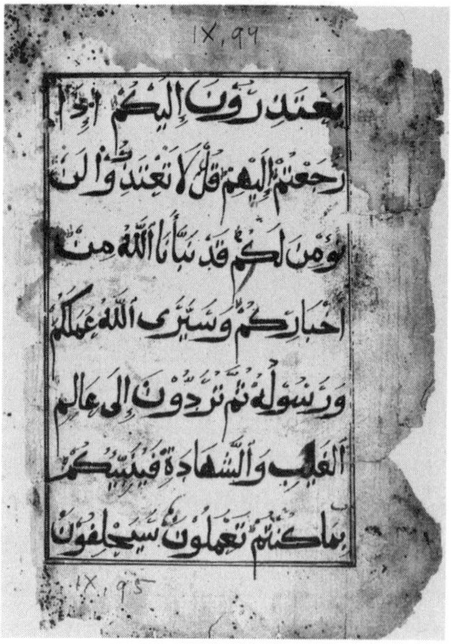

يعتذرون إليكم إذا
رجعتم إليهم قل لا تعتذروا لن
نؤمن لكم قد نبأنا الله من
أخباركم وسيرى الله عملكم
ورسوله ثم تردون إلى عالم
الغيب والشهادة فينبئكم
بما كنتم تعملون سيحلفون

FIG. 3.8 Qurʾān fragment from Ḍūrān, dated 1151/1738–39.

After a short trip to Sanaa, he returned to Mocha. Between 1142/1729 and 1145/1732 he traveled between Mocha and Mecca often. In 1145/1732 he decided to make his residence in Mocha, where he quickly married and had two sons, ʿAbd Allāh and Muḥammad. He remained in Mocha under the sponsorship of Aḥmad Khazindār until he completed his work, *Nuzhat al-jalīs*, and presented it to the governor's son, ʿAbd Allāh, on the fourth of Shawwāl 1148/1736. Al-Mūsawī died in 1180/1766–67.

During his years of travel he made notes about the people he met and the places he saw. Wherever he went he won the favor of the notables by offering them his eloquent verses. The twentieth-century editor of his volume, Muḥammad Mahdī Khurasān, differentiated al-Mūsawī from earlier geographers and travel writers because his work was largely personal and his observations were detailed, specific, and immediate, rather than comprehensive and formulaic.[119] Its chapters interspersed descriptions of cities such as Mecca, Kūfa, Baghdad, Isfahan, Nishapur, Ṭūs, Shiraz, Surat, and Mocha with biographies of the notables al-Mūsawī met in those places and anecdotes about strange occurrences and details of his travels. Although al-Mūsawī's account was unique, the geographical dimensions of his tour were not. Rather, he was representative of a significant group of Arab and Indian Muslim scholars who traveled between South Asia, Yemen, and the Ḥijāz in this period, in search of diverse religious training and teaching.[120] Al-Mūsawī's volume describes the cultural and scholarly dimensions of the trade routes at the time, pointing to a significant overlap between the itineraries of religious learning and the channels of commercial profit in the eighteenth century.

It was under the sponsorship of Faqīh Aḥmad Khazindār that al-Musawi completed the writing of *Nuzhat al-jalīs*, which served as a major source for this study. Its perspective is that of a transplanted resident of the city of Mocha. Al-Mūsawī wrote, "My master Faqīh Aḥmad honored me and granted upon me his favor when I was far from home in Yemen. He appointed a salary for me from the Muslim treasury."[121] From 1145/1732 to 1148/1736 Khazindār supported al-Mūsawī and his family with this stipend, thus allocating at least some of the fruits of the trade from the treasury to support this literary and historical effort. Certainly Khazindār was aware that his sponsorship of the writer would allow him to maintain an overwhelmingly positive historical profile. He was right: al-Mūsawī completely omitted the scandalous events that were attributed to Khazindār by the local merchants, and coincidentally, he finished the work before the French bombing of the city in 1737 prompted the removal of the controversial governor. Al-Mūsawī also spoke highly of ʿAbd Allāh b. Aḥmad Khazindār, who was deputy governor in place of his father for extended periods in the 1730s. It is fitting that Khazindār sponsored a tome describing the Indian Ocean world from the perspective of a traveler of the Arabian Peninsula in the first half of the eighteenth century.

Governors as Patrons

This review of biography, architectural construction, and cultural patronage reveals that the governors of Mocha in the second half of the seventeenth century and the first half of the eighteenth were geographically and socially mobile members of Qāsimī society. Each of the governors featured here maintained strong connections throughout Yemen as he held the governorship. He could stay in the good favor of the imam only if he maintained close contact with him and his wazirs in highland Yemen. And Mocha was by no means an end point in the careers of these administrators; the governorship of Mocha was linked to the eventual or concurrent appointment to the position of wazir for Jaḥḥāf and al-Ḥuraybī. For Khazindār, two periods in Mocha punctuated either end of a stint as governor of Sanaa.

The shift in the identities of Mocha's governors is also important. Over the decades under consideration, status and elite pedigree became less important than loyalty, military prowess, and administrative experience. Under al-Mutawakkil Ismāʿīl, in the mid-seventeenth century, two governors from notable families of *sayyids*, descendants of the prophet, held the post, Sayyid Zayd b. ʿAlī Jaḥḥāf and Sayyid Ḥasan b. al-Muṭahhar al-Jurmūzī. In the eighteenth century, non-*sayyid* appointees dominated, men such as al-Ḥuraybī and Khazindār, whose pedigrees were markedly less prestigious.[122] As Haykel noted, the full administrative transformation of the Qāsimī imamate took root by the beginning of the eighteenth century, when the imam turned away from the established local elites and began to appoint people he trusted, particularly slave *amīrs*, in key administrative positions as military commanders and governors.[123]

The governors I have discussed used their Mocha profits for pious and charitable contributions, for private buildings and public works, for the endowment of Qurʾān manuscripts, and for the authorship of a significant text. Yet traces of this patronage in Mocha are scanty, particularly because the governors' local contributions were directed mainly toward immediate, practical, and functional necessities such as fortifications, towers, and wells. One must look outside Mocha to find the monumental mosques, luxurious houses, and Qur'ān manuscripts that emerged from Mocha's riches under the patronage of the city's preeminent governors. Unlike their Ottoman predecessors, who were active in major architectural efforts and monumental building in the city, the Qāsimī governors used their Mocha profits to build in the heartland of the empire, primarily in the northern highlands. In Mocha their efforts were largely routine and defensive, despite their long periods of residence in the city.

4 *Merchants and Nākhūdhas*

The merchants of the coastal trade are more elusive subjects than the governors of Mocha because they were often omitted from the larger historical record of Yemen, focused as it was on local religious scholars and the legacies of the imams. Left out were more mobile, and often foreign, economic elites whose lifestyles were unsuited to the traditional format of Zaydī biography.[1] The European sources mention the trade activities of Mocha's merchants on a daily basis, but with scant discussion of their identities, their biographies, or the details of their larger trade profiles. Piecing together the cultural dynamics of Mocha's merchant community is much more difficult than the task of the preceding chapter.

Nelly Hanna and André Raymond, scholars of Ottoman Cairo, have laid the foundations for critical study of the cultural and economic activities of early modern merchants, who took on elite roles that previously had been restricted to the ruling class.[2] In Hanna's work the merchant Ismāʿīl Abū Ṭāqiyya appears as a major power broker and significant urban renewer of sixteenth- and seventeenth-century Cairo. Raymond has highlighted the legacy of the coffee merchant and *shāhbandar al-tujjār*, or head of the merchants' guild, Qāsim al-Sharāʾibī, whose net worth exceeded that of the military elites of the time.[3] Although the merchants of Mocha cannot be discussed at the same level of detail, I do adopt the formats used by Hanna and Raymond, who placed the merchant within the economic, social, and cultural world from which he emerged, in which he participated, and to which he contributed. As people who animated the city, moved along its roadways, and dwelled in its residential quarters and houses, merchants are essential to understanding the lived dimensions of Mocha's urban space. The sketches that follow provide cultural and social profiles of some prominent members of this elusive and transient community.

Commercial Worlds

Many ships arriving at Mocha's port carried mixtures of goods of all sorts—some destined for the wholesale market and others for the retail market, luxury goods packed in with everyday necessities. The social makeup of Mocha's trade community was more rigidly segmented. In his monograph on the merchants of the Moroccan port city of Essaouira, Daniel Schroeter made a clear distinction between the types of commercial groups one might find in Arab commercial capitals by identifying the *tājir* as a wholesaler, separate and distinct from the more numerous retail shopkeepers.[4] Writing about Cairo, Raymond described a similar but more complex breakdown among the ranks of artisans and merchants in this bustling, early modern commercial city. There, too, the important wholesale merchants, or *tujjār*, formed a cohesive social and economic class separate from the local retailers, or *bā'iʿ*s.[5] In regard to an earlier era, S. D. Goitein stressed that the designation *tājir* "was reserved for those enormously versatile men who dealt in a great variety of goods," as opposed to retailers and more specialized wholesale merchants.[6]

Likewise, at least two classes of merchants coexisted in Mocha. The high-volume overseas merchants, *tujjār*, dealt in large quantities of wholesale goods such as textiles, coffee, spices, and metals that were intended for or originated in the international market. The goods they purchased at Mocha were either transshipped to another maritime destination or sold to a broker for entry into the Yemeni inland market. Operating from their small stores in the bazaar, local retail merchants belonged to a different mercantile class. They dealt in small quantities of the aforementioned import items as well as other commodities for daily use, local distribution, and regular consumption. As I describe in chapters 5 and 6, wholesalers and retailers conducted business in different sectors of the city in different types of establishments, and their commercial worlds only rarely intersected.

Historical contextualization of the Jidda gap from 1635 through the first half of the eighteenth century is extremely important for an accurate understanding of the cultural profile of Mocha's wholesale merchant community. A review of some of the major merchants in the city confirms that Mocha's foreign commercial class was composed primarily of merchants who hailed from ports to the south and east of the Jidda gap. The most important merchants were from Surat, Mocha's twin city of trade across the Arabian Sea. Indeed, it is difficult to speak of a merchant as belonging exclusively to Mocha's commercial class when most of the major merchants of the city participated in the Mocha-Surat trade route and their affiliations were thus more cross-regional, mobile, and shifting than a single urban attachment might suggest.

Although Surat and Mocha shared many transient residents who traveled between the two ports, they diverged in regard to the relationship between the merchant community and local authorities. As M. N. Pearson has described, Gujarati port cities functioned as relatively autonomous zones in which merchants commanded and managed their trade free from the intervention and obstacles posed by governing bodies.[7] Merchants there had the upper hand in handling commercial conflicts and settling trade agreements, using their economic muscle and social standing as leverage. This balance of power worked in western India such that merchants reaped the benefits of their political clout but also shouldered the brunt of losses from the risky business of maritime transit. Although this model of merchant primacy appears to have had wide-reaching significance in other Indian Ocean ports, in Mocha merchants lacked such autonomy. They attempted to control their own affairs, but the city's authoritative governor, as agent of the wazir and imam in the highlands, kept close watch over individual negotiations and intervened whenever he saw fit.

In Mocha, as in most other Indian Ocean port cities, merchants were not organized into guilds. Instead, ethnic connections and religious affiliations largely defined a person's professional possibilities and the scope of his commercial investments. As Philip Curtin suggested, members of diasporic communities maintained strong connections to compatriots while trading abroad.[8] These community ties allowed groups to form hardy coalitions when needed to respond to the inequities and injustices that overseas residence could entail. Some groups and affiliations overlapped and shifted according to the needs of the moment. For instance, the Ismāʿīlī and Sunnī Bohra merchants from Surat each looked after the needs of others from their subsect and may be identified as tight and cohesive groups that dominated the shipping sector. Yet at times the major Muslim merchants of

Mocha banded together as an organized coalition that superseded subsect interests and regional affiliations and included local, Indian, Persian, Turkish, and Arab merchants, both Sunnī and Shīʿī.

The best case of such community solidarity in Mocha is that of the Baniyan brokers. They were Hindu and Jain merchants from western India who held a monopoly over land-based trade brokerage by facilitating the transfer of goods from the hands of maritime merchants into land-based markets, overseeing currency exchange, and maintaining the local deferred payment schedule.[9] As the primary cogs in a well-defined and hierarchical system of brokerage, these Baniyan intermediaries were in contact with all the different types of merchants in Mocha and served as the city's middlemen in all commercial affairs. Early modern brokerage in the western Indian Ocean was complex, however, and the role of broker had a certain amount of functional flexibility.[10] A broker could specialize in a certain commercial good or work for a specific merchant or trading company, either freelance or as a continuing employee. At Mocha one sees examples of all these types of brokers among the Baniyans. Many brokers seem to have played more than one role at a time and to have shifted roles from one season to the next. The Baniyans wielded enough power to collectively withhold their services from their clients, who included the city's multitude of wholesale merchants, in order to protest an unreasonable demand of remittance from the governor or the persecution of a member of their community.[11] Their strategic strikes brought Mocha's trade to a standstill, as I describe in chapter 7.

Three types of merchants were engaged in the trade along or traveled the Mocha-Surat pipeline: the shipowner, the *nākhūdha*, who acted as ship's captain and agent representing the shipowner, and the land-based merchant. These categories overlap with those Ashin Das Gupta identified as the key types of Indian maritime merchants, with one slight difference. He divided the merchant community into "substantial merchants" of great wealth, agents of merchants, and small-scale merchants.[12] In the case of Mocha's merchant class, one may discuss "substantial merchants"—namely, Indian Ocean shipowners—and their agents, the *nākhūdhas*. Small-scale merchants were numerous in Mocha, because many who were destined for Mecca stopped at the port en route to the Ḥijāz. Little is known, however, about these transient and often nameless travelers, so I do not discuss them. Rather, I add another category to Das Gupta's list—the land-based merchant. In Mocha, land-based merchants participated in the Indian Ocean trade by channeling Asian goods into the center of Qāsimī territory in Sanaa.

Their networks were largely distinct from those of the maritime class, but they constituted an important block of merchants in the port city.

Indian Ocean Shipowners and Their Agents: The Family of Mullā ʿAbd al-Ghafūr

Mullā ʿAbd al-Ghafūr (d. 1718) was the greatest shipowning merchant of Surat in the late seventeenth and early eighteenth centuries. At the height of his fleet he owned around twenty ships that frequented Indian Ocean ports. This number is considerable, given that the wealthiest Indian Ocean shipowners usually possessed and operated no more than two ships.[13] At least one of his ships could always be found in Mocha's harbor during the trade season, and sometimes as many as five.[14] Usually he shipped from Surat and Gogha and docked at all points in the southern Red Sea, but he also shipped from Bengal. His shipping volume was so great that he owned a private wharf in the village of Athwa at the mouth of the Tapi River, the riverine gateway to Surat. The wharf was prominently located directly upstream from the imperial Mughal dock.[15]

ʿAbd al-Ghafūr, who was a Sunnī Bohra, is often invoked as an iconic figure who managed to thrive economically despite the encroaching presence of European trading companies.[16] Considering his prominence in the Mocha trade, it is surprising that he never appeared on Mocha's shore in person. He represents the sedentary shipowning entrepreneur of the Indian Ocean, whose fortunes were tied to the sea but who apparently never crossed it himself. His *nākhūdhas*, the captains of his ships, served as his representatives in the Red Sea, carrying the status of the family name. Regardless of his physical absence in the city, his reputation was well known in Mocha. Ships owned by him were identified by his name, as was his grand house in the city, even after his death in 1718.[17] When he died, ʿAbd al-Ghafūr left a reputed eight and a half million rupees in cash, a garden in the northern suburbs of Surat, two houses in the city, a mosque, the wharf in Athwa, and some property on an island in the Gulf of Cambay.[18] One of the houses was located in the elite merchants' neighborhood called Saudagarpura, in the subdistrict named Mulla Chakla, probably after Mullā ʿAbd al-Ghafūr himself.[19] The suburban garden housed the family plot and was used as a fresh-air retreat to entertain guests and business partners outside of the city.

Although ʿAbd al-Ghafūr's son, ʿAbd al-Ḥayy, died shortly after him,[20] his legacy was sustained by his grandson Mullā Muḥammad ʿAlī, who continued the family business of shipping from 1720 until his death in 1733. According to Das Gupta, Muḥammad ʿAlī, who aspired to a princely lifestyle, was considered "virtually the governor of Surat, in all but name."[21] This status was clearly recognized by the imam of Yemen, who honored Muḥammad ʿAlī yearly by engaging in a ceremonial practice of elaborate international gift exchange with him and his *nākhūdhas*. For instance, on May 21, 1729, the ships of Mullā Muḥammad ʿAlī brought the normal yearly presents to the imam and court notables. The gifts were transported from Mocha to Sanaa on camels. Clearly the load was large, for it had to be supervised by two servants and eight laborers.[22] In return, Muḥammad ʿAlī received honored and valued objects that were to be accepted by his *nākhūdha* and carried back to Surat. At the end of Ramaḍān in 1724, the imam sent two horses to Mocha's governor, ʿAlī b. Amīr Rizq, in addition to one for the *nākhūdha* of the ʿAbd al-Ghafūr family ships and another for the *nākhūdha* of the rival Chalabī family. The two Surati *nākhūdhas*, along with the governor, were the only people in the whole city who were honored with the imam's gifts at that time, an exclusive right linked to the unique primacy of their sponsors in the city.[23]

Das Gupta's comparison of Muḥammad ʿAlī to his grandfather ʿAbd al-Ghafūr reveals a major generational gap between the two merchants. ʿAbd al-Ghafūr rose to the level of long-distance merchant and shipowner from a humble background. Accordingly, he lived a fairly modest lifestyle, although he became extremely wealthy and powerful. Muḥammad ʿAlī, on the other hand, accustomed to the wealth that surrounded him from birth, strived for political power and the representation of his independence. Das Gupta referred to him as "the prince among merchants."[24] Contemporary onlookers described at length his drawn-out yet failed struggle for administrative power in his political alliance with the governor of Surat, Sohrab Khan.[25]

Unlike his grandfather, Muḥammad ʿAlī did travel the Mocha-Surat route, but only once, as documented in 1727.[26] When he arrived in Mocha, the Dutch merchants identified him as "the next heir of ʿAbd al-Ghafūr" and observed that he was received with "all of the signs of the city's government."[27] He stayed in Mocha for only a few days and soon left for Jidda to perform the pilgrimage with more than 1,200 other pilgrims. Muḥammad ʿAlī had three sons, Muḥammad Ḥusayn, Amīn al-Dīn, and Fakhr al-Dīn.

Muḥammad Ḥusayn served as his father's *nākhūdha*, and Fakhr al-Dīn attempted to maintain the family business after his father's death. Muḥammad ʿAlī's ships arrived yearly at Mocha until 1733, when his unpopular politics resulted in his murder by poisoning in Surat. His death marked the end of his family's prominence in the Red Sea trade.

During his thirteen years as head of the shipowning family, Muḥammad ʿAlī asserted himself along the western Indian Ocean coast in visible and conspicuous ways. He built monumental structures in Surat and Mocha that reflected his pious commitment or enhanced his commercial activity. In 1723 he built a mosque in Surat that catered to his subsect, that of Sunnī Bohras, and still stands today.[28] In a bold move, he expanded the wharf that his grandfather had built in Athwa and developed a strongly fortified satellite port center there, a venture that lured shipping and commerce away from Surat. Unabashedly he appointed officials, armed the city, and even minted his own coins. This venture stirred the suspicion of the local authorities and onlookers, who saw Athwa as a rival port to Surat and a military threat.[29]

Muḥammad ʿAlī's building activities in Mocha paralleled those in Surat. Unsurprisingly, he owned a great house in Mocha, originally the property of his grandfather. A house was necessary for any high-profile trader in the port city, because such men did not stay in public quarters. The city's major Muslim merchants often met at Muḥammad ʿAlī's house to discuss local problems as a coalition. He also added to the broader landscape of the city with conspicuous public contributions that went beyond those of ordinary merchants. In 1139/1726–27 he ordered the reconstruction of the minaret of the Mosque of al-Shādhilī (fig. 4.1), the centerpiece of the city's religious structures, erected by the Ottomans in the late sixteenth or early seventeenth century.[30] Clearly the patron wanted to improve upon the original Ottoman minaret, which was described as "marvelous, the highest, the slimmest, the most beautiful, and the most unique."[31] The minaret must be seen as more than a pious contribution, for it was a tall and vivid symbol of the city and was often used as a navigation tool by boats approaching Mocha from the Red Sea.[32] It was Mocha's most visible monument from both land and sea. Muḥammad ʿAlī did not supervise the effort but rather entrusted his *nākhūdha*, ʿAbd al-Raḥmān b. ʿAbd al-Qādir, to oversee the project while he was in Mocha.[33] It is likely that he undertook the project after his first and only visit to the city in March 1727, when he seized the opportunity to identify the most prominent monument of Mocha's landscape and its potential to serve as a symbol of his maritime empire.

FIG. 4.1 Mosque of al-Shādhilī, Mocha. Photograph by Hermann Burchardt, 1909.

A year later, in 1140/1727–28, Muḥammad ʿAlī continued his pious contributions in Mocha by building the mosque of Shaykh Jawhar, outside the city wall.[34] The tomb of this saint already existed at the site, but Muḥammad ʿAlī ordered the addition of a new, adjacent mosque. Again it was executed by his *nākhūdha*, who was Muḥammad Saʿīd that season. This tomb and the associated mosque built by Muḥammad ʿAlī no longer stand today, so it is difficult to reach any conclusions about their visual attributes.[35] Muḥammad ʿAlī probably built the mosque to cater to the practices and linguistic needs of Mocha's transient but significant Indian Sunnī Bohra merchant community, as he had done in Surat a few years earlier. Another mosque, also ruined today, called Masjid al-Buhra, already stood within the city walls, but this mosque would have served the Ismāʿīlī Bohra community. By associating the new Bohra mosque with a local saint and choosing a site outside the city wall, Muḥammad ʿAlī would have set his community apart from the Ismāʿīlīs, who were also prominent merchants in Mocha. It is notable that a private merchant who visited the port only once was so engaged with the embellishment, renovation, and expansion of Mocha's major religious monuments while the local governors and Qāsimī administration contributed little to this realm.

The family of ʿAbd al-Ghafūr controlled the Red Sea shipping of Surat for several decades, but not without competition from other leading Muslim merchants, particularly from the west coast of India. Its biggest rival was the Chalabī family, which was originally Turkish, probably from Iraq, but had lived in Surat for generations. Throughout the late seventeenth and early eighteenth centuries they shipped to Mocha and Jidda, but their shipping activity in the Red Sea was always less significant than that of the ʿAbd al-Ghafūr family. Both families competed in the Persian Gulf market as well.[36] Muḥammad Ṣāliḥ Chalabī was a contemporary of ʿAbd al-Ghafūr's, and ʿUthmān Chalabī took over the Red Sea routes during the time of Muḥammad ʿAlī.[37]

ʿAbd al-Raḥmān Sulaymānjī was another Bohra shipowner who lived in Gujarat, although he was originally from Sindh, and frequented Mocha's harbor. And beginning in 1729, Sīdī Surūr II (d. 1732 or 1734), also known as Sīdī Yāqūt Khān II, sent one ship to Mocha from the port of Danda-Rajpuri yearly.[38] Sīdī Surur II was the leader of the Sidi clan of Janjira (the island opposite Danda-Rajpuri, south of Mumbai), a group descended from former African slaves and seamen who were brought to or arrived in India as early as the twelfth century. Although they were known primarily for their strong navy, which the Mughals mobilized against the Marathas in the seventeenth century, the Sidis also used their maritime fleet for the trade.[39] In 1730 the *nākhūdha* of the Sidi vessel, a man named Ambar who likely was also a Sidi, went to visit the imam's court in Sanaa and returned with gifts from the imam and his brother in Taʿizz to carry back to India. It is clear that the Sidi *nākhūdha*, a relative latecomer to Mocha's harbor, was treated with the same respect and honor that was accorded to the other established Muslim merchants from the west coast of India.

Local Shipowners and Merchants: Qāsim al-Turbatī and Saʿd al-Dīn al-ʿUdaynī

Considering the transience of merchants and merchant groups around the early modern Indian Ocean, it is unwieldy and anachronistic to ascribe national identities to them. In the case of Mocha, no major merchant was local in the sense of being native to the city, and the majority did not come from the southern Arabian Peninsula at all. Every major merchant of Mocha came from somewhere else—Surat, Basra, Jidda, or Sanaa, for example. Yet it is clear that each merchant had a place he called home. Some made Yemen their home base and overwintered there, spoke Arabic as their main language, and maintained strong ties to the centers of power of the Qāsimī dynasty. Of these merchants, whom I call local, the most prominent was the shipowner Qāsim b. Ṭāhir al-Turbatī,[40] who was considered the "leading merchant" in the city from at least 1699 until he died in 1738.[41] In 1704 the Dutch labeled him "a reliable Arab merchant," and the next year, a "favorite of the governor [Ṣāliḥ al-Ḥuraybī] who normally deals with the foreign merchants of the city."[42] He was called upon to serve as a mediator between the local administration and the Europeans in many instances. In 1723, when an English soldier spent the night out of the residence and was jailed for trying to rape an indigent woman, al-Turbatī acted as the middleman between the governor and the English factor.[43] He was called upon to play this intermediary role because he was capable of communicating with the European merchants and apparently was familiar with their practices. Al-Turbatī dealt with more than just the European merchants, though, and carried out significant business transactions throughout the city.

His wealth and status were conspicuous among Mocha's merchant elites. In 1719 the Dutch resident Abraham Pantzer indicated that al-Turbatī lived in a house that was more expensive than any other merchant's, with many wives, slaves, and concubines.[44] Al-Turbatī, like other merchants who diversified their investments, also owned real estate in the city. His houses could easily be rented out during the annual high trade season, when lodging became scarce in the city.[45] Although al-Turbatī was firmly established as a Mocha resident, he owned at least two ships that traveled the Indian Ocean trade routes and allowed him geographic mobility.[46] In 1714 he went with his family to live in Surat for a short period, indicating that he was well connected across the Indian Ocean and more mobile than some of his Gujarati counterparts.[47]

Al-Turbatī's trade, like that of all successful merchants, was a family business. His son ʿAlī worked as a *nākhūdha* on his ships.[48] His other son, Muḥammad, was described as one of the leading merchants in the city in 1723.[49] One of al-Turbatī's daughters was married to a Mocha merchant named Zayd Muṣṭafā, who traded with the Dutch in 1712.[50] Yet al-Turbatī's prosperity, however conspicuous, did not endure throughout his lifetime. Later sources from the 1720s focus on his growing debts to the VOC, the English East India Company, and the French Compagnie des Indes. Al-Turbatī never repaid these debts, to the chagrin of the Dutch residents, who visited him periodically about the outstanding loans.[51] According to the VOC registers, al-Turbatī would respond with a hopeful "*in shāʿ allāh*," but he produced nothing except meager sums.

Qāsim al-Turbatī was never formally elevated to the position of governor of Mocha, although he did hold minor official posts such as second to the governor in the late 1720s and royal merchant (the imam's *wakīl*) in the 1730s. For these duties the imam paid him a small monthly stipend of ninety Spanish riyals.[52] Regardless of the insignificance of his official appointments, at times his control in the city was more considerable than that of the named officials. From 1724 to 1727 the English believed it was al-Turbatī who actually held the power in the city and that the young governor, ʿAlī b. Amīr Rizq, was merely a pawn. They said that al-Turbatī "influences the Governor upon all occasions being a kind of tutor to him, not chosen, but imposed by the King and esteem'd by all men, a cunning and plodding old fellow."[53] Later they added, "The Governour of Mocha Emir Ally Rizuk has only the name, but old Turbatty a creature of the Viziers and vakeel or Agent to the Emaum, has the sole direction and at the same time is the Chief Merchant of the Place."[54] Al-Turbatī's strong influence on the city's administration was confirmed when the governor, ʿAlī b. Amīr Rizq, married his daughter in 1726.[55]

Like al-Ḥuraybī, al-Turbatī maintained close relations with the highland court through the wazir to uphold his commercial standing and his local preeminence. Indeed, the English believed all their letters of complaint regarding al-Turbatī's debts were intercepted by the wazir, the illustrious Muḥsin al-Ḥubayshī, who consistently hid them from the imam.[56] Al-Turbatī, like the governors of the city, visited the imam yearly, and he generally was well received.[57] Strategically, he also maintained close ties with the brother of

Imam al-Manṣūr Ḥusayn, Amīr Aḥmad b. al-Mutawakkil Qāsim, who held authority over a semi-independent princedom in and around Taʿizz in the mid-eighteenth century. Al-Turbatī may have engaged in economic ventures with Amīr Aḥmad, for he claimed that the prince owed him 13,000 Spanish riyals in 1727. When al-Turbatī embarked on his yearly visit to the imam in Sanaa, he would stop by Amīr Aḥmad's court in Taʿizz and spend time with him there. In 1738 Qāsim al-Turbatī died, leaving his family to settle his unpaid accounts.[58] Notably, his preeminence in Mocha spanned the reigns of three imams and several governors.

Shaykh Saʿd al-Dīn b. ʿAbd al-Walī al-Yamanī al-ʿUdaynī was another important local merchant who was active through the middle of the eighteenth century. Zabāra is silent about where he was born and the exact date of his birth, but his *nisba*, or byname, places his roots in al-ʿUdayn, one of the major coffee growing regions to the east of Ḥays. Al-ʿUdaynī's biography recounts a classic rags to riches tale. Before he entered the city of Mocha in 1141/1728, he was a humble coffee husker.[59] That a rural laborer could become a major merchant in Mocha gives a sense of the ways in which the commercial activity at the port allowed for the transgression of certain social norms that dominated Yemeni society.

Despite his modest beginning, al-ʿUdaynī became a skilled merchant and extremely wealthy in Mocha while maintaining continuous residence in al-ʿUdayn. The historian Jaḥḥāf claimed, "If he had aimed to sell dust, he could have made his livelihood from it and it would have made him very rich."[60] There are few details about his commercial activity in the biographical account, although it is known that he dealt in textiles in Mocha. One story recalls how he bought some low-quality textiles being sold from the estate of a Baniyan merchant who had died.[61] The treasury of Mocha would seize the estates of Baniyans who passed away in the city in order to settle any outstanding accounts. Al-ʿUdaynī was coerced into buying the textiles on credit for 3,000 riyals, paying 600 riyals up front. Soon after completing the purchase, he decided to sell some of the cloth in order to distribute largesse to the poor, as was his routine. When he inspected the rough pieces of cloth closely, he found valuable luxury textiles worth thousands of riyals wrapped inside those of poorer quality. The deceased Baniyan merchant had evidently tried to mask the true value of the sumptuous goods from the local inspectors, perhaps to evade taxes or confiscation by the governor. This tale is important because it highlights the trade activity of an inland merchant who was filtering Indian Ocean goods and their associated revenue into the land-based networks of Yemen, whereas the European trade documents disproportionately highlight the maritime commercial activity at the port and its associated gains and losses. In this case, the profits obtained through the exchange of Indian textiles were intended for a local charity purpose.

Although their family was not of distinguished origins, both Saʿd al-Dīn al-ʿUdaynī and his brother were able to enter the merchant and elite class, often traveling between Mocha, Taʿizz, al-ʿUdayn, and Sanaa. Indeed, the two were called to the court of Amīr Aḥmad b. al-Mutawakkil in Taʿizz in 1162/1748–49. They regretted the invitation because they knew they would have to bring a great gift. Eventually they set out for the city with 30,000 Maria Theresa thalers, but by the time they reached the city walls, the announcement of the *amīr*'s death rang throughout the city—a timely occurrence for the brothers, who were spared the loss of their money. On a later occasion, Imam al-Mahdī ʿAbbās called upon al-ʿUdaynī for a visit to his court in Sanaa. Al-ʿUdaynī was one of the first to pledge allegiance to al-Manṣūr ʿAlī b. al-Mahdī ʿAbbās when he declared himself imam in 1775. Clearly, Saʿd al-Dīn's reputation was widespread, for the famed scholar Ibn al-Amīr wrote a *qaṣīda*, or laudatory ode, to him that is recorded in his biographical entry.[62]

Al-ʿUdaynī represents the ideal of the pious merchant. He was learned in *fiqh*, or Islamic jurisprudence, and was a notable scholar of the Shāfiʿī school of law. He dutifully channeled portions of his profits from the trade to charitable causes. Jaḥḥāf praised his generosity, stating that he never skipped giving a large sum of alms to the needy every morning.[63] He built a charity house to lodge the poor and the sick in an unnamed location.[64] It was said that he brought a box full of money to this place every day and read the Qurʾān with the inhabitants. He would not leave until the entire box of money had been dispersed to the needy. Al-ʿUdaynī went blind in his later years and died in 1192/1778–79.

Al-Turbatī and al-ʿUdaynī were both members of the wealthy local *tujjār* class of Mocha in the first half of the eighteenth century, and they both dealt in textiles, among other commodities. Both were in contact with the imam's court, as well as the court of Amīr Aḥmad in Taʿizz. But the historic traces of their trade activities diverge significantly. Al-ʿUdaynī was not mentioned in the contemporary European documents, whereas al-Turbatī was profusely acknowledged. The disparity is due to al-ʿUdaynī's having been a land-based merchant who focused his commercial ventures on the inland transfer of goods. Qāsim al-Turbatī, a shipowner who sent vessels across the Indian Ocean, traveled the maritime routes himself and developed strategic relationships with European merchants. Although it is possible that al-Turbatī's goods, like those of the European merchants, ended up eventually in al-ʿUdaynī's hands, it would have been through the third-party intermediation of a Baniyan broker rather than by direct contact. By avoiding the customs house of Mocha, a merchant such as al-ʿUdaynī eluded contact with the Europeans and other maritime merchants.

Conversely, al-Turbatī is absent from the Arabic biographies and chronicles of Yemen, even though he held high standing at the imam's court, on a par with the governors of the city. Al-ʿUdaynī, on the other hand, merited inclusion. He did so because he conformed to the model of the pious merchant who used his profits for charitable contribution and because he was a Sunnī, who could trade with less stigma than his Zaydī cohorts.[65] Zaydī historiography disdains the worldly affairs of the merchant; those who were involved in commercial activity are often omitted from the local historical record, despite the fact that many were closely tied to the imam's court. Hence al-ʿUdaynī's biographical record is a unique and fortuitous inclusion in Yemen's textual record. The parallel biographies of al-Turbatī and al-ʿUdaynī reveal the sharp social rift between the world of the seafaring, shipowning merchant and the world of the land-based merchant of Qāsimī Mocha. Although both were motivated by the fortunes of the Indian Ocean, their worlds remained distinct through the well-structured system of brokerage that dominated Mocha's trade.

The Imam's *Nākhūdhas*: Amīr Rizq Allāh and His Successors

The Qāsimī imams of Yemen possessed no naval fleet, but they sent two trading ships to Surat yearly, as documented since the time of Ṣāḥib al-Mawāhib.[66] Although the Yemeni sources of the time do not allude to the Qāsimī commercial vessels, the Dutch sources document the seasonal arrival and departure of the imams' ships.[67] Dynastic involvement in the trade was not a new development in Yemen. The Rasulid and Tahirid sultans also owned ships that traveled the Indian Ocean, and they benefited directly from the profits of the trade, although they used Aden as the primary royal port.[68] As shipowner, the imam entrusted the transfer of his valuable cargo and the maintenance of his ship and crew to his *nākhūdha*, the captain of the ship. The royal *nākhūdha* appears in the records as an important person who played a singular role within the elite merchant class of Mocha and as the imam's representative in India.

The position of *nākhūdha*, from a Persian term, appears in Arabic texts as early as the eleventh century.[69] Its early meaning was fluid, as was demonstrated by the Geniza scholar Roxani Margariti, who showed that the medieval term was used to refer to either the shipowning merchant or the captain, not distinguishing between the land-based and maritime roles.[70] By the seventeenth century the role of *nākhūdha* in the western Indian Ocean was fixed as a seafaring post that was mainly commercial and social rather than technical. The *nākhūdha* possessed no skill in maritime navigation but rather acted as the agent of the merchant at the port and held authority over the crew, the passengers, and the cargo on the vessel. A man who was called the *muʿallim*, the *rubbān*, or the *sarang* filled the specialized navigational role of pilot.[71] Both the *nākhūdha* and the navigator carried their own cargoes and engaged in trade at the point of destination. In the Indian Ocean trading world of eighteenth-century Mocha, the most important merchants, such as al-Turbatī and ʿAbd al-Ghafūr, owned large private ships and hired the services and expertise of *nākhūdhas* for each season. The *nākhūdhas* served as the representatives of shipowning merchants or royal patrons, who were often sedentary.

Instead of having technical nautical skills, it was important that the *nākhūdha* be trustworthy, loyal, socially respectable, and aware of the protocols of commercial interaction. For that reason, many major shipowning merchants enlisted their sons as *nākhūdhas*. Emphasizing status as a major attribute, Das Gupta vividly described the *nākhūdhas* who traveled the Indian Ocean trade routes, each as "a little god on his own ship" who displayed "the waywardness of immortals."[72] High-ranking officials were sent as *nākhūdhas* of the royal Mughal fleet, an example in 1712 being Mirza Ṣāḥib, who was described as an "Indian nobleman, a commander of five thousand horses, and, it was said, a former governor of Gujarat."[73] That elite visibility was central to this role is clear when one looks at the lavish entry ceremonies that were held for the *nākhūdhas* of Indian Ocean ships, particularly those owned by the great Muslim shipowners of Surat. Further, as C. G. Brouwer noted for the early seventeenth century, under the Ottomans, Indian Ocean *nākhūdhas* were important enough to receive seats on the city council, appointed by Mocha's governor.[74]

Among the Qāsimī imam's *nākhūdhas*, Amīr Rizq (d. 1721) is an important yet murky character in Mocha's history who rose to the rank of governor of the city.[75] Nothing is known of his origins because he was referred to only by title, an abbreviation of Amīr Rizq Allāh, which designates his post rather than his birth name and *nisba*.[76] His historical record begins in the early eighteenth century, when he was first assigned as Mocha's *amīr al-baḥr* and then appointed as *nākhūdha* on Imam al-Mahdī Muḥammad's ships. Thus he was directly involved in the Indian Ocean society of trade, traveling yearly along the Mocha-Surat route as the imam's representative.

In 1715, Imam al-Mahdī called Amīr Rizq back from Surat to help him in his struggle against his nephew's challenge for the imamate.[77] Amīr Rizq returned from Surat to support al-Mahdī but soon shifted allegiance to his competitor, the future Imam al-Mutawakkil Qāsim. Amīr Rizq obviously held significant military rank, judging from al-Mutawakkil's entrusting him to lead the effort to win over the Mocha garrison in his name in 1716.[78] Immediately after taking over the city, he demanded money from the merchants in order to send much-needed funds to the new imam. This hostile seizure angered and alienated many of Mocha's leading inhabitants, including the Dutch, who accused him of orchestrating an attack on their house in February 1717.[79] His participation in al-Mutawakkil's struggle for dominance throughout Yemen gained Amīr Rizq the new imam's favor, resulting in his promotion to the governorship of Mocha in 1718. His extensive experience in the trade made him a fitting candidate for the position.

Amīr Rizq's high profile as the imam's *nākhūdha*, before his appointment to the governorship, is clear from the great pomp and ceremony that welcomed him along Mocha's shores when he returned yearly from Surat. On May 20, 1705, the imam's ships, both commanded by Amīr Rizq, were seen in Bāb al-Mandab, and by the evening of the next day they were visible in the harbor. When they dropped anchor, shots were fired from the bastions around the city and from the ships in the harbor. The governor sent two boats out to the harbor to bring in the crews of both ships. Both "high and low" officers of Mocha came out to welcome Amīr Rizq.[80]

He was well established in Yemen and also maintained connections on the other side of the Arabian Sea, particularly through relationships with the shipowners and merchants of Surat. The Dutch call him a "duke" and a "landowner" in Yemen, indicating that he owned significant properties there in addition to his house in Mocha. When he was al-Mahdī Muḥammad's *nākhūdha*, the Dutch considered him to be a good friend of the VOC.[81] Yearly he acknowledged their presence in Mocha with gifts, camaraderie, and even information about their countrymen from Surat.[82] After he allegedly orchestrated the 1717 attack on the Dutch house and then became governor, they became more critical of his actions, comparing him to the governor al-Ḥuraybī in the way he maintained a monopoly over goods and acted as the city's chief merchant.[83]

Notably, as they observed his governorship, the Dutch wrote in detail about his excessive drinking habits, claiming that he lived a "godless and improper life" and that "people swear that outside of wine, he requires a half bottle of brandy in the morning and another half in the evening everyday."[84] This habit tied him to the European merchant community, because no alcohol was produced or sold in Mocha except the date palm wine made by Jewish vintners to the south of the city, which was considered unpalatable by people accustomed to European varieties.[85] The European ships that came to the harbor yearly brought alcohol for the residents, supplies meant to last a full year until the next shipment arrived. The English usually furnished Amīr Rizq's needs, but the Dutch were also strategic about his alleged addiction.[86] They would request supplies of white or red wine or French brandy from Batavia specifically to suit the governor's taste. When they needed to meet him for a request or to settle an agreement, they would bring a bottle along. Although this heavy drinking cannot have been condoned in Yemen, the Dutch claimed that Amīr Rizq's habits were well known in the city.

After Amīr Rizq was elevated to the governorship in 1718, the imam replaced him with someone named "Mansie" as the royal *nākhūdha*.[87] Later, in 1723 and 1724, Hajjī Muḥammad Mulūd took the position.[88] But these appointments were temporary. On July 24, 1725, news circulated that the imam had appointed a new *nākhūdha* who was on his way to Mocha from Sanaa.[89] When he arrived at the port the Dutch were disappointed. They found that it was Sīdī Ṣāliḥ Ḥalabī, with whom they were familiar enough to describe him as "a bad payer who has been in debt to us for two years."[90] This comment indicates that Ḥalabī was a commercial figure with previous experience at the port. The imam's new *nākhūdha* traveled the Mocha-Surat route for nearly six years until his death in Surat on May 30, 1731.

ʿAlī, Amīr Rizq's son, followed in his father's footsteps by serving as the imam's *nākhūdha* temporarily and then taking over the governorship of Mocha from 1724 until 1727, during which time he married the daughter of Qāsim al-Turbatī.[91] ʿAlī b. Amīr Rizq's short tenure as governor was unsuccessful and ended in his dismissal in 1727 when he refused to take money from Mocha's treasury to pay Imam al-Manṣūr Ḥusayn so that he could fight off the contender to his imamate, Muḥammad b. Isḥāq. ʿAlī was replaced by Shaykh ʿAmr al-Mughallas, who, as governor of Zabid, had given the imam a great gift the year before.[92] In a moment of weakness, ʿAlī took the side of Muḥammad b. Isḥāq when he wielded temporary control of Mocha in his bid for power. When al-Manṣūr's brother surrounded the city, it became clear that Mocha would go back to the imam, and in panic ʿAlī fled on an English ship to Surat. He returned only after Imam al-Manṣūr sent a horse to Mocha as a token that he had pardoned his betrayal.

The imam chose his royal *nākhūdhas* because they displayed cosmopolitan sensibility and a familiarity with commercial practices, maritime routes, and the international world of seafaring. They formed part of a spectrum of merchant communities in Mocha, communities that operated within a clearly articulated structure of functional roles. Merchants stayed within expected spheres of engagement, though all of them worked to encourage the growth of the trade, and one of them even sponsored major city monuments. Many high-profile figures whose businesses dominated the city's trade rarely or never appeared on its shores, such as the famous Gujarati shipowner ʿAbd al-Ghafūr and his grandson Muḥammad ʿAlī. Rather, their *nākhūdhas* represented them abroad, accepted all the signs of their sponsors' privileges, and crystallized their legacies in overseas ports. The Yemeni maritime merchants who traveled the seas, such as Qāsim al-Turbatī, were conversant with larger Indian Ocean culture and comfortable with their European counterparts. Those who worked in the inland trade of Indian Ocean goods, such as Saʿd al-Dīn al-ʿUdaynī, operated in a commercial world largely distinct from that of maritime travel. Together, the stories of the merchants who animated the trading houses of Mocha render the early modern routes of exchange and travel within the Mocha trade network tangible and visible.

5 The Urban Form and Orientation of Mocha

The harbor of Mocha took the shape of a crescent, with a shoreline stretching from south to north and two arms of land jutting from either end into the Red Sea. As ships entered the sheltered haven, multistoried, whitewashed buildings appeared along the shore, punctuated by towering minarets rising high above the skyline. Many visitors mentioned, however, that the city's architectural landscape was more impressive from the water than from within the city itself, where modest houses with conical thatched roofs surrounded decrepit buildings in ruin. The monumentality of the shoreline vista deceived the first-time visitor to Mocha because the most imposing structures bordered the waterside, like a façade to the city, obscuring the interior with its humble, low, mud and thatch settlements and brick structures in disrepair.[1]

The rhythms of city life were determined by Mocha's harsh weather. Excessive heat brought daytime activity to a standstill during the summer months, when even merchants shuttered their houses until the cooler evening hours. Several months of strong winter winds followed during the more temperate season, when sand continually whipped through the air, impeding vision and traffic. Indeed, most of Mocha's merchants tried to escape the city's heat and oppressive weather by spending time in country houses in the more hospitable town of Mawzaʿ to the east and in pleasure gardens built to the south of the city in an area filled with shady palm groves.

All the sources indicate that the walled city of Mocha was modest in dimensions and in the size of its population. At the city's shore, the extent of the walled area reached only half a mile from north to south, and the semicircular wall that wrapped around the city to the east measured only one mile in length.[2] Although there were a number of extramural residential quarters, the city's main houses sat inside the wall. Many of them were fully inhabited only during the high trade season, for the population fluctuated as merchants, pilgrims, and seafarers came and went. Additionally, any political instability in the area invited a surge in the local population as soldiers from the imam's army arrived for temporary residence.

In January 1709, when the French captain La Merveille arrived in Mocha, he noted that the city had 10,000 inhabitants, of which 500 to 600 were soldiers.[3] January marked the beginning of the trade season, and the number of residents was sure to grow over the next months with the arrival of ships from the east. But even after accounting for the influx of traders from abroad, it is clear that Mocha's eighteenth-century population had declined severely from its Ottoman height in the early seventeenth century, a time for which C. G. Brouwer estimated 23,000 transient and settled residents.[4] Comparing Mocha with other Indian Ocean ports with which it was in communication, one sees that it was much smaller than Basra, which had an estimated population of 50,000 to 60,000 at this time, but around the size of Bandar ʿAbbās, which was closer to 9,000.[5]

Most of Mocha's notable residents during the late seventeenth and eighteenth centuries were not native to the city. Governors, city scribes, money exchangers, religious scholars, and the major merchants and *nākhūdhas* were African, Indian, Persian, and Arab, the last from other cities on the Arabian Peninsula. Within the Indian trading community were a number of subgroups, such as the Gujarati Muslim merchants, some of whom were Bohras, and the Hindu and Jain Baniyans. Muslim Lotia merchants, from the Kathiawar Peninsula in India, constituted another subgroup.[6] Armenian merchants are mentioned occasionally in the records but appear not to have constituted a significant block of merchants in the city. English, Dutch, French, Austrian, and Swedish merchants represented Europe. Large communities of Jews and Somalis lived in two residential quarters to the south of the city. The cross section of Mocha's Muslim population reveals a great deal of sectarian diversity, including Sunnīs, Zaydīs, Bohras, and Twelver Shīʿīs, and religious multiplicity encompassing Hindus, Christians, and Jews.

In sharp contrast, Mocha today appears to the visitor a forgotten and depopulated outpost, its brick monuments reduced to crumbling mounds of ruins covered by sand and rubble. The fate of the Mosque of Sayyida Zaynab (fig. 5.1) revealingly illustrates the extent of the city's decay. In 1909 the German traveler Hermann Burchardt photographed the small, flat-roofed mosque with its modest, low minaret, located in what was once the city's center. Even at the time Burchardt's Yemeni companion, Aḥmad b. Muḥammad al-Jarādī, wrote that only twenty stone and brick houses remained standing in the city, reminders of Mocha's bygone commercial heyday.[7] One hundred years later, the crumbling minaret of the Mosque of Sayyida Zaynab (fig. 5.2) stands desolately as a single monument, teetering on a shaky foundation after having lost its adjoining prayer hall amid mounds of ruined debris.[8] Other major public, religious, and private structures have suffered the same destiny as this small mosque. Any analysis of the city's layout, then, hinges upon a thorough reconstruction of the city's monuments and their past spatial coordinates.

Drawing on historical maps, textual sources, aerial photographs, extant evidence from Mocha, and the memories of current residents, I have reconstructed the city's plan from 1683 through 1748, as summarized in map 5.1.[9] The map serves as a reference throughout this chapter, in which I explore the spatial dynamics of Mocha with a focus on the layout of its major built elements and an analysis of its orientation. My breakdown of Mocha's urban shape assumes that geographic, political, and economic systems played important roles. I believe the port city served as a shared location where systems overlapped and required spatial and tangible translation for those who crossed from one to another. I privilege Anthony King's understanding of urban systems, which "emphasizes the symbiotic relationship between the material and spatial aspects of cities, their built environment, and architectural form, and the social, economic, and cultural systems of which they are a part."[10] As a central node between the empire of the Zaydī imam and its Indian Ocean trading partners, Mocha facilitated the meeting of interior hinterland and maritime foreland. Both political worlds and economic systems defined Mocha's city life and its urban form, through tangible, visible, built markers. This relationship of part to whole was complex and fixed in time, and it requires historical recovery.

FIG. 5.1 Mosque of Sayyida Zaynab (now destroyed), Mocha. Photograph by Hermann Burchardt, 1909.

FIG. 5.2 Ruins of the minaret of the Mosque of Sayyida Zaynab, Mocha, 1996.

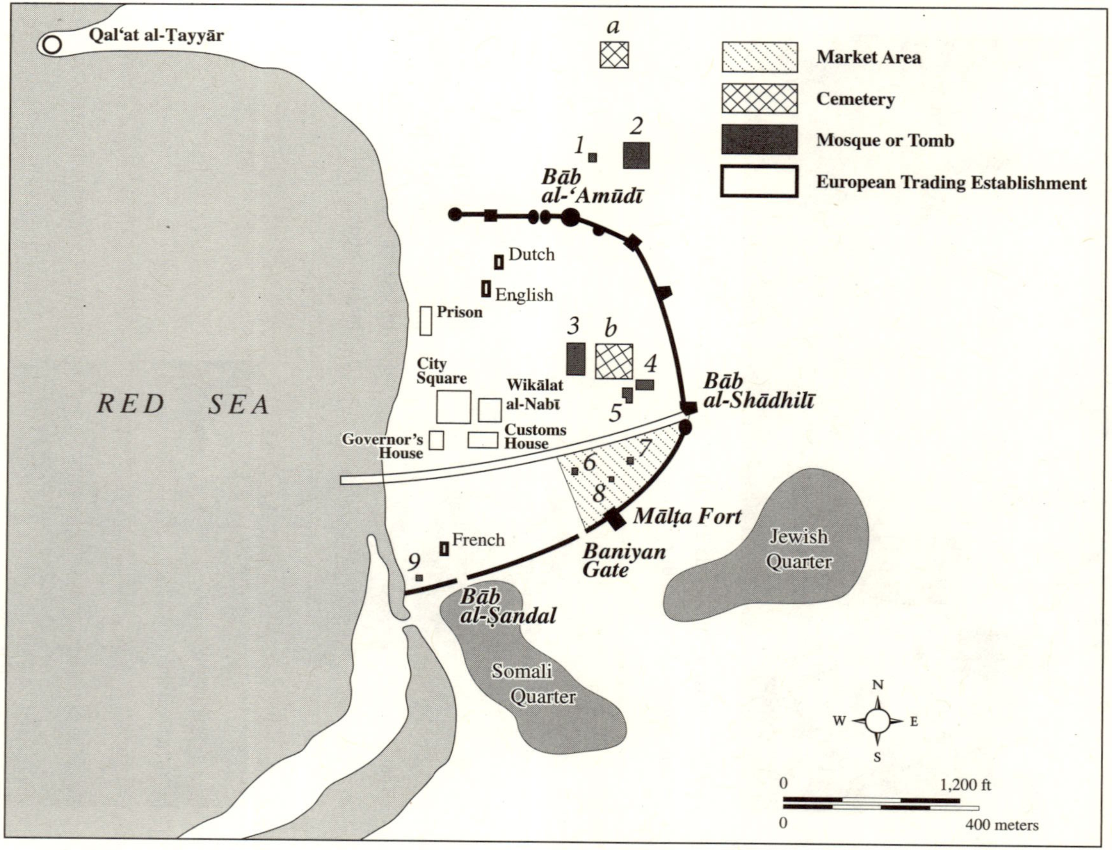

MAP 5.1 Author's reconstruction of Mocha in the late seventeenth and early eighteenth centuries.

1 Tomb of al-ʿAmūdī
2 *Muṣallā*
3 Great Mosque
4 Mosque of al-Shādhilī
5 Tomb of al-Shādhilī
6 Tomb of Ḥātim al-Ahdal
7 Mosque of Sayyida Zaynab
8 Tomb of Shaykh Ṣiddīq al-Shādhilī
9 Mosque of al-Ṣandal
a European cemetery
b Cemetery of al-Shādhilī and the Great Mosque

A Shaykh and the Legend of Mocha's Rise to International Renown

The legend of Mocha's rise, as recounted by the mid-eighteenth-century German traveler Carsten Niebuhr, combines the city's best-known elements—the famous Sufi saint Shaykh ʿAlī b. ʿUmar al-Qirshī al-Shādhilī, the legacy of coffee, and the city's reputation as a major international port:

> Mokha is not an ancient city. It was built about four centuries since. It, like many other cities in the Tehama, owes its origin to a saint, the celebrated *Schech Schoedeli*. This Schech [*shaykh*] acquired at that period so great a reputation, that persons eagerly resorted from the most distant countries to receive his instructions. Some of his devout disciples built huts round his hermitage, which stood on the sea-side. A small village arose on this spot, and was by degrees enlarged into a city. . . . A ship bound from India to Jidda cast anchor, one day, about four hundred years since, in these latitudes. The crew, observing a hut in the desert, had the curiosity to go and see it. The Schech gave those strangers a kind of reception, and regaled them with coffee, of which he was very fond himself, and to which he ascribed great virtues. The Indians who were unacquainted with the use of coffee, thought that this hot liquid, might cure the master of their ship, who was ill. Schaedeli assured them, that, not only should he be cured by the efficacy of his prayers, and of the coffee, but that if they would land their cargo there, they might dispose of it to considerable advantage. Assuming at the same time the air and tone of a prophet, he told them that a city should one day, be built upon that spot, which was to become an eminent mart of the Indian trade.[11]

Since Niebuhr, many other writers, mostly Western, have repeated the story in travel narratives and studies of the city.[12] By aligning the diverse and disparate details that have become associated with Mocha's history, the story presents itself as an archetypal urban myth. It gives coherency to the city's rise from its humble origins to its status as an international port, and it assigns a key role to an important religious figure.

Indeed, al-Shādhilī is the appropriate starting point for any discussion of Mocha's early life, because the city hardly appears in historical chronicles or topographical texts before he settled there in the fourteenth century.[13] He was born in a village called al-Qirshiyya al-suflā, in Wādi Rimaʿ near the lowland city of Zabid, but he made Mocha his home and the locus for his *zāwiya*, or Sufi lodge, and his following after having traveled to the Ḥijāz and Abyssinia. His pious legacy and lengthy career in Mocha brought notice to the city during his lifetime, for many outsiders seeking knowledge and blessings came to visit the *shaykh* in this seaside village. He died on the first of Safar 828, or December 23, 1424, and his tomb marks Mocha's former city center.[14]

Al-Shādhilī has also been credited with the introduction of coffee consumption to the Middle East, although the stories differ on the details of his involvement, and some cite other Sufis as the proposed originators. In his study of the Sufi beginnings and dissemination of coffee consumption, Éric Geoffroy called into question this fundamental link between Mocha's al-Shādhilī and the roots of the global habit.[15] Although sources dating long after the famous saint's death abound with references to al-Shādhilī as the introducer of coffee, none of his contemporary Arab biographers mentioned his relationship to coffee, although they extolled his other accomplishments at length. Hence the common characterization of Mocha's patron saint as coffee's first inductee was clearly posthumous and embellished to match the city's later reputation. Al-Shādhilī's life, however, has become a site for the conflation of a multiplicity of legacies: the legacy of coffee consumption as linked to Sufi practice, the primacy of the international trade of the city of Mocha, and the importance of Yemen as the global home of the coffee bean.

Despite the fancifulness of Mocha's origin tale and the web of coffee legends that surrounds it, the urban myth of Mocha's founding, told by Niebuhr and many after him, does correspond to an important element in the city's history. It is that Mocha witnessed two major stages of growth, first as a village built around a Sufi saint's legacy and then as a major international port, in response to two very different sets of historical needs. The inland village that grew out of al-Shādhilī's popularity and the international port district that stretched along the seaside eventually became integrated into the unified early modern port city. Yet both sectors retained strong and unique qualities within the city's changing social and economic landscape.

The Eastern Core

Although Mocha's early history, before Shaykh al-Shādhilī's arrival in the early fifteenth century, is shrouded in historical debate, it is clear that the city was "a most insignificant port prior to 1500," as Brouwer determined by drawing on a comprehensive pool of evidence.[16] Even after the saint's settlement, sometime in the first or second decade of the fifteenth century, Mocha was described as a modest village, or *qarya*, focused on the saint and later on his legacy and tomb, but not as a major commercial center.[17] During this early period, before the rise of Mocha's port, building in the city was focused on an inland core east of the coastline. Fisherman dominated the coast itself, and no fortified wall protected the city's inhabitants.

The Ottomans, who entered Yemen in 1538, were responsible for shaping much of the early modern city, more than 100 years after the death of al-Shādhilī in 1424. Notably, they developed the port and stimulated new growth along the city's previously undefined shoreline. The Ottoman governor Aydin Pasha produced a new internal dynamic in the urban space by building the city wall around the eastern side in 1037/1628.[18] The fifteenth-century inland core of Mocha thrived in the following centuries, even enclosed within the semicircular wall. In this area one found the major retail institutions and a group of religious structures related to the legacy of al-Shādhilī.

The southeastern part of the wall enclosed the marketplace (map 5.1). This market has since disappeared, but textual sources and maps confirm that it consisted of two parts, a market for nonperishable commodities such as textiles, tools, pottery, and spices and a market that specialized in perishable foods, particularly fruits and vegetables.[19] The market for nonperishables took a built form comparable to that of the well-preserved Tihāmī market of Zabid (fig. 5.3), where individual stalls rise on high, brick-built plinths and segments are covered by a perforated roof that offers shade from the sun's heat while allowing light to filter in.[20] In 1683, Dutch merchants counted a thousand shops in this market, which stretched from west to east and eventually led to Bāb al-Shādhilī, the main gate of the city.[21] The fruit and vegetable market ran along the perimeter of the wall, between the Baniyan Gate and Bāb al-Shādhilī, in an open-air space dedicated for the purpose, as marked on a map published by Jacques Bellin in 1763 (map 5.2).

Many references suggest a wide-ranging public character for this southeastern area, which included numerous coffee shops.[22] In the late seventeenth century, Dutch observers wrote, "There are an unbelievable number of coffee houses, built of straw and bamboo. One can find them filled with Arabs during the whole day (although namely in the mornings and evenings)."[23] A source from the early nineteenth century refers to the *minzila*, or coffee house, that was located in this area by the eastern gate and served as a place for the many maritime men of the city to pass the hot evenings.[24]

This *minzila* apparently disappointed its Western visitor, for it was little more than a rustic meeting house with high, wood frame beds, or charpoys, and water pipes for smoking. Hermann Burchardt's early-twentieth-century photograph (fig. 5.4) captures the modesty of this type of establishment, an unornamented stall along Mocha's brick-built market.

Steps away from this commercial area, important religious structures such as al-Shādhilī's tomb (fig. 5.5) dominated the intramural city's north-eastern portion.[25] The patron saint chose the location of his own tomb, or *qubba*, which was built soon after his death.[26] Builders who came from the area of Yāfiʿ, to the north of Aden, erected the domed structure that marked and adorned the site of his burial.[27] Today his vaulted cenotaph stands prominently within the tomb chamber. Others joined al-Shādhilī in his tomb, such as his son ʿAbd al-Raʾūf, who died on the third of Ramaḍān 857, or September 7, 1453.[28] When Abd al-Raʾūf, the inheritor of his father's legacy of teaching in the city, was buried next to the great saint on the northern side of the chamber, both teak cenotaphs were draped in textiles. Another religious scholar, Faqīh Aḥmad b. Muḥammad al-Zabīdī al-Muqrī, was buried there in 1505.[29]

The tomb underwent a major expansion, from a single-celled domed building to a larger edifice, as detailed by al-Mūsawī, who provided information about the chronology of the enlargement.[30] In 999/1590–91, Ḥasan Pasha, the Ottoman governor, ordered Aḥmad Chalabī, the Syrian translator who was in charge of Mocha at the time, to build a monumental tomb for al-Shādhilī.[31] The promotion of Sufism and the visitation of saints' tombs constituted a major part of the Ottoman effort to garner support and heighten anti-Zaydī sentiment, a particularly potent strategy in the Sunnī lowlands.[32] Hence it is no surprise that the Ottomans would link their authority to the foremost Sufi saint of the city by expanding his tomb. This linkage was reinforced in 1016/1607 when the Ottoman governor of Yemen Sinān Pasha Kaykhiyā (not to be confused with Koca Sinān Pasha, the wazir) died at the port unexpectedly during his return trip to Istanbul and his son, Mehmed Bey, buried him in al-Shādhilī's enlarged tomb.[33] Today, nineteen subsequent burials can be counted in the *qubba*, some of which are unidentified. More recent burials lie in the expanded mosque section in the northern part of the tomb.[34] The sanctity of the *shaykh*'s burial has been maintained continuously, and people travel in large numbers from all over Yemen to perform the yearly *ziyāra*, or ritual visitation to holy sites, of al-Shādhilī on the fifteenth of Safar.

FIG. 5.3 The *sūq*, Zabid, Yemen, 1996.

FIG. 5.4 A stall in the *sūq* (now destroyed), Mocha. Photograph by Hermann Burchardt, 1909.

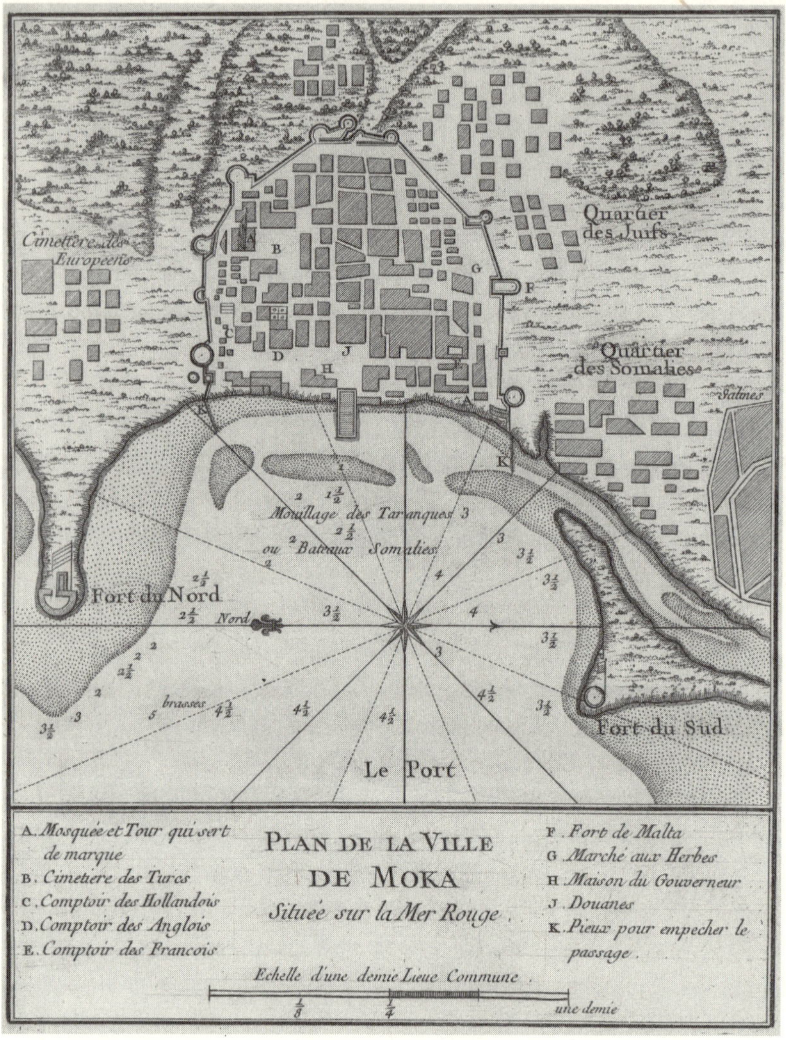

MAP 5.2 "Plan de la Ville de Moka." Reproduced from Jacques Bellin, *Le Petit Atlas Maritime*, 1763.

In regard to the monumental, nine-domed Mosque of al-Shādhilī (see fig. 4.1), al-Mūsawī wrote that it was built after the expansion of al-Shādhilī's tomb, again under the sponsorship of the Ottoman governor Ḥasan Pasha in his effort to promote the saint's legacy in the city.[35] At this time a *minbar*, or pulpit, of green stone was added to the prayer hall, and a high minaret, later restored in the early eighteenth century by the Gujarati Bohra merchant Mullā Muḥammad ʿAlī, crowned the skyline. According to al-Mūsawī, after construction of the al-Shādhilī mosque, Friday prayer took place there, suggesting that the newer domed mosque replaced the larger Great Mosque in this function.[36]

The older Great Mosque stood to the northwest of the pair of al-Shādhilī monuments. An exact date for the structure is unavailable, but it probably dates to the time of al-Shādhilī, when the saint and his followers would have required a large mosque for congregational prayer.[37] Furthermore, it seems unlikely that the Ottomans would have built this large, hypostyle, flat-roofed structure, so different from their other, domed mosques in Yemen. Italian shelling destroyed the Great Mosque during the Turkish-Italian War in 1911, along with several other sites along Yemen's Red Sea coast.[38] The only visual reminder of its form survives in a single photograph taken by Hermann Burchardt in 1909 (fig. 5.6).[39] Its exterior was white-washed and lined with grilled windows and blind arched niches. Inside, imported, faceted wooden columns supported its ceiling.[40] Its single, tapered minaret, with rows of carved relief ornamentation in plaster, served as the model for the minaret of the al-Shādhilī mosque.

In the seventeenth and eighteenth centuries, the two religious structures named for al-Shādhilī, along with the Great Mosque, or al-Jāmiʿ al-Kabīr, made up a religious sector in the eastern part of the city. A cemetery for Muslims, located near the mosques, further defined this portion of the town.[41] Contemporary observers, however, never mentioned burials taking place in this intramural cemetery. It appears that by this time, extramural burial grounds had taken over the functions of the small, overcrowded cemetery situated close to the saint's tomb.[42]

Smaller religious structures sat within the market area. Nestled in the town's commercial core, the single-celled, unadorned Tomb of Shaykh Ṣiddīq al-Shādhilī stood out with its conical dome, which is extant today but in poor condition. Local residents claim that he was one of al-Shādhilī's three sons, perhaps Zayn al-ʿĀbidīn, who died in the fifteenth century.[43] The Mosque of Sayyida Zaynab (fig. 5.1) was located nearby, interwoven with

FIG. 5.5 Tomb of al-Shādhilī, Mocha, 2000.

FIG. 5.6 The Great Mosque (now destroyed), Mocha.
Photograph by Hermann Burchardt, 1909.

the commercial sprawl of the *sūq*. Two travelers mentioned the presence of the Mosque of Sayyida Zaynab in 1835, but it probably had been part of the city's landscape for far longer.[44]

Preceding the development of the port in the sixteenth century, the commercial sector and the religious precinct to its north functioned tightly as a unified public core, with residential neighborhoods surrounding it. Although none of the houses from this early period still stands, one can determine where some residential quarters were situated. Today, a modest, low, whitewashed building with a flat roof (fig. 5.7) marks the burial site of Ḥātim b. Aḥmad al-Ahdal al-Yamanī, the famous poet.[45] He died in 1013/1604, having lived in Mocha for thirty-seven years.[46] The present location of his tomb, in the center of the city next to Bayt al-Akhḍarī, a house built in 1326/1908–9, provides information on the location of residential quarters in the late sixteenth century, for he was buried in his own house at the western edge of the commercial quarter. The present tomb's shape suggests that al-Ahdal lived in a small, single-story building now masked under several layers of lime plaster. When al-Ahdal lived in Mocha, in the late sixteenth century, his house would have been one of many in a residential neighborhood north of the *sūq* and west of the religious precinct. Another major residential area was located north of the Mosque of al-Shādhilī. In the early twentieth century a majestic house, Bayt Sīdī Nūnū (fig. 5.8), stood there amid sand mounds representing the traces of past houses. Residents finally abandoned this quarter by the end of the twentieth century, when extensive decay instigated migration to other quarters both inside and outside the city wall.[47]

The majority of Mocha's population resided in modest thatch dwellings, or *ʿushshas*, both intramural and extramural. Although few details exist about the way these simple houses were built and used, contemporary examples and historic drawings (fig. 5.9) provide some clues.[48] The houses were generally circular in plan and built around a raised, packed mud floor. The walls and the conical roof were thatched and held in place with a net of knotted ropes. Entry was made through a wooden door frame, and the interior mud surfaces were often decorated with built-in shelves and radial painting that accentuated the rise of the cone-shaped roof. Such houses were rarely freestanding but rather constituted the main structure within a larger enclosure of mud walls that included an open courtyard for utility functions.

It is clear that a large number of these modest thatch dwellings and enclosures shared the town's intramural space with more stately buildings

FIG. 5.7 Tomb of Ḥātim al-Ahdal, Mocha, 2000.

FIG. 5.8 Bayt Sīdī Nūnū (now destroyed), Mocha.
Photograph by Hermann Burchardt, 1909.

of stone and whitewashed brick. Indeed, Brouwer claimed that mud and thatch settlements constituted the majority of city structures in the early seventeenth century.[49] This distribution seems to have been maintained through the early eighteenth century, as affirmed by a Dutch source from 1701. It states that the city had "many poor huts" and around 450 stone houses that were not inhabited year-round but rather were rented out when the merchants were in residence during the high trade season.[50] Although the records provide few details about the exact locations of the perishable settlements within the city, it does not appear that they were segregated from the stone and brick houses.[51] The majority of residential neighborhoods in Mocha included both types of dwellings.

In the late seventeenth and early eighteenth centuries this inland core persisted, although it lost its integrity as a village and was transformed by many Ottoman monumental additions, the seventeenth-century wall and its corresponding gates, the central roadway that cut through the city, and the shoreline development that I discuss next. Through the nineteenth century, however, this key area, the original heart of the city, still functioned as the local retail market and sanctified core of Mocha.

The Shoreline Strip

In 1616 the Dutch merchant Pieter van den Broecke visited Mocha and published the earliest descriptive observations of the Ottoman port. Describing the inland core, he referred to the port city as a mere "fisher's village" before the Ottomans set up trading facilities there during the sixteenth century.[52] Drawn to the mobility that the Red Sea provided, the Ottomans developed the western, seaside portion of the city (fig. 5.10) for the trade by placing their major administrative buildings and defensive structures along the water. Besides developing Mocha's shoreline for their burgeoning trade, the Ottomans used it as the launching point for administrative activities related to the maintenance of Ottoman Yemen, for which Mocha served as a central place of embarkation and disembarkation. The Ottomans privileged the functional livelihood of the trade and navy as well as the maintenance of communication with other Ottoman territories.

The city square, the governor's house, the customs house, and the *wikāla*, a caravanserai, on the shore constituted the nucleus of an area of development that stretched along the seaside, separate from the established interior. These administrative buildings have long since collapsed,

FIG. 5.9 View of Mocha from the north, showing ʿushshas, or circular thatch houses, nineteenth century.

FIG. 5.10 Artist's rendering of the south quarter of Mocha, nineteenth century. The Mosque of al-Ṣandal stands in the center.

so their precise dates of establishment are impossible to ascertain. That the Ottomans founded administrative facilities in the city by the mid-sixteenth century is supported by a coin minted in the port of Mocha and dated 970/1562–63.[53] Because the Ottomans were minting Mocha coins at that time, we can assume that they had established their other administrative and official functions in the city by then. By the end of the sixteenth century the port was functioning with all the necessary facilities of a major harbor, as is confirmed by an anonymous Arabic source detailing the rise of Mocha and Aden's associated decline as the central port at the mouth of the Red Sea.[54]

In the late seventeenth and early eighteenth centuries this Ottoman public core persisted. The Qāsimīs made no effort to alter the existing order of the port but rather chose to work within the fixed Turkish infrastructure. Mocha's governors during the Qāsimī period made few changes to the city's urban landscape and funneled their resources back into the highlands of Yemen. For that reason Mocha appeared majestic from the seaside, with its large, Ottoman-period buildings lining the coast, while the interior of the city resembled the more ephemeral appearance of port cities of the Persian Gulf such as Muscat and Kung, which were dominated by houses in mud and thatch and buildings in disrepair.[55]

The Ottoman city square, or *maydān*,[56] defined the center of the western seaside strip, surrounded by public buildings and lines of merchants' houses stretching along the shore. The open square hosted the important ceremonial functions of presentation and reception, as well as military inspection. Every day the city's soldiers waited in the square to escort the governor from his palace to the mosque for the noon prayer, with flags and music.[57] Cavalry exercises were conducted in the square every Friday after congregational prayer at the mosque and occasionally to celebrate a religious feast day.[58] On ʿĪd al-Aḍḥā the governor slaughtered animals and distributed fresh meat to Mocha's residents in this public area.[59] He often ordered his soldiers to line up in the square for inspections.

The governor's house, located on the shore north of the jetty, was the most impressive monument of this open square. The Ottomans had built the palace, which differed from an ordinary Mocha house only in size and luxury, not in general plan, building materials, or type of decoration. The house remained the official residence of the city's governor through the early nineteenth century, when the rebellious governor Sultan Ḥasan built an opulent replacement. The governor's house was more than just a residence; its main hall served the official purposes of reception and audience, thereby functioning as the seat of the administration. Textual references indicate that its interior must have been generous. In 1727 the new governor of Mocha, Shaykh ʿAmr Mughallas, arrived in the city with his ten wives and concubines, as well as many bags.[60] Apparently the palace was large enough to accommodate such a retinue while housing all necessary official functions.

The customs house, or *furḍa*, was situated immediately inland from the jetty beyond the Sea Gate, a coastal surveillance building, to the east of the governor's palace.[61] This large square structure was surrounded on all sides by a continuous storage shed. Brouwer described the institution as both "a weighing house and a tollhouse, called the *alphandigo* by the Dutch, a Portuguese corruption of the Arabic term for a trading house, *al-funduq*."[62] The customs house was a requisite stop for almost every merchant and traveler who entered the port.

The other main public building on the square was Wikālat al-Nabī, a caravanserai built by the Ottoman governor Mehmed Pasha (r. 1616–21).[63] Although the name *wikāla* might suggest that it was a commercial structure, in the Qāsimī era its use was limited to lodging traveling peddlers and pilgrims, who arrived in large numbers en route to the Holy Cities. This modest structure sat across the square from the governor's palace.[64] Pack animals that could be hired for inland transportation were tethered in the square next to the *wikāla*. These three public structures—the governor's house, the customs house, and the *wikāla*—all built by the Ottomans to accommodate local administration, the trade, and pilgrimage, formed the center of a new western shoreline band of the city in the sixteenth century, upstaging the previous inland center near the *sūq* and the city's major mosques.

From the seventeenth through the nineteenth century, Mocha's prison was located along the waterside north of the city square.[65] Contemporary daily accounts mention the prison often, because the governor was accustomed to placing important members of the community, including merchants and officials, in jail temporarily to forcibly procure loans and advance payment of tolls. The imam used the island of Zaylaʿ, across the Gulf of Aden in modern-day Somalia, for exile and remote confinement of criminals and outlaws who threatened the stability of his rule—men such as Muḥammad b. Ḥusayn al-Kawkabānī, who spent almost a year there in 1724–25 as punishment for his participation in Muḥammad b. Isḥāq's rebellion against Imam al-Mutawakkil Qāsim.[66] These prisoners traveled from the highlands through Mocha, usually spending at least one night in its prison before being sent by boat to the island's isolated jail. That the size of Mocha's prison was considerable is demonstrated by the fact that fifty-nine prisoners who were on their way to Zaylaʿ spent the night there on June 30, 1725.[67] Zaylaʿ was part of the imamate, under the jurisdiction of Mocha, and the seaside location of the Mocha prison served as a visual marker of that overseas relationship.

The Turks strove to incite local dissatisfaction with their Zaydī opponents by supporting local interest in the cult of saints throughout the Shāfiʿī regions, as is demonstrated by their sponsorship of the expanded Tomb of al-Shādhilī and the new mosque bearing his name. Aside from these two structures, only one other mosque in the city bears the Ottoman mark. The Mosque of al-Ṣandal stood on the southern coastline, within the city wall. Previously domed, this structure held both a prayer hall and the tomb of Shaykh al-Ṣandal. Today a flat-roofed, modern mosque stands in its stead, so analysis of its historic organization is impossible.[68] All that remains of its original form is its historic minaret (fig. 5.11), which reflects a local style in its tall, rounded, whitewashed shaft, a balcony supported by rows of sawtooth bands, and low-relief carved niches on its surface. A nineteenth-century print (fig. 5.10) shows that the original mosque had a dome, which sat on a wide, low, polygonal drum. It is impossible to determine whether the dome covered the prayer hall in a standard Ottoman form or whether the domed chamber surmounted the saint's tomb with an adjoining prayer hall. But in either form, this single shoreline mosque expressed Ottoman expansionist notions in its visible location and distinctive profile.[69]

When one turns to locating private structures, the task of reconstruction becomes more difficult, because the monumental homes of the seventeenth- and eighteenth-century merchants crumbled long ago. Although the general European experience in the city does not necessarily reflect the practices of all merchants, the Europeans followed local protocols for housing and trade in this noncolonial city in which they never held positions of great power. Because one can pinpoint the locations of their houses with a great deal of precision, the European residential pattern must serve as an example of housing patterns for the merchant class.

The Europeans' houses, which also functioned as their trading establishments, were all situated along the seaside strip. Although many European merchant companies changed residences over the years, this axis was their major area of housing. Map 5.1 identifies the Dutch, English, and French company establishments as they were located in the early eighteenth century. The practical advantage of living along the seaside was obvious—proximity to all the important administrative buildings and the port. Furthermore, the fresh breezes off the water cooled the homes, offering relief from the unbearable heat of the humid city. These whitewashed, multistory houses of stone and brick that stretched from south to north dominated the shoreline. Within this area also stood a large number of low, single-story warehouses that resident merchants used as storage facilities. Even the imam had a dedicated storehouse in the city, referred to as the imam's *wikāla*, where commodities were kept before being transported to Sanaa.[70] Beyond this front line, the rest of the city appears to have been mixed in distribution, including the more modest, less permanent structures of ordinary residents.

Defense and Surveillance

Historical documentation offers extensive information about Mocha's defensive structures, allowing one to reconstruct the shape of the city wall and its fortified towers with great accuracy. Built in 1628, the wall represents the Turks' last effort to hold onto Yemeni territory before their imminent expulsion.[71] Their priorities were directed toward defense against landward attacks rather than seaside offense. The wall was composed of a mixture of materials, with stone and baked brick foundations and upper levels of sun-dried brick and packed mud.[72] A Dutch observer in 1701 reported that its height reached between ten and twelve feet.[73]

The extent, condition, and height of the city wall changed continually over time as restoration efforts responded to current threats and political instability. For instance, in the early eighteenth century the governor Shaykh Sāliḥ al-Ḥuraybī raised the existing wall by twenty *dhirā*ʿ, or cubits, and added the Mālṭa Fort to strengthen observation points toward the south.[74] In 1726, when the city feared unrest because of the future imam al-Manṣūr Ḥusayn's rebellion against his father, Mocha prepared itself for a possible attack on its eastern side by repairing the city wall and the main battery at Bāb al-Shādhilī. The labor for such public endeavors was sought from the ranks of the army, led by the governor and his advisors, and often paid for by the city's merchants.[75]

Four gates pierced the semicircular wall.[76] In the east, Bāb al-Shādhilī, named for the saint whose tomb and mosque lay directly inside the wall next to the gate, was the largest entryway to the city. Europeans referred to it as the Great Gate. Bāb al-ʿAmūdī was named after Shaykh Muḥammad b. Saʿīd al-ʿAmūdī, who was buried to the north of the city outside the wall in a domed tomb that still stands today.[77] To the southeast was the Baniyan gate, also called al-Bāb al-Ṣaghīr, the Small Gate, which led directly into the market. The gate situated in the southwest, close to the shoreline, was called Bāb al-Ṣandal, for the saint buried in the nearby tomb and mosque.[78] The major city gates were equipped for defense, each with a draw gate and a battery, making it possible to seal off the city from the east completely. Unsurprisingly, the most strategic point from the inland side, Bāb al-Shādhilī, was the best equipped.[79] This gate was closely monitored, not just for defensive purposes but also so that goods arriving from or leaving for inland Yemen could be closely supervised and taxed. A nineteenth-century French print of Bāb al-Shādhilī (fig. 5.12) reveals that it had a bent entrance, so that one entered from the southeast and not directly from the east. Two circular, crenellated towers flanked the central doorway, and canons and artillery were directed from second-story windows and openings. Projecting windows provided surveillance points from above.

Forts embedded in the city wall at strategic points between the main gates added to Mocha's defensive capacity. They included the three forts between Bāb al-ʿAmūdī and Bāb al-Shādhilī, overseeing the area outside the northeast quadrant of the city. The Mālṭa Fort, between the Baniyan gate and Bāb al-Shādhilī in the southeastern sector, was the largest fort that was not freestanding. Adding to the defensive infrastructure targeting inland aggression were towers placed at strategic points outside Bāb al-Shādhilī along the main eastern transit route to Mawzaʿ, Taʿizz, and Sanaa. These towers, built by the governor Aḥmad Khazindār, allowed the al-Shādhilī wells to be managed and protected, for water was precious in this dry city with only brackish supplies.[80] They also served as lookout posts so that the city could be warned of oncoming enemies from the east.

There was no continuous city wall along the seaside in the early part of the eighteenth century, but the Sea Gate, called Bāb al-Sāḥil, Bāb al-Baḥr, and Bāb al-Furḍa, was a freestanding surveillance site that monitored entry into the city from the jetty. It contained a large reception area where the *amīr al-baḥr* often sat.[81] Such a surveillance point allowed for initial inspection of goods before they entered the customs house, and it gave the governor (by way of the *amīr al-baḥr*) the opportunity to identify potential merchandise for purchase immediately upon its arrival. Merchants and their goods could

FIG. 5.11 Minaret of the Mosque of al-Ṣandal, Mocha, 2000.

FIG. 5.12 Bāb al-Shādhilī, Mocha, nineteenth century.

be held in this waterside gate before embarkation if the governor was not prepared to release them. The square fort Qalʿat al-Faḍlī, built by the Ottoman governor Faḍlī Pasha (r. 1622–24) during the first Ottoman period and located to the north of the Sea Gate, bolstered seaside defense.[82] A fort also stood next to the jetty. It was built by the governor Sayyid Ḥasan al-Jurmūzī in the late seventeenth century, probably as an effort to control the pirate attacks that were a constant menace at the time.[83]

The city was shaped like a sickle with its northern and southern tips extending into the water, each crowned with a fort (map 5.2).[84] The fort known as Qalʿat al-Ṭayyār, on the northern tongue of land, mirrored Qalʿat ʿAbd al-Raʾūf, at the endpoint of the southern tongue of land.[85] Together they formed a unified line of defense against enemies who sailed into the curved harbor. When the French took Qalʿat ʿAbd al-Raʾūf in 1737, they gave precise measurements of its interior, noting that it was sixty feet in diameter and eleven feet high inside, with a bench in the interior raised to seven feet, as well as a parapet at four feet with many holes.[86] Following the French attack on the city, the governor built a bridge from the shore across to the southern promontory, which became an island at high tide, so that his troops could reach the southern fort quickly in the case of another military siege.[87] These two forts stood at strategic points, so an enemy who claimed either of them would have unrestricted access to the city by land when the tide was low.

Visitors to the city, who were often keenly concerned with its military facilities, described these defensive structures in great detail. They indicated that the city wall and its concentrated surveillance structures echoed the duality of its intramural sectors. Although the walled perimeter allowed for overall protection of the city, the two poles—the inland path pointing out of the city along the road to Taʿizz and culminating at Bāb al-Shādhilī and the extended strip along the seaside—required the greatest defenses. The layout of the city's defensive elements emphasized this organization of urban elements. Defensive structures stretched along the shore in the west and out into the bay, and inland forts followed the city wall in a rough wedge pointing east at Bāb al-Shādhilī.

A Divided Marketplace

Looking at the reconstructed plan of Mocha (map 5.1), it is clear that one main axis dominated the city, a roadway stretching from west to east and linking the city's seaside and inland sectors. This road was a major topographical feature for many centuries, defining the flow of visitors into and out of the city. Brouwer confirmed that it already existed in the early seventeenth century: "In the heart of al-Mukhā a long street led as straight as an arrow from the jetty, alongside the south walls of palace and *furḍa*, to the east. This slightly wider road may be considered the main street of the city."[88] It was wide enough to accommodate the pack animals that moved along its length in great numbers, transporting goods to and from the shore. Traces of this main axis appear even in a twentieth-century photograph of the city, long after Mocha's trade had waned and caravans no longer frequented the roadway.[89]

Although a central street is not a feature unique to this city, the arrangement of elements along it deserves further discussion. In Mocha, important official, public, and religious structures punctuated either end of the axis rather than being organized into a unified public sector. The retail world of the everyday bazaar was physically linked to the religious realm and the local circuit of saints, whereas the wholesale world of trade lay at the city's other pole and maritime gateway. This spatial split between the maritime wholesale and local retail sectors diverges greatly from the layouts of other commercial cities, such as those described by the urban historian Donatella Calabi, who emphasized the centripetal shaping force of the marketplace in early modern Europe. In examples such as Venice, Barcelona, Paris, London, Amsterdam, and Antwerp, the market square and its related elements magnetized other commercial and economic facilities, resulting in a multifunctional economic zone.[90] Such an expectation about the spatial centrality and functional cohesion of the market applies not only to early modern European capitals but also to the Arab world during the same period. There the market often appears as a central site for commercial activity, both long-distance and local, that is linked to religious and public institutions.

The capital of Qāsimī Yemen, Sanaa, provides an example of the ways in which markets took on central and unified shapes, in contrast to the situation in Mocha. A continuous path wove through the fabric of the intramural city of Sanaa, its endpoints punctuated by the major gates Bāb al-Yaman to the south and Bāb Shuʿūb in the north (map 5.3). In Sanaa, however, unlike in Mocha, the main roadways converged in a cluster in the center of the city, where the most important religious and commercial institutions were situated in a single, cohesive public district. These institutions were closely linked economically as well as spatially, because *waqf*, or pious endowment,

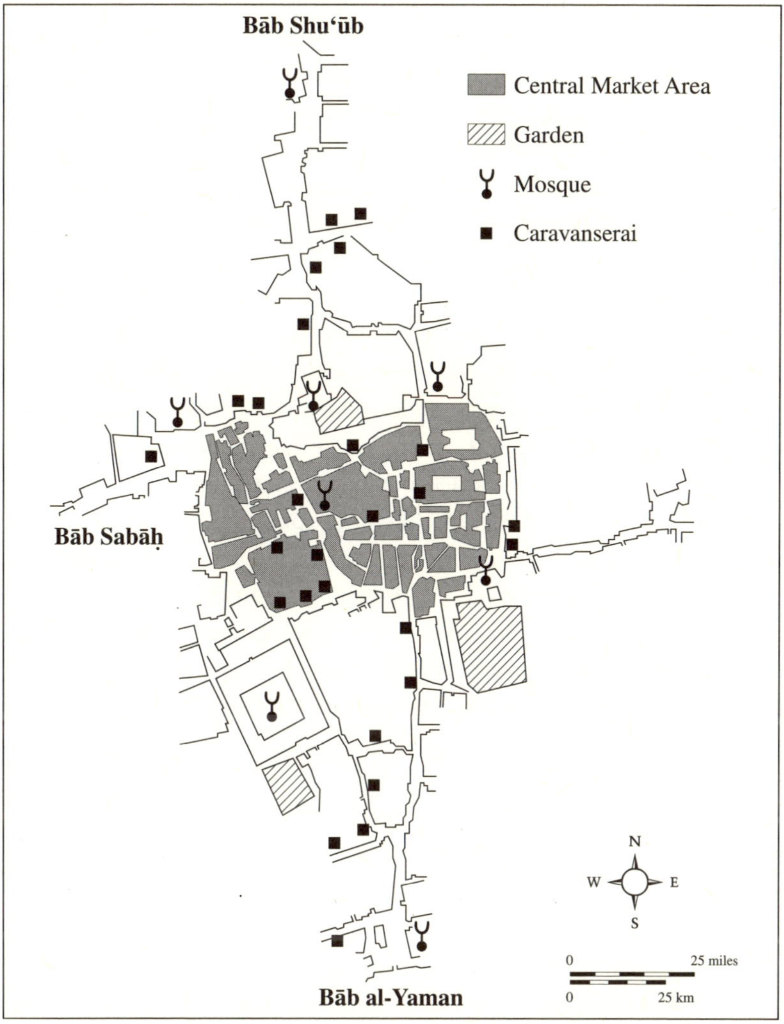

MAP 5.3 The central market area, Sanaa.

revenues from commercial institutions often supported the maintenance of religious ones. Large wholesale buildings were seamlessly interwoven with the smaller stores in the retail market to form a tightly knit commercial area, particularly in the eighteenth century, when many *samsaras*, or wholesale trade structures, were newly built. Artisans populated the *sūq*, linking production with sales and distribution. The more private *ḥāras*, or residential neighborhoods, surrounded this central core. Such a layout established a clear distinction between the public and the private while maintaining an integration of wholesale and retail functions, as well as artisanal production, within the public commercial domain. Notably, in the eighteenth century the imam's palace was located to the west, outside both realms.

In the case of Mocha, the seaside point of the axis was marked by the official structures that administered the wholesale overseas trade of the city and the merchants' houses, in stone and whitewashed brick, which added to the everyday functional operations of the long-distance trade. The eastern quadrant of town, with its multiple mosques, tombs, and intramural cemetery, served as a well-trafficked public retail region and religious precinct that catered to the needs of the local community. Public, religious, and official institutions at each end defined the length and the extent of the city's east-west axis and roadway, stretching along the shore in the west and clustered at the inland point of convergence in the east, rather than being gathered at the center of the city. This organization was not planned but resulted as a function of the city's development over time and changing urban character.

A City in a Network

Mocha in the late seventeenth and early eighteenth centuries offered visitors two facades. Travelers entering from the seaside through the gate on the shore, Bāb al-Sāḥil, saw first the nearby governor's house, the customs house, the caravanserai, and the monumental stone houses of the merchants, all of which emphasized the official nature of this entry point and the prominence of overseas trade and pilgrimage. Those who entered by Bāb al-Shādhilī in the east saw first the *sūq* and the most important religious structures of the city, which were named for its patron saint. Appropriately, the seaside entrance fostered an initial urban experience that privileged contact with the world of maritime and international wholesale trade. The inland entrance introduced the city by displaying the familiar elements of the Yemeni lowland village—the retail market and recognizable religious structures. The two sets of spatial and built elements facilitated a transition between the realms of the Indian Ocean maritime network and the Zaydī highlands of the Qāsimī imamate, mediated by the landmarks of a lowland Sunnī village. One may understand the city as functioning like a directional signpost, indicating the course of the trade routes through a varied combination of visual and structural signals. On its western edge, functions related to its trade identity and links to overseas locations predominated, including the prison, which signaled a relationship to Zaylaʿ across the Red Sea. On its eastern edge, links to the city's inland counterparts and the local concerns of a Yemeni Muslim community were the most visible and recognizable features. The concentration of defense and surveillance structures mirrored this urban bifurcation by imposing upon the city the form of a funnel opening toward the sea in the west and closing in on the east, pointing like a needle toward the highlands.

Although architectural and urban forms have long been discussed under the rubric of cosmological concepts, art historian Suzanne Blier's treatment of worldview, creation myths, and the formation of meaning in the Batammaliba house in West Africa is particularly helpful as a model for conceiving of the relationship between larger global systems and the shape of the built environment.[91] Using relational terms such as "directional affiliation" and the "condensed metaphor," Blier described the translation of cosmologic concepts into visual and built icons within house form, highlighting aspects of directionality and orientation in her analysis of part in relation to whole. The circular shapes that echo throughout the Batammaliba house evoke the originary circular form of the earth, as conceived in local mythology. The supporting beams aligned from east to west take on emblematic qualities, recalling the movement of the solar deity's passage throughout the day. What is significant about Blier's analysis is that the house does more than simply represent the shape of the earth or point to the details of its creation myth. Rather, its parts allow residents to "bridge the conceptual chasm between the highly abstract and remote realm of the larger cosmos and the practical, lived experiences of the world. These metaphors, like metaphors everywhere, serve to clarify the unclear and familiarize that which is foreign."[92]

Although Mocha's landscape was shaped by commercial and administrative necessity rather than by ritual resilience within a fixed belief system, Blier's notions contribute to the understanding of the role Mocha played within its larger trade network. The city functioned as a scaled-down diagram of the commercial and political network that defined its coordinates, its economic livelihood, and its administrative dimensions. Much as in the city of Surat, called the "Gateway of Mecca" and "the door to the house of God" by Mughal rulers who saw in its shape a directional impulse that collapsed thousands of miles of maritime distance, the built features of Mocha evoked through their layout the signals of both local and faraway places.[93] The city played an instrumental role as a built tool of spatial translation for those who experienced the urban fabric after arriving from either faraway inland or overseas sites and who struggled to cope with the dislocation that accompanies long-distance travel.

Central to this discussion are the shaping forces of movement through the urban sphere, however fleeting they may be. In the case of commercial cities in early modern Europe, Calabi noted that "the city absorbs, uses and regenerates every form of movement," and "one gets the impression that the market's configuration was more heavily determined by the norms dictating spaces of movement and pause . . . than by building design.[94] In Mocha the locations and orientations of major buildings, streets, and gates mapped out the trade routes while facilitating the flow of merchants and their cargo along part of the lengthy route from Indian Ocean ports to Sanaa, the highland capital. The main roadway formed a political and economic channel linking the port to the inland, accommodating and marking the movement of people, revenue, and goods into and out of the Arabian Peninsula. The buildings at either end framed the urban experience of those who passed through the city's gates. The programmatic ways in which inhabitants used the space reinforced the ongoing and dynamic relationship between foreland and hinterland, with the port city the threshold between the two realms.

Mocha's urban shape must be viewed in relation to the processes by which it was formed. Indeed, the map of the city is meaningless without a consideration of the unique urban development that brought about its shape. One must remember both its beginnings as a small seaside village that sprouted around the *zāwiya* of a famous Sufi saint and its later dimensions as a major international port. These two distinct shaping elements led to a spatial bifurcation of the city and its marketplace, but both parts were used and instrumentalized by the Qāsimī administrators, the city's merchants, and its residents in the seventeenth and eighteenth centuries.

6 *Trading Spaces*

At its most essential, the role of the maritime port city is to facilitate the movement of goods from the sea onto dry land and from the interior into maritime networks. At Mocha the transfer of goods entailed an extended process and involved many players. Small lighter boats left from the jetty to bring in cargo from the larger Indian Ocean, Persian Gulf, and Red Sea vessels that had newly arrived. Merchants hired day laborers and pack animals from the port to carry the bundles to the customs house. After the imam's inspectors and scribes had thoroughly scrutinized the goods and recorded their weights and quantities, they released the cargo into the merchant's possession. From that point the goods entered the free market, where they were sold or traded by the merchant's broker and then either returned to the maritime sphere, to be sold again somewhere else, or sent into the interior of Qāsimī Yemen for local consumption.

Because the import and export trade was the major business of the city, one might expect that the structures that traveling merchants used for their business negotiations, lodging, and storage were numerous and heavily trafficked during the peak season. But eighteenth-century Mocha calls into question the dominant paradigms for conceiving of spaces of trade in the Arab world. Its commercial practices collapse a rigid understanding of form and function, and the needs of its flourishing trade blur the boundary between public and private spaces as traditionally cast. Mocha serves as a significant example in which textual sources—namely, the Dutch Dag

Registers—provide daily documentation of trade throughout the city and in which extant architectural remains permit insights into the spatial and architectural context of such activities.

Commercial Architecture in Arab Capitals

In his comprehensive study of Middle Eastern markets, Mohamed Scharabi articulated a general typological framework for commercial architecture that provides a structure for the conventional understanding of market organization in the historic Islamic world. Supported by examples from North Africa, the eastern Mediterranean, the Turkish and Persian worlds, and the Arabian Peninsula, Scharabi's straightforward framework is useful, because the terminology for commercial architecture is often slippery, misleading, and historically unstable.[1] A single term may refer to several types of structures with various functions, and standard types go by many different names according to subregion.

As an ordering mechanism, Scharabi posited three broad categories of commercial buildings: the *sūq*, the *qayṣariyya*, and the *khān*. The retail *sūq* consists of street-level stretches of stores that can be opened individually and cater to the general public. Shop owners lease these stalls to sell goods, and craftsmen use them doubly as workshops and as retail sites to vend their finished wares. The *qayṣariyya* is a freestanding structure or an area within the market, without any lodging facilities, dedicated to the production and sale of specialized merchandise for the retail sphere. The *khān* is a structure for wholesale, bulk trade, intended for the use of the merchant community, with lodging and storage facilities. The three types of buildings meet in a spatially unified market center that addresses the multiple needs of commercial communities and their clients.

Of the three kinds of commercial structures, the *khān* is of primary interest here because it was the most important type of building in the Arab world that played a role in large-scale international trade. Often translated as caravanserai, the *khān* as a generic type may take many different names depending on region, date of construction, and subtype. Some other lexical possibilities from the Arab world include *wikāla* and *funduq*. In highland Yemen the term *samsara* appears widely.[2] Despite the diverse names, these structures were used in a fairly consistent manner historically and maintained a standard built form with slight variations. I use the term "urban *khān*" to refer to the general type of metropolitan, wholesale public structure that encompasses all the subtypes just named and is distinct from the caravanserai found along rural pilgrimage and trade routes. Although the rural caravanserai shares structural qualities with the urban *khān*, its functions and clientele diverge, so it should be treated separately.[3] Although the terms *khān*, *funduq*, and *wikāla* may also be associated with official or governmental institutions, I identify the urban *khān* as a public structure intended for the use of local and itinerant merchants and not as an administrative establishment.

Located in the heart of Sanaa, the *khān* known as Samsarat al-Naḥḥās (fig. 6.1) provides a good example of the layout and organization of an urban *khān*.[4] With a single entrance that could be securely locked at night, the lower level was subdivided into small stalls rented by individual merchants to store their goods. The stalls were organized around a ground-floor central courtyard that served as a common room for trade, exchange, and discussion. In this communal open space, officials disseminated news concerning the trade, and merchants made prospects for deals. From there goods were filtered into the Sanaani retail market or bought in bulk for redistribution to other cities around Yemen. All merchants arrived in Sanaa by land, and their pack animals were tethered on the ground floor. The upper two levels (fig. 6.2), subdivided into temporary living units and also arranged around the central courtyard, provided basic washrooms and additional warehouse space. Addressing multiple needs within a single structure, Samsarat al-Naḥḥās took on the role of warehouse, hotel, stable, and showroom for the traveling merchant in Sanaa.

In his survey of Arab cities during the Ottoman period, André Raymond showed the extent to which scholars consider the multifunctional urban *khān* a dominant structure within the realm of wholesale trade in the early modern Arab world. According to Raymond, the urban *khān* exclusively governed the volume of bulk exchange, so the number of *khāns* in a given city serves as an absolute indicator of its large-scale commercial activity.[5] Indeed, the urban *khān*, with its retail counterparts the *qayṣariyya* and the *sūq*, presents an ordered image of the workings of the trade in which functional roles are linked to formal structures in a distinct and binding fashion. In this system, international and high-volume trade is situated in the public sector, in wholesale establishments nestled within the retail *sūq* and starkly distinct from private, residential space. This model of economic function

FIG. 6.1 Street-level view of Samsarat al-Naḥḥās, Sanaa, 2000.

FIG. 6.2 Roof-level view of Samsarat al-Naḥḥās, Sanaa, 2002.

and architectural response assigns a functional exclusivity to building types, emphasizing the traveling wholesale merchant's unwavering reliance upon the urban *khān*.

But the urban *khān* model, like all archetypes, is problematic because it suggests uniformity in merchants' status and denies variations in practice among the traveling merchants of the historical Arab world. Even within the walls of the urban *khān*, class-consciousness must be factored into an understanding of merchants' choices of lodging. For instance, Samsarat al-Majja, situated in the heart of Sanaa's marketplace in the vicinity of Samsarat al-Naḥḥās, had special domed suites on the roof that were larger than the rest of the standard, flat-roofed rooms.[6] These rooms were positioned far above the busy central courtyard with its boisterous stable and were strategically isolated from the traffic of the stairwells. The size, prime location, and visual demarcation of these special rooms made them roomy, privileged, short-term residences for elite merchants and spatially confirmed their occupants' status. The clear gradation of room standards at Samsarat al-Majja suggests that certain merchants had expectations about the quality of their temporary lodgings and that in at least some cases they had the means and desire to be differentiated from less prominent merchants as well as from ordinary travelers and pilgrims.

Along the same lines, scholars using the Geniza documents, which provide minute details about tenth- to thirteenth-century trade in the Mediterranean Sea and Indian Ocean from the perspective of Jewish traders, also suggest that traveling merchants were not a singular, cohesive cluster in their temporary housing practices in medieval commercial cities. Questioning the centrality of the urban *khān* for the many purposes of all traveling merchants, S. D. Goitein argued that the high-profile merchants of Cairo did not use the urban *khān* as a place of lodging, although they may have stored goods there and visited the building in the interest of conducting negotiations. Citing the unsavory reputation and uncomfortable accommodation of the urban *khān*, he wrote that "distinguished visitors from overseas and better-class merchants would seek more comfortable quarters than a noisy caravanserai. Wealthy traders possessed houses in the different countries they frequented or would exchange hospitality with relatives and intimate business friends."[7]

Drawing on the same pool of evidence for medieval Aden, a port that holds great relevance for Mocha, Roxani Margariti suggested a complete absence of the urban *khān* as a commercial auberge, although public institutions were used for the purposes of wholesale trade and negotiations. Elite merchants opted for the more luxurious and private accommodations of a local associate's house or a rented residence in this Arabian Sea port, for both lodging and storage.[8] Separate warehouses were numerous and widely available for lease by individual merchants to contain their surplus goods during the peak season. Some less prominent merchants went back to their ships to sleep and came ashore to conduct trade during daylight hours.[9]

Essentially, Goitein's and Margariti's findings from the perspective of these intimately detailed trade documents suggest that architectural form and commercial function in medieval Arab trading centers were more elastic than the dominant urban *khān* paradigm implies.[10] By abandoning the notion of the urban *khān* as the primary or singular institution used by merchants for lodging, trade, and storage, one can begin to disassemble its multiple functions. Rather than being localized within the urban *khān*, the diverse needs of a single traveling merchant might have been accommodated at different sites, including private houses and public institutions.

Historian Olivia Remie Constable's work on the *funduq* as a pan-Mediterranean institution sheds light on the geographic scope of the urban *khān* paradigm. Her encyclopedic study traces the medieval Arab *funduq* from its ancient roots as the Greek *pandocheion* to the development of its later counterparts, such as the Byzantine *foundax* and the Venetian *fondaco*. By characterizing the Arab *funduq* as one of a Mediterranean "family of institutions," Constable breaks down the religious boundaries that often characterized the establishment.[11] The *funduq* is not cast as a uniquely Muslim institution or entirely "associated with oriental influence," as others have posited, but rather is one type within a shared genre of public facilities that took on various features in diverse locations through time and place around the Muslim, Jewish, and Christian rim of the Mediterranean.[12] If the *funduq*, and by extension the commercialized urban *khān*, is conceived of as part of a large and broadly defined family of Mediterranean institutions, then we can begin to understand the limits of its applicability to the southern Arabian Peninsula, particularly in a region such as coastal Yemen that looked away from the Mediterranean and toward the Indian Ocean geographically and culturally.[13] Margariti has suggested in regard to Zurayid and Ayyubid Aden that a difference might have existed "in the organization of transient residence between the Mediterranean and the Indian Ocean."[14] It remains to be seen where the Red Sea lies in this division of maritime space.

Although the urban *khān* has traditionally been conceived of as the key structure for trade, lodging, and storage for merchants in historic economic capitals of the Arab world, notable exceptions undermine the urban *khān*'s comprehensive scope. The actual habits and customs of merchants, recorded in everyday trade documents, reveal a wider variety of urban practices. Following on the framework provided by the medieval Geniza documents and the conceptual span of Constable's cross-cultural synthesis, in the rest of this chapter I examine the place of trade in early modern Mocha, moving away from the realm of public facilities as the key sites for such an exploration.

In Search of the Urban Khān

Following the urban *khān* paradigm, many scholars have voiced the expectation that urban *khān*s should be found in Mocha. As discussed in chapter 2, researchers have sought to locate the former site of a wholesale coffee market in the city, misled by an oft-repeated error in reading an eighteenth-century French narrative. But in fact there were no urban *khān*s in Mocha. In his encyclopedic monograph on the early-seventeenth-century city, the Dutch historian Cees Brouwer remarked with amazement that "the mere existence [of *samsaras* or *khān*s] is not mentioned in the sources."[15] Brouwer assumed that functional urban *khān*s must have been used in Mocha, given the volume of its trade, but simply were not mentioned in the wide-ranging archival documents he consulted. A review of the most prominent public commercial structures in the city corroborates Brouwer's initial suspicion and verifies the conspicuous absence of public structures used by the international wholesale merchant class in the eighteenth century as well.[16]

The customs house, or *furḍa*, was the most important official building in Mocha related to the trade. No negotiations took place there; it was the site for official and administrative functions connected to the trade and overseen by the governor of the city and other officials, who served as deputies of the Qāsimī imam at the port. Commodities coming ashore from overseas were inspected, weighed, and cleared for taxes and customs in this building and sometimes were stored there temporarily. The space served as the single common room for the overseas trade in the city. Most merchants needed to pass through it, and as they observed the required rites of entry, they kept tabs on the daily passage of others' goods in the interest of their own trade. During the eighteenth century the European company merchants and some major Gujarati merchants gained the privilege from the imam of bypassing the customs house. The governor agreed that they could bring their goods on land and directly to their houses, where an official would go to inspect them. Still, they were aware of daily activity at the customs house because their brokers often reported to them about notable occurrences there.

Mocha had a single caravanserai, built by the Ottoman official Mehmed Pasha between 1616 and 1621 and called Wikālat al-Nabī, or the Prophet's Caravanserai.[17] Despite the name *wikāla*, which might seem to indicate a commercial function, in the early eighteenth century this caravanserai did not function like the urban *khān* I described earlier, meant for use by traveling merchants.[18] The structure was simple and provisional, with a single entrance leading to a four-sided, open courtyard with a gallery around its perimeter. It offered visitors no luxuries and was hardly suitable for the long-term lodging of upper-class merchants, shipowners, and *nākhūdhas* for the entire trade season, which lasted several months. Pilgrims en route to Mecca and unaffiliated travelers and peddlers were the primary, albeit temporary, residents of this caravanserai.[19] Because Mocha was one of the last major stops for pilgrims coming from the south and east, the volume of this intermittent traffic was significant during the peak season.[20]

Travelers who stayed at the caravanserai said little about its qualities, but their record of occupancy reveals its unsuitability for continuous residence. When the Meccan traveler and poet al-Mūsawī first arrived in the city in the early eighteenth century, he stayed in the house of a local resident and then in the *wikāla*, which he called "a pleasant *funduq*."[21] It appears, however, that the *wikāla* was not pleasant enough to warrant an extended stay. After a few short days he moved to the house of a well-known *qāḍī* in the city. When the Czech missionary Remedius Prutky, who was unaffiliated with any European trading company and was heading for the court of the Ethiopian emperor Iyasu in Gondar, arrived in Mocha in the mid-eighteenth century, he, too, was directed to stay in this *wikāla*. He described it as "the lodging-house of the Prophet Mahomet, so-called, which was like a huge tenement block laid out in many hundred separate cells where accommodation was rented to all strangers without discrimination of race or religion."[22] Although Prutky and his associates did not criticize the facility explicitly, it is clear that they were not entirely satisfied by it, for they stayed only a short time. Their alternative accommodations were no more satisfactory, though; they rented "a dark cell with no window" in a house owned by a Muslim "holy man."[23]

Along with the caravanserai, there were many independent warehouses in the city, but they were not used as primary sites for negotiation, either. Rather, they were built to accommodate surplus cargo at the height of the trade season and usually were rented short-term, only to be emptied out with the departure of the ships. Of these warehouses, the Dutch singled out one as the royal storehouse, the imam's *wikāla*. The imam conducted large-scale trade in the city, sending two ships to Surat yearly. In his physical absence, his representative, or *wakīl*, conducted trade on his behalf, and the goods were placed in this dedicated structure.[24]

Found along well-traveled routes in lowland Yemen, the *miqhāya*, alternatively called *maqhā* and *maṭraḥ*, was a coffee house that doubled as a humble rest house. The architectural scholar Ronald Lewcock called the Tihāmī *miqhāya* "little more than a large shelter on poles with charpoy beds, cool in the hot weather, and a cabin or two for the proprietor and his family," like the one in Zabid photographed by the French sculptor Auguste Bartholdi in the nineteenth century (fig. 6.3).[25] Whereas the caravanserai of Mocha accommodated long-distance maritime travelers, the city's *miqhāya* catered to a local clientele that arrived by land. In 1909, when the German photographer Hermann Burchardt visited Mocha on a journey from the Yemeni highlands, he stayed in the house of the Italian consul, Gaetano Benzoni. His Yemeni companions, including the scribe Faqīh Aḥmad b. Muḥammad al-Jarādī, stayed in the *miqhāya* of ʿAlī Jābir, which included a safe place to tether the pack animals.[26] This urban *miqhāya* was a modest establishment for overnight stays of travelers by land, not a trade establishment for the wholesale merchants in the city. Nor did it cater to the many pilgrims who arrived by boat.

When one examines the context of commercial class and status in Mocha, it is clear that the simple public lodging facilities of Wikālat al-Nabī and the *miqhāya* could not have served as accommodations for high-profile merchants or notable visitors to the city. For instance, when Sayyid Qāsim Amīr al-Dīn, a representative of the contender to the imamate Muḥammad b. Isḥāq, came to the city in September 1727, he stayed at the home of the wealthy Gujarati merchant ʿAbd al-Ghafūr, as arranged by the governor.[27] Thirty soldiers were placed at the door of this residence to protect him. In another case involving a notable guest, the historian Abū Ṭālib described the visit of Safavid Shah Ḥusayn's messenger and his retinue to the imam's court in 1113/1701–2. After returning to Mocha from their visit to Imam al-Mahdī in al-Mawāhib, the Persian diplomatic group set up a temporary settlement of royal tents before they departed by sea.[28]

FIG. 6.3 A *miqhāya*, Zabid. Photograph by Auguste Bartholdi, 1856.

Although one might expect that overseas merchants operated out of the city's *sūq*, this was not the case in Mocha. The major international wholesalers would not have conducted their business affairs in the modest local *sūq*, which was dominated by small-scale establishments that provided everyday goods to a local clientele. No urban *khān* existed in the *sūq* in the eastern part of Mocha, far from the port.[29] Moneychangers were the only persons associated with the long-distance trade who had shops in the *sūq*, but their shops were used not as depots for merchandise but simply as bureaus of exchange. In the 1730s the head exchanger, ʿAbd al-Razīq, sat in his small shop, as did the Baniyan exchanger for the Dutch, whom they called "Deeuwkraan."[30]

Thus, public structures fulfilled none of the daily functions of the overseas trade in Mocha except for customs inspection and clearance, banking, and currency exchange. Indeed, because the high-profile merchants viewed the opportunity to forgo a visit to the *furḍa* as a major trading privilege, it appears that public structures were seen as generally inappropriate for the use of the more elite ranks of the commercial class, although small-scale merchants and even ordinary travelers were required to stop at the customs house and reveal their belongings to the city's officials.[31] Although one might expect to find many urban *khāns* established for the use of the trade, the major overseas merchants at Mocha did not conduct their trade in them, and they were conspicuously absent from the city's landscape.

The Merchant's House

The sources from the first half of the eighteenth century consistently describe trade activity, commercial meetings, lodging for merchants, and storage of commodities as taking place in the houses and residential complexes of the merchants. Houses took on the multiple functions of warehouse, trade establishment, and residence and served as the primary centers for negotiations among participants in the overseas trade. Some merchants rented extra warehouse space to accommodate overflows of goods, but most of the time a single house served multiple purposes.

The contemporary Arabic texts are silent on the everyday functional details of commercial interaction, but a close analysis of the sparse references suggests the mode of organization just described. The sources never indicate the presence of public structures for the facilitation of trade in Mocha, not even in passing reference, whereas they often mention the *samsaras* and *khāns* of Sanaa and other highland cities. Furthermore, one account describes the house that served as the residential trading establishment of the French Compagnie des Indes in Mocha as a "*dukkān*," which refers specifically to a small retail shop.[32] This label, although imprecise, suggests a dual commercial and residential nature for the merchant's house. The reference, probably transmitted via a highland historian, indicates the lack of a specific term for a structure or institution that encompassed both public and private roles, a functional duality otherwise unobserved in Yemeni highland cities.

The European sources, which contain more abundant references to everyday trade activity, provide the clearest information. In all of their eighteenth-century records of transactions with both local and other foreign merchants, spanning more than twenty years of daily documentation, the Dutch described the domestic localization of trading practice. A few entries serve as a sample. On January 5, 1706, some Bohra merchants from Ahmedabad, India, entered the Dutch house asking the VOC representatives for help in getting some confiscated money returned to them.[33] A few days later, on January 8, the broker of the governor of the city visited the Dutch at their house to tell them that the governor was interested in purchasing some goods. On April 15 that year a group of Baniyan brokers paid a visit to the Dutch residence to complain about the poor quality of the pepper they had bought from the Dutch, which was mixed with much dirt. The next day the Dutch went to the house of those Baniyans to take account of how much dirt was mixed in with the shipment. On another occasion the Dutch chief resident stopped by the house of Qāsim al-Turbatī, the local merchant who often entertained the favor of the imam and his officials, and found two other major Muslim merchants there with him.[34] From a reading of these and other accounts, it is clear that merchants' residences served as the sites for all negotiations, trade interactions, and storage of goods, not to mention lodging and social exchanges.

This domestic localization of the trade encompassed the upper stratum of the overseas merchant class. But whereas the European houses were described in great detail, only passing references were made to the houses of non-European merchants. For example, one sees only sporadic mention of the house of the active trader Qāsim al-Turbatī or the residence of Muḥammad Yāsīn, a major merchant from Basra who had permanently relocated to Mocha. The merchants of Muscat held at least one house in the city, but probably more, judging from the number of merchants who would have been in residence during the high trade season. The merchants from Kung, on the Persian coast of the Gulf, also held at least one residence in Mocha. The sources do not specifically mention the houses of merchants from Jidda or Basra, but there must have been at least one for each of these mercantile groups and probably many more, because several ships from those cities called at the port each season.[35] The governor, whose personal standing was inextricably linked to the overall success of the trade, had his brokers and officials bring objects to him at his palace for inspection.[36] Any meetings among the major Muslim merchants of the city—a diverse group of Arabs, Persians, and Indians—took place at their houses. This often occurred at the house of the Surati merchant ʿAbd al-Ghafūr.[37]

The Baniyan brokers also conducted business, including negotiations, storage, and lodging, out of their homes. The residents of many Baniyan households worked together, as in the household of a man named Vira who, with his many sons, served as the primary broker to all Europeans in the first part of the eighteenth century. It is well documented that Baniyan women never traveled with their husbands or other male relatives to participate in this émigré lifestyle, so the brokers' houses could serve as business facilities without conflict over family privacy. In the early eighteenth century, European merchants even lodged in Baniyan residences temporarily.[38] Unlike Europeans and prominent Gujaratis, Baniyans were not accorded the privilege of bypassing the customs house.[39]

The Europeans conformed to local practice, visiting other merchants at their homes (or sending their brokers) and welcoming other merchants into their own residences daily. In general, European merchants chose to follow local standards of trade and interaction rather than introduce outside practices. For instance, in 1721 William Phipps, the English East India Company official who visited Mocha to check on the status of the company's trading establishment there, wrote to the Court of Directors in Bombay complaining of the excessive cost of living in the city, particularly the upkeep of the company's large house. He explained that he had made great efforts to cut the daily costs of the establishment's maintenance, but "it may be necessary that such a publick way of living be maintained to preserve respect from these country people, which I find practiced by other European nations."[40] Out of desire to uphold a high profile and positive reputation in the city, the English, like other European merchants, mimicked the lifestyle of the local elite merchant class.

A perusal of European sources and studies might appear to contradict this understanding of the merchant's house as the locus for the trade, because the commercial documents and the modern historians who rely upon them often use the term "factory" to describe early modern European trading establishments in Indian Ocean cities, including Mocha. To modern readers, however, the term, which denotes the residence of the factor, is misleading. The European "factories" at Mocha were mere houses that were rented and used as trading establishments. In fact none of the European companies in Mocha ever built any kind of dedicated structure. They simply followed the mode of conducting trade in the city as modeled by the dominant merchant class. European residences carried no visual or structural markers to distinguish them from other stone and brick houses in the city, except for their flags, a right the imam had granted the European companies in their trade treaties.

Several of the larger houses were enclosed within perimeter walls, together with an area to house animals and perhaps extra warehouse space, thus making up a complex. The historical texts are misleading in this regard, too, because they seem to suggest that several distinct structures fulfilled the various purposes associated with the trade. For example, the Dutch might comment about their "warehouse" and then in another instance mention their "residence," which implies two separate structures. All these functions, however, were housed in one and the same complex or building, and the scattered references relate to different parts of the house rather than to separate structures. Although independent warehouses existed in the city, it is clear that the ground-floor warehouses of the merchant's house were the safest and easiest to guard.

Bayt al-Maḥfadī and the Idāra Building

A nineteenth-century photograph by Auguste Bartholdi shows the façade of a house that has since disappeared from Mocha's landscape (fig. 6.4). With exquisite woodwork adorning both the door frame and the primary *rawshan*, or projecting casement window, the house serves as an icon of Mocha's domestic architectural style, which is largely lost from the ruined city today.[41] Like the one featured in the photograph, the whitewashed houses of Mocha ascended two or three stories and were arranged closely together to enclose narrow streets and shade passersby from the sun. Elaborately screened wooden *rawshans* extended into the streets at the upper levels, allowing inhabitants to peer out from their houses unbeknownst to pedestrians below.[42] Carved plaster bands delineated each level along the façade, and decorative arches crowned the doorways and windows. The towering merchants' houses stood out distinctively from the masses of mud and thatch houses, or *ʿushshas* (fig. 6.5), that made up the majority of Mocha's intramural and extramural settlement.

Echoing in its functions the plan of the general Yemeni tower house, the ground floor of the Mocha merchant's house served not as living space but as a warehouse, easily accessible for the transfer of goods and a safe place for storage. All such houses in Mocha had more than one entrance to the ground-floor space, which was subdivided into distinct areas that could be closed off and separated from one another. Household animals were also kept on the ground floor and fed from built-in troughs and bins. The second floor, above the ground level, served as the major living space of the house, used by the family or residents for everyday cooking, eating, and sleeping. There was no interior courtyard, but an open-air light well brought sunlight and cool breezes into the enclosed rooms on the upper

FIG. 6.4 House, Mocha (now destroyed). Photograph by Auguste Bartholdi, 1856.

FIG. 6.5 *'Ushsha*, mud and thatch dwelling, al-Riṣāṣ, northern Tihāma, 2000.

level. Each house had a living space on the roof that often served as an outdoor bedroom on hot summer nights.[43]

The house pictured by Bartholdi has long since fallen to ruin, and none of the historic houses still standing in Mocha—fewer than ten of them in the spring of 2000, when I conducted a survey—can be dated definitively to the period before the nineteenth century.[44] But the layouts of the extant houses serve as the only remaining data that can illuminate the organization of earlier houses. All these later houses exhibit consistent features, many of which are corroborated in early texts, so one can make a strong case for a stable tradition of building that dates back to earlier decades as well. An examination of the existing historic houses in the city, along with a reading of the sources that document trade interactions, allows for a spatial analysis of how and where commercial transactions took place.

Located in Ḥārat al-Ṣandal, Bayt al-Maḥfadī (fig. 6.6) is one of the few historic houses that still stands and is inhabited today. According to the residents of the house, Ḥasan Ismāʿīl Luṭf al-Maḥfadī, for whom the house is named, moved to Mocha from Sanaa in the early 1930s when he was assigned to the city as a customs official.[45] As such, al-Maḥfadī represents a modern continuation of the structure of authority of the Qāsimī period, when highland officials channeled an uninterrupted flow of revenue and information from their coastal stations back to the capital. The two lower floors of the house date to the late nineteenth century or earlier, and the rooftop rooms date to 1351/1932–33, as is indicated by an inscription outside the top floor *majlis*, or sitting room, added by al-Maḥfadī. Positioned near the shore, the house would have been surrounded by many other prominent stone and brick houses when Ḥasan al-Maḥfadī purchased it. Since then, most of the houses around it have collapsed.

The foundation of the house is a damp-proof course of stone, and the upper levels are constructed of baked brick. Each exterior and interior surface is covered with a thick coat of *nūra*, or lime plaster. Twentieth-century restoration has transformed the house, which now has a coat of gray concrete all over its exterior façade (fig. 6.7), but its fabric reflects traditional techniques, particularly on the bottom two floors.[46] The main entrance, marked by double doors and the primary (and only existing) wooden *rawshan* above them, is located in the northern façade. Although this *rawshan* is badly worn today (fig. 6.8), it was carved elaborately with rosettes and roundels in relief, traces of which are still visible. Many of the smaller panels once swung open but are now boarded shut. The building's exterior

FIG. 6.6 Bayt al-Maḥfaḍī, Mocha, 2000.

FIG. 6.7 Northern façade, Bayt al-Maḥfaḍī, Mocha, 2000.

surface ornamentation, in brick, consists of bands of sawtooth decoration and continuous, linked horizontal diamonds. Windows are crowned with arched hoods in the form of blind niches, some pierced with single- or triple-rounded or arched oculi. On the second floor of the eastern façade, another window in brick, smaller than the coastal type of *rawshan* in wood, projects out to accommodate a jug of water for cooling.

Historically, the designs of Arab houses had to integrate family privacy and gender segregation, both major concerns. In Mocha the needs of the trade complicated these domestic considerations. Much writing about gender segregation in the Arab house has focused on fixed divisions within domestic space, following the assumption that separate men's and women's quarters provided the most convenient built response to the issue of family privacy. Speaking from a contemporary anthropological perspective with a focus on Sanaa, Gabriele Vom Bruck rejected the notion that built features unconditionally defined gender relations within the Yemeni house. She contended that daily practices and temporal interventions allowed family members to strategically maintain gendered distance within domestic space, avoiding both physical and visual contact.[47] In some cases the house became a largely female or male space for a particular event, such as an afternoon *qāt* chew, when large numbers of men or women from outside the family entered. In the case of a men's *qāt* chew, the female family members might move to a single room far from the social activity and go to great lengths to avoid encounters with the visitors. In other cases, the house might be turned over completely to a gendered gathering, with the others leaving the house altogether. In either circumstance, house space was not fixed by immutable built boundaries, nor were spaces unconditionally labeled male or female. Rather, temporal and shifting factors instigated strategic responses to the need to keep men's and women's realms separate.

In eighteenth-century Mocha, temporally determined gendered spaces and fleeting strategies to avoid physical and visual contact with visitors were also pertinent. The plan of Bayt al-Maḥfadī illustrates how domestic space might have been employed to accommodate merchants' interactions while maintaining distance between family members and guests. Of the upper rooms in Bayt al-Maḥfadī that constituted the main living space for the original merchant and his family, the *dīwān* on the north side of the second floor (fig. 6.9) is the largest. It would have been furnished with a ring of cushions and bolsters laid along the four walls. Its *rawshan* is about a meter deep, and family members could have sat inside the projecting box to catch breezes from the street on warm days without being seen. The *dīwān* could also have been reserved to accommodate more formal events, such as the elaborate entertainment of a visiting merchant. In these cases the women of the house might have left the area and ascended to the roof, out of view. Figure 6.10 shows a drawing of a nineteenth-century roof apartment that was sufficiently cut off from the rest of the house to be used on such occasions.[48] Alternatively, the women could leave and visit a neighbor or friend, allowing the house to be used freely by the male family members and their guests. In line with a common practice still alive in the Tihāma today, women in Mocha often left the house in the cool hours of the night to engage in a rotating social ritual of evening visitation with female neighbors and friends, leaving the house empty to be used by the men of the family.[49]

Many commercial transactions in Mocha, however, clearly were unannounced and completed rapidly, rather than planned. Merchants appeared at each other's houses to examine goods or to make bids without advance notice. Brokers stopped by merchants' houses several times a day with news of price shifts, political unrest, or the arrival of ships in Bāb al-Mandab. For those cases, the organization of the ground floor offered a number of ways in which merchants could interact with one another while avoiding physical and visual contact with the family. The complex division of the ground floor storage space of Bayt al-Maḥfadī suggests that multiple functions might have taken place there, most of them public and commercial rather than private and family oriented.

Entering through the primary northern entrance, one may ascend directly from the entry vestibule to the upper floors, enter the storage spaces to the left and right, or head straight into the large central warehouse area (fig. 6.11). All the house's inhabitants probably used this main entrance for access to most of the house's spaces. Another entrance, at the southeastern end of the building (fig. 6.12), opens into a small, well-fenestrated reception chamber. From it merchants had immediate access to the main storage chamber, in order to examine goods or pick up merchandise without disturbing the family members.[50] Although the room is small, it certainly could have accommodated the ceremonial customs related to the execution of trade transactions, such as the sprinkling of rosewater, the burning of aromatics, and the offering of coffee—traditional rites that accompanied any visit. The room's potential for male socialization was demonstrated by one of the contemporary residents, ʿĀdil al-Maḥfadī, who expressed the

FIG. 6.8 Detail of the primary *rawshan*, Bayt al-Maḥfaḍī, Mocha, 2000.

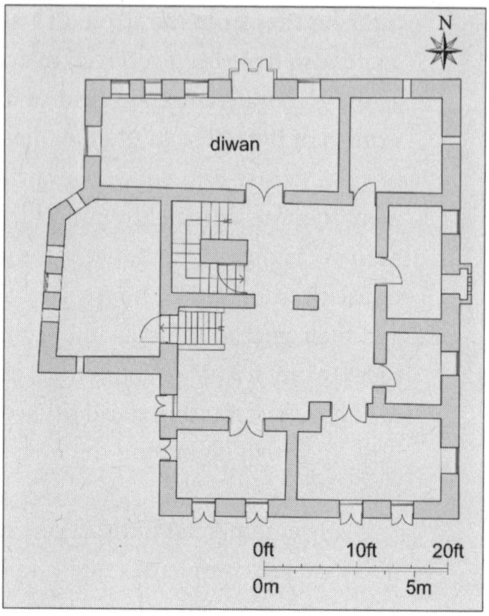

FIG. 6.9 Plan of the second floor of Bayt al-Maḥfaḍī, Mocha.

FIG. 6.10 "L'appartement des femmes, Moka." Sketch by Auguste Bartholdi, 1856.

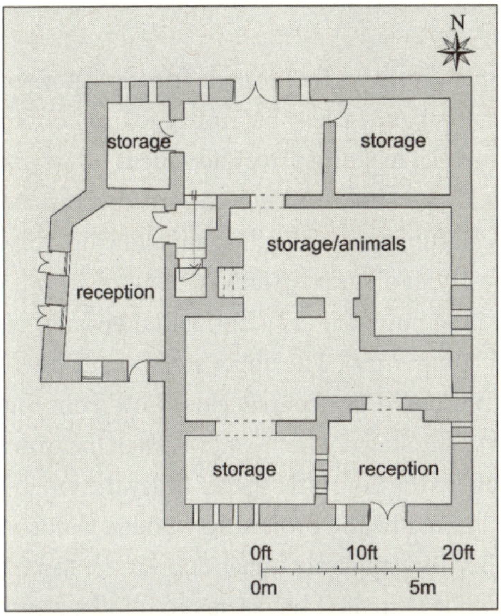

FIG. 6.11 Plan of the ground floor of Bayt al-Maḥfadī, Mocha.

FIG. 6.12 Southern view, Bayt al-Maḥfadī, Mocha, 2000.

desire to refurbish the space to hold *qāt* chews for his male friends. Another room, located on the mezzanine level and accessible from the front door, might also have served as a commercial meeting place and a locus for negotiations. With its many windows, larger size, and modest ornamentation, it could have accommodated social functions as well, again allowing nonfamily males to enter the house without disturbing family members above.

Bayt al-Maḥfadī, then, offered the potential for a horizontal division of house functions, residential and commercial. The upper stories, inhabited and used collectively by the family, could be securely closed off from the lower level by the door at the top of the stairs, which—rather than the front door—served as the true threshold to the domestic space. Today the inhabitants leave the front door, highlighted by the projecting wooden window above it, unlocked and open. They lock the only upper door at the top of the stairs, which is smaller and unornamented but seems to fulfill a more central function as a social boundary. Although the division of space in eighteenth-century merchants' houses in Mocha was ordered with concern for the social needs of the family, it was equally ordered with concern for the trade. The ground floor, with its complex subdivision of storage space and its dual entry system, functioned as a semipublic site in lieu of the urban *khān*, allowing a flow of everyday traffic that did not disturb family life.[51] Still, the concerns of family privacy were dealt with in a number of ways, temporal as well as spatial, and merchant activity could be taken to the upper floors if the appropriate arrangements were made.

Of course not all merchants conducted their trade transactions in the same way. In eighteenth-century Mocha, many of the residences of the traveling merchant class housed only male merchants during the trade season.[52] European merchants in the city, who rented houses with their fellow male merchants, described how they invited other merchants to the upper levels of their houses to share meals and discuss business, without intrusion into family space.[53] Some European merchants wrote with delight about being invited into the upper *dīwān* of a local residence and catching fleeting glimpses of the women of the house.[54] But the layout of houses such as Bayt al-Maḥfadī allowed for restricted access to family-oriented spaces if the residents so desired. For example, Qāsim al-Turbatī, who lived with his family in Mocha, might have sealed off his upper floors from the more public spaces of the lower level, giving the family ample room to use without entering the sphere of negotiation or having to meet strangers within the domestic sphere.

Many of the ground-floor storage spaces were composed of units that had their own doors that could be locked, suggesting that whole areas could be segmented and potentially rented to a nonresidential merchant.[55] Some overseas merchants maintained separate storage facilities in addition to those in their main residences, facilities needed especially during the peak season when they experienced overflows of merchandise. On July 12, 1730, the private English merchant Mr. Harnett had to rent "three great houses including their warehouses" in order to store for the winter all the goods he had brought to Mocha and failed to sell.[56] In another instance the Dutch rented a small additional warehouse to store their goods while the ground-floor warehouse of their residence was being repaired.[57] This secondary storage space might have been a dedicated free-standing structure or part of a house.

Bayt al-Maḥfadī provides a clear example of the spatial organization of the Mocha merchant's house and the potential use of its interior spaces for purposes of trade in the absence of public commercial structures. Other extant houses, too, reveal a complex division of warehouse space and multiple ground-floor entryways, confirming the presence of such features in a wider spectrum of Mocha's merchant houses. The official building that I call the Idāra building now houses the municipal administration (fig. 6.13). The current residents of the building are government employees who are not from the city, so they live and work in the official structure.[58] Much contemporary restoration, again in concrete, has masked many of the Idāra's premodern features. According to the current residents, the building used to be the residence of an Italian coffee merchant. During Hermann Burchardt's December 1909 visit to the city, his Yemeni companion called the Italian consul in Mocha "al-Banzūnī." From other sources we know that Gaetano Benzoni worked as an Italian consular agent in Mocha from 1905 to 1909, during a moment when Italy was attempting to expand its scope to Yemen's Red Sea coast from its stronghold on the African side.[59] Burchardt's photographs, which show the consular sign above the front door, confirm that the Idāra was Benzoni's house and consulate building and provide a glimpse of the house's nineteenth-century state (fig. 6.14; compare 6.15). Judging from the timetable of Burchardt's visit, the house can be dated as pre–twentieth century, built and inhabited before Benzoni's arrival in the city. Both Burchardt and Benzoni were mysteriously killed soon after leaving Mocha together.

FIG. 6.13 Idāra building, Mocha, 2000.

FIG. 6.14 *Rawshan* above the doorway, Idāra building, Mocha. Photograph by Hermann Burchardt, 1909.

FIG. 6.15 *Rawshan* above the doorway, Idāra building, Mocha, 2000.

Located in Ḥārat al-Furḍa, the residential district southeast of the now-destroyed jetty, this house was strategically placed across from the customs house and near the palace of Sultan Ḥasan, in the vicinity of the main square of the city. Its exterior surface articulation, like that on Bayt al-Maḥfadī, consists of windows with hoods pierced by triple oculi and bands of saw-tooth ornament. The main doorway is oriented to the north, with three majestic *rawshans* adorning the primary façade. The front doorway had a scalloped arched hood decorated with carved rosettes and stars in plaster relief, which did not survive the modern renovation. The woodwork on this house is of fine quality, although worn over time, particularly in the double doors on the northern façade, the lintel of the main doorway (fig. 6.16), and the three *rawshans*. Burchardt's photographs show how the main *rawshan* above the doorway would have looked in its original state, with rounded projecting sections that have now been replaced by glass.

As in most traditional houses in contemporary Mocha, the entire ground floor is no longer in use. Subsequent reconstruction surrounds the whole northeastern base of the structure, blocking access to the original doorway on the northern side. Now, entrance to the building is made through the modern doorway and stairway that were cut from a window on the east façade of the second floor. Regardless of these contemporary changes, one can still detect the past organization of the ground floor, which, like that of Bayt al-Maḥfadī, is complex and subdivided into smaller units, one of which was accessible from the exterior by a door on the east side (fig. 6.17). Although the newer building that supports the eastern staircase has obscured the passageway between this eastern chamber and the rest of the ground floor, one can still see a segmented commercial space that allowed entry along a different axis from that of the front entrance and also blocked lines of sight beyond the commercial quarters. With their distinct ground-floor plans and scales, Bayt al-Maḥfadī and the Idāra building are examples of the ways in which Mocha houses were built to accommodate trade while maintaining both physical and visual distance between resident family members and visiting merchants.

Continuities in the Maritime Sphere

For a major merchant in Mocha, it was essential to have one's own house, in order to carry out trade in the manner that dominated locally. This practice differed greatly from the standard model of Arab urban trade, which

FIG. 6.16 Detail of the lintel above the main door, Idāra building, Mocha, 2000.

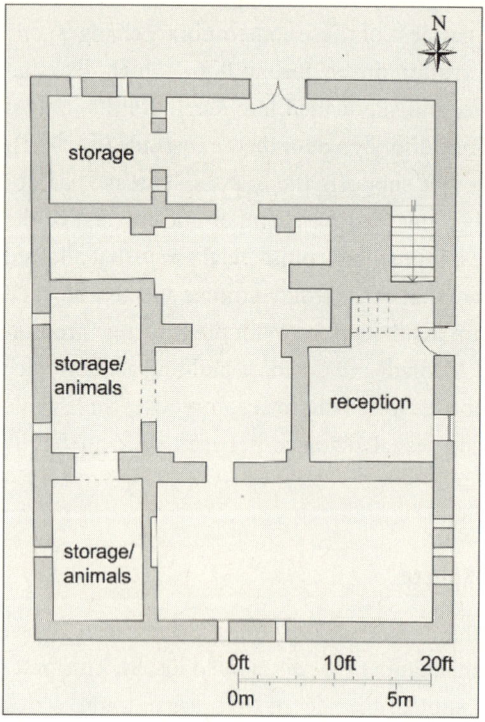

FIG. 6.17 Ground-floor plan of the Idāra building, Mocha.

was oriented around the urban *khān* and was observed in most Arab cities in North Africa and the eastern Mediterranean, as well as Sanaa. But Mocha was not unique as an early modern city in which the needs of profit-seeking merchants and entrepreneurs motivated creative responses to traditional housing concepts. For instance, the *rab*ʿ, or collective housing unit, which came to be widely proliferated in Ottoman Cairo, functioned as an apartment building. The upper units were leased out to unrelated families, and small-scale merchants and artisans rented separate spaces on the ground floor for commercial purposes.[60] The *rab*ʿ, a unique mode of communal housing in the early modern Arab world, was found in areas of "high economic activity" in Cairo, away from zones populated by private homes.[61] Built during a period when intense financial growth instigated the construction of many new buildings, the *rab*ʿ collapsed commercial and residential demand into one and the same structure in a busy merchant city where space was in short supply. Such an example indicates how the commercial impulses that shape economic centers wield the potential to change the typical functional role of the residence—just as happened in Mocha.[62]

Because the expected functional paradigms for domestic and commercial architecture in the Arab world are unaccommodating as tools with which to conceive of the built dimensions of Mocha's trade, one must look in other directions. Again, Constable's work on the *funduq* as a pan-Mediterranean institution is instrumental. Following her recasting of the *funduq* in a maritime light as an institution shared by cultures across modern national boundaries, one can begin to map the dimensions of trade relations and commercial practices around bodies of water rather than within bounded regions defined by language, ethnicity, or religion. Most significantly, in describing the *funduq*'s dispersal around the coasts of the Mediterranean, Constable did not employ terms of foreign influence or cross-cultural transfer but rather provided a framework for the functional transmission of a commercial institution that moved from one place to another as a result of the routines, practices, and patterns of cross-regional trade and travel, which intrinsically require the translation of local functions for visitors and merchants from other cities.[63] By looking at such processes in a maritime setting, Constable suggested that the coastal communities and inland hubs of transit that merchants visited tolerated a certain amount of practical flexibility that allowed new and different modes of commercial functions to flourish.

Mocha diverged significantly from its distant northern Arab counterparts because it was fully entrenched in another system of trade interaction, and the merchants who frequented the port—*nākhūdhas* and merchants from Gujarat, the Persian Gulf, and other southern Red Sea ports—were accustomed to a mode of commercial interaction that did not correspond to the practices of Arab Mediterranean centers. I next investigate the role of the house in a number of port cities that Mocha's merchants may have come from or traveled to, in order to gain an understanding of the expectations for the organization of trade practices at these sites and to highlight the continuity of maritime commercial procedures. The examples I discuss date to the nineteenth or early twentieth century, roughly contemporary with Bayt al-Maḥfadī and the Idāra in Mocha.

While calling into question standard notions about commercial architecture in the Arab world, Mocha's trade structure also addresses assumptions about the nature of the Arab and the Arabian Peninsula house. As Paul Bonnenfant has emphasized, citing a cross section of French studies, the inward-facing courtyard house is often cast as the dominant house type of the Arab world, aptly suited to the climatic and social needs of North Africa, the eastern Mediterranean, and Iraq.[64] Although this type exists on the Arabian Peninsula, it is far from the only or the dominant house type in Yemen, where each region has an individual style and draws on local materials, which produces a great deal of diversity in domestic architecture. The tower house, seen ubiquitously throughout the Yemeni highlands and the Ḥaḍramawt, is characterized by the replication of the upper-story plan on each level. Each floor functions as a complete living space dedicated to a single unit of an extended family. A large penthouse room with a view, called the *mafraj*, crowns the house and is intended for the collective use of the inhabitants. Other house types are found in the Tihāma, including the enclosed brick house complexes of the city of Zabid and its neighbors, the mud and thatch houses, or *ʿushshas*, of the Tihāmī lowlands, and the so-called Red Sea house, found in Mocha, al-Ḥudayda, and al-Luḥayya but also in the Ḥijāz and across the Red Sea in Sawākin and Massawa. The Red Sea house type, however, is unified by formal features such as whitewashed exterior surfaces, elaborate plaster relief work, and ornamental wood carving of windows, doors, and their frames, and not necessarily by internal organization.[65] The historic Mocha house, as I have described it in this chapter, is a unique type in its internal organization and plan, although specific features of its elevation resemble those of houses in other, nearby coastal towns.

To the north of Mocha, the port city of al-Luḥayya offers an alternative example of the commercial possibilities of the Red Sea house in Yemen. Al-Luḥayya participated as a key port in Mocha's trade network and catered to merchants from Jidda who came to Yemen in search of the coffee bean. Houses in al-Luḥayya, too, offered spaces for the trade within the merchant's residential realm.[66] An example documented by Paul Bonnenfant and Jeanne-Marie Gentilleau in 1990 is the early-twentieth-century house Bayt al-Wadūd, formerly inhabited by a merchant and shipowner who was active in the Red Sea and the Persian Gulf.[67] It included a full-service commercial ground floor. A sitting room close to the main entryway, outfitted with an adjoining closet for commercial documents or precious goods, served as an office for the merchant and a convenient surveillance post from which to monitor people's ingress and egress. Unlike houses in Mocha, Bayt al-Wadūd's multiple storerooms encircled an open-air courtyard on the ground floor (fig. 6.18), so that the house took on the spatial format of the urban *khān* at its base level. Of the many entrances, some took visitors directly to the ground-floor commercial areas, and others brought family members immediately to the stairwells to ascend to the living quarters just above the courtyard. The ground floor was the most frequently trafficked and convenient space for commerce, but the profusely decorated upper-level reception room, with its elaborately painted ceiling, called the *salāmlik* by Bonnenfant and Gentilleau, was also used for social functions. Its own dedicated stairway in the southeastern corner of the house allowed guests to ascend without meeting family members. This house in al-Luḥayya, although ruined today, presents a plan that served for trade negotiations, storage of goods, and the formal reception of merchant cohorts. As at Bayt al-Maḥfadī, several features, such as multiple entryways and ground-floor storage and meeting rooms, allowed for the domestic overlap of commercial and residential family functions, although here the spatial layout and courtyard plan differ greatly from the plan of the Mocha house.

An example from the East African coast of the Red Sea constitutes another appropriate comparison. The Sudanese port city of Sawākin thrived during the Mamluk period and was revived in the mid-nineteenth century under Egyptian rule. There, the historic merchant's house functioned similarly to the Mocha house, with a commercial ground floor that played a singular role for the resident merchant in the absence of a network of urban *khāns*. The ground floor of the house of ʿUmar Effendi ʿUbayd (fig. 6.19)

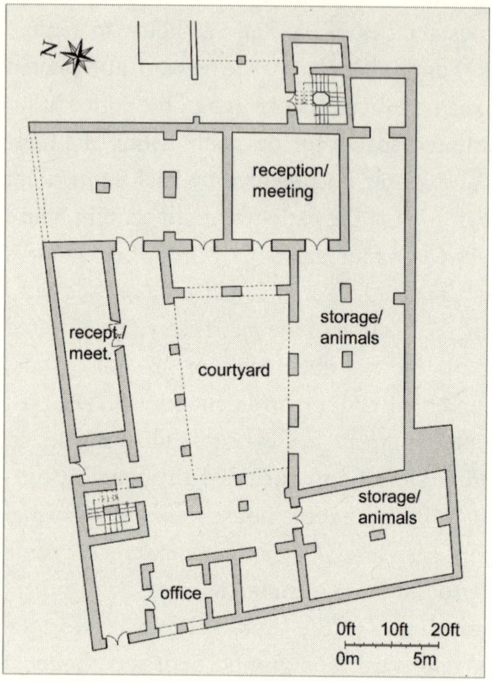

FIG. 6.18 Ground-floor plan of Bayt al-Wadūd, al-Luḥayya.

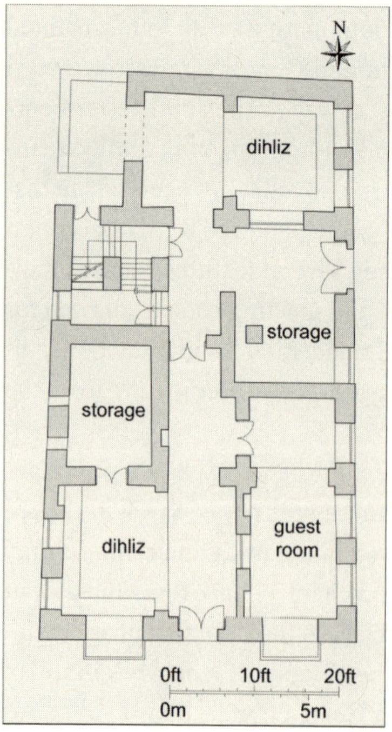

FIG. 6.19 Ground-floor plan of the house of ʿUmar Effendi ʿUbayd, Sawākin, Sudan.

had an articulated *dihlīz*, or foreroom to the storage area, located directly inside the main street entrance on the south. This meeting space was outfitted with built-in benches for visitors and ample adjacent space for storage. Some Sawākin houses, such as this one, featured guest rooms and latrines for the temporary lodging of commercial cohorts.[68] According to Derek Matthews, the commercial sections of such houses were even equipped with small cooking stoves in order to entertain guests with a proper reception of coffee and the wafting aroma of incense ignited on hot coals.[69] In many of Sawākin's nineteenth-century houses, such ʿUbayd's, one also sees a dual entry system in which the family entered via a back entrance (on the west side of the house in this case) that led directly to the living spaces on the upper floors, out of sight of any visitor. The front entrance on the south fulfilled a more public function, giving immediate access to the ground-floor commercial meeting rooms and their associated storage spaces.[70] Before the establishment of modern public institutions such as banks and company buildings, the merchant's house in Sawākin serviced all types of wholesale overseas trade negotiations and activities. An Egyptian merchant, obviously transplanting ideas about trade that were native to his homeland, built the single *wikāla* of the city in 1881.[71] Jean-Pierre Greenlaw emphasized that this foreign institution did not replace a previous trade structure but rather the *nuzl*, the open space where camels were unloaded of their goods, so it was a new structural concept in a city that had never housed the urban *khān* as a commercial establishment.

In Jidda, known for its towering houses in coral, merchants' houses also served as sites for commercial negotiations and storage.[72] Although the Jidda house shares stylistic features with the houses already described, such as projecting wooden *rawshans*, intricate plaster ornament on the interior, and elaborately carved wooden doors and door frames, its plan differs from those of the others.[73] In Jidda, the lofty tower house dominates. A stairwell that serves as the central axis and vertical core of the building links multiple floors of similar plan in a spiraling upward progression. In the past, the ground floor accommodated the commercial and social needs of merchants by means of a *maqʿad*, which Bonnenfant described as "both a reception room and an office that permitted the owner of the house to receive guests and commercial partners while remaining in close proximity to the entry and the movement of goods."[74] In some cases the reception rooms on the lowest level of the house were ornamented with *rawshans* on the outside, which allowed in light and cool breezes. Unlike Mocha and its other lower Red Sea counterparts, however, Jidda maintained an articulated network of urban *khāns* in addition to residential trade establishments.[75] Whereas Jidda and Yanbuʿ to its north, like their Mediterranean counterparts, prominently featured the urban *khān* as a space of trade, the urban *khān* virtually disappeared as a trade structure in port cities south of the Jidda gap.[76]

A further journey, to the eastern edge of the Arabian Sea, points to another node of connection, Gujarat, which was closely linked to Mocha by the movement of ships, *nākhūdhas*, merchants, and commodities. The architectural scholar V. S. Pramar noted that the house served as the domestic locus for most professional activity in Gujarati cities and that "few buildings were designed for commercial use."[77] He wrote:

> Although the Gujarati town was known for its extensive commercial activities, there was no provision for any permanent market place and commercial buildings, no place of adjudication, no place for public assembly even of merchants, no town hall, and almost no inns. The Muslim *sarai* existed only in a few major towns and was obviously an imported concept; the Hindus had no equivalent. The reason for this lies in the nature of Hindu commerce and manufacture, which were carried out strictly within the domestic sphere.[78]

In Gujarat, not only did merchants use their houses for trade activity, but also local craftspeople and artisans considered house space as analogous to the workshop. According to Pramar, such an organization was derived largely from the Hindu caste system, which prevented the development of an open institution such as the urban *khān* that housed a mixed group of itinerant strangers, even temporarily. Muslim traders based in Gujarat adopted this usage of the house for business purposes as well.

In urban Gujarat, prominent merchants inhabited the *haveli* house, a local type of half-timbered mansion marked by cantilevered facades and elaborate woodwork on projecting balconies, doors, and windows. Although the *haveli* house took various shapes in different parts of the region, the general layout allowed the family-oriented spaces to remain separate and undisturbed by commercial and professional activity, although this concern was monitored more rigidly in the Muslim domestic context than in the Hindu. Arranged around an internal courtyard as the main built module, the *haveli* house was organized so that the inhabitant could move pro-

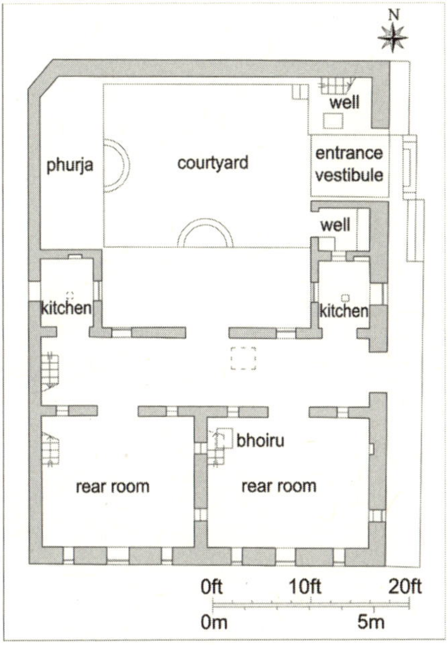

FIG. 6.20 Ground-floor plan of the Mehta house, Gogha, India.

gressively from spaces used for commercial activity to spaces dedicated to the everyday happenings of the family.

As an example, the Mehta house (fig. 6.20) of coastal Gogha presents a progression from the outside to the internal realm, which becomes increasingly private and family oriented. The front veranda of the house, on its northeast corner, serves as a raised, covered space for social interaction and a sheltered extension of both street and house. From the first internal intermediary space of the house, the entry vestibule, guests and visitors can be taken to the *phurja*, the casual, multi-use room situated across the courtyard. More honored guests are led up to the *diwankhanu*, the elaborately decorated and well-furnished main reception room on the second story, by way of a staircase next to one of the house's interior water wells near the entry. A second entrance, less prominent than the primary one to its north, leads to the back of the house, which is defined by two rear rooms that constitute the inner sanctum used by the family, each with a kitchen and secret spaces to store valuables. This rear area constitutes the family living space, which extends up to the second floor, where the general plan below is replicated. Each section of the house, front and back, uses the two main living levels of the house, but they remain spatially delineated, with separately accessible staircases that keep the two lines of traffic from intersecting.

The shores of the lower Red Sea and the closely connected northwestern coast of India present multiple models for trade interaction in which the residential house was the primary locus for merchants' public activities in the nineteenth and early twentieth centuries. In each case the house offered concrete, structural responses to the needs of the trade, whether through a multiple-entry system or reception rooms with dedicated modes of access and built features tailored to the commercial functions they anticipated. Yet the plans represent different ways of coping with the need to balance commercial and private life—the courtyard plan in al-Luḥayya, the tower house model of Jidda, and the progressive axial plan of the Gujarati *haveli*.

The house types of al-Luḥayya, Sawākin, Jidda, and Gujarat share distinctive formal and decorative features with Mocha examples. In all of them one sees projecting windows and balconies with highly ornamental carved wooden brackets and screens or interior walls pierced by configurations of carved arched niches. These features bear the visible yet historically elusive marks of the cross-cultural exchange of artisans, visual motifs, materials, and techniques of production. Other scholars have endeavored to identify the origins of some of these features in the Red Sea region—for example, the finely carved brackets shown in figure 6.4, which undoubtedly derived from Gujarati prototypes.[79] It is almost impossible, however, to move beyond stylistic comparison and presumptions about the manufacture of such designs, which might have been made by Indian artisans living in the Red Sea region, shipped from India as pieces of worked wood, or crafted on the model of Indian originals by local artisans. For this reason I have avoided looking closely at the particularities of individual house parts and instead have concentrated on the house as a functional whole accommodating practices of the trade.

This functional correspondence between structurally distinct examples of houses suggests that in the spatial logic that characterized the Mocha trade network, traveling merchants expected to conduct negotiations in their houses rather than in public structures, but they held no expectations about the way these houses needed to be organized.[80] The focus was on replicating a mode of commercial practice rather than imitating the physical receptacles of those practices. By examining the routines and patterns of the trade, one can trace the extent of this shared understanding along the trade routes leading to and emanating from Mocha.

The Stone House

The Mocha house, however, was more than simply a site for trade. It also functioned as a built signifier of worth and economic status in a coastal society in which trade was conducted on a system of trust and credit and a merchant's reputation and social standing were his most valuable assets. The southern Red Sea and northwest Indian examples I have already described may be amplified by cases of commercialized houses from other cities along the Swahili and Abyssinian coasts. These cases support the notion of a larger Indian Ocean tradition of the domestic localization of trade while pointing to the close links between the house and social and economic standing in the western Indian Ocean port city.

Case studies and textual sources from ports on the Swahili coast and in the littoral region of the Horn of Africa and Abyssinia reveal a pervasive system of trade sponsorship that used the house as a key commercial tool. For Massawa, the Eritrean port city closely linked to Mocha by the transit of ships, the historian Jonathan Miran described the East African coastal practice in which any merchant who arrived at Massawa's port from the hinterland or overseas had to engage a local broker for a fee.[81] This broker acted as an all-encompassing sponsor for the foreign merchant throughout his sojourn in the city, by hosting the merchant at his home and facilitating all of his dealings with local merchants. In return, every foreign merchant was required to entrust the entirety of his business affairs to the broker, including storage of his goods at the broker's residence, because local merchants refused to deal directly with outsiders. In Massawa, as in Mocha, with no urban *khān* or other public structure as a site of commercial facilitation, the house took on the role of commercial structure, warehouse, and residence for the traveling merchant, but in this case only under the supervision of the local sponsor. By assuming lodging in a local house, a foreign merchant indicated that he had become part of Massawa's trade system and agreed to participate by its rules. By sponsoring the foreign merchant, the local broker assumed responsibility for the outsider's transactions at the port, including any financial liability. Many travel writers, such as Ibn Battuta, identified this system of sponsorship as a distinctive practice in cities up and down the Swahili coast and along the southern part of the western Red Sea coast as early as the thirteenth century.[82]

The coastal East African built environment was shaped to foster and facilitate this system of trade sponsorship. Both archaeological and extant built evidence reveals the prominence of the merchant's stone house as a feature of urban port development in cities such as Massawa, Shanga, and Lamu. The architectural historian Thomas Gensheimer identified the key role that merchants' houses played: "The design and grandeur of stone houses served both economic and social functions, because formal market structures with specialized building types were virtually unknown in medieval East Africa. . . . Because the conditions of interregional trade were largely determined by social relationships, independent market institutions and formal commercial structures were not needed to facilitate exchange. Instead commercial affairs were carried out in the stone houses, with domestic architecture developing specific features to accommodate such activities."[83] The houses of medieval Shanga and early modern Lamu include numerous examples of guest rooms cut off from the rest of the house and available for the use of a sponsored foreign merchant in residence.[84]

Yet along the East African coastline, the house was intertwined with merchants' activity in a twofold manner. For local merchants who dealt in the long-distance trade, ownership of stone houses was a privilege linked to their status as the elite commercial class, distinct from other locals who lived in low, wattle and daub structures. Traveling merchants established their legitimacy through their relationships with these high-profile merchants in a world of trade in which strangers and foreigners needed to be integrated into a highly stratified and clearly defined social system as a mark of their economic reliability. The stone house, in its size, obvious expense, and durability, made a visual declaration on the urban landscape. In regard to the city of Shanga, the archaeologist Mark Horton stressed, "If one did not own a stone house, then trade was impossible. Stone houses were constructed and occupied as a symbol of aristocracy and permanence. Permanence implied creditworthiness, and in a society based on trade this was essential to the successful merchant."[85] Thus the stone house generated a type of social merit, again integrally linked to the practice of trade on the Swahili coast. The stone house doubled its purpose, serving as both a site for trade and an appropriate investment for a well-to-do merchant. It was a stronghold of wealth and a safe, defensible place to store goods, which also confirmed that its owner and his associates would not evade payment or flee the city.

Although this strictly controlled system of trade sponsorship was not in place at Mocha, one may use its Swahili and Red Sea coastal counterparts to approach an understanding of the larger significance of its stone and brick houses. Standing apart from the low-lying mud and thatch settlements both inside and outside the city wall, the towering, fortresslike Mocha house communicated a sense of permanence and stability in a city where fires and attacks from outside were common. In general, Yemenis place structural and decorative emphasis on the exterior facades of their houses and on their front doorways as outward modes of representing the success and high standing of the owners.[86] Mocha's sculpted doorways, crowned with ornate, projecting wooden windows, aptly fulfilled that function. In Mocha, where almost everything was bought and sold on credit in an imaginary currency, the Mocha dollar, such signs undoubtedly held importance. In a city where strangers arrived daily from faraway locations, the strength and permanence of the house (even a rented one) assured the trustworthiness of the merchant and confirmed that he was indeed of high standing, rather than an ordinary peddler who would spend the night in the city's short-term *wikāla*. As Philip Curtin has highlighted, cross-cultural trade inherently entails "problems of cross-cultural understanding," and for that reason "special institutional arrangements to help guarantee the mutual security of the two sides" were developed around trading networks.[87] The merchant's stone house, of a considerable size and located within the safe, defensible walls of the town, served as one such institution, as both the site for this trading lifestyle and built confirmation of the inhabitant's economic reliability.

7 *On the Politics of Inside and Out*

Although much has been written about the status and social standing of Jewish and Christian communities under Muslim rule in the Arab world, little is known about the smaller and less widespread religious minority group, the Hindu and Jain Baniyans of the Arabian Peninsula. The Baniyans of Mocha appear in every account of the city, but often in murky terms, as transitory translators and conscientious intermediaries who served the needs of the city's merchants. It is difficult to learn anything concrete about the community's practices and social standing beyond the oft-repeated ethnographic observations and stereotypical descriptions left by their European clients, who focused on their keen business acumen, their exceptional compassion toward animals, their strict adherence to a vegetarian diet, and their staunch observance of nonviolence and rites of purification.[1]

In this chapter I explore the Baniyans as an economically central yet socially marginalized merchant community in multiethnic Mocha during the first half of the eighteenth century. Their social status and legal position in Qāsimī Yemen were greatly intertwined with those of the Jewish community, although in Mocha their urban standing and residential practices differed significantly from those of the long-settled Jews. Each group was defined by its relationship to the city wall of Mocha, which marked the limits of the urban landscape and established distinct residential realms. Other hierarchical systems, too, were mapped in the urban matrix of the city, and the dynamics of the trade, together with occupational identities, economic roles, and religious affiliations, had a strong effect on the definition of the social order of Mocha.

The Baniyans of Mocha

The Baniyans are a caste-vocational group that encompasses a number of Hindu and Jain subcastes as well as members of other, higher-caste merchant groups.[2] Irfan Habib noted: "When one speaks of the Banya one means everyone who describes himself as such."[3] In the case of the early modern Indian Ocean, the economic cohesion and social solidarity offered by the Baniyan professional affiliation served the needs of many merchants, particularly abroad, allowing some Baniyans to cross strict and fixed notions of caste or sect divisions. Invariably associated with commerce, Baniyans from the northwest coast of India worked as trade brokers, commercial middlemen, and economic intermediaries around the shores of the southern Red Sea, the Arabian Sea, and the Persian Gulf, in cities such as Massawa, Sawākin, Muscat, and Basra. It has been suggested that this group—referred to by the term "Bāniyān" or the collective designation "al-Hunūd" in the Arabic sources—may have lived and worked in Yemen long before the Islamic conquest.[4] The earliest historical documentation is considerably later, dating from the fourteenth century.[5]

The largest Baniyan communities of Yemen lived in the lowlands, in cities such as Mocha, Aden, al-Luḥayya, al-Ḥudayda, Bayt al-Faqīh, Zabid, and al-Shiḥr in Ḥaḍramawt, and in interior commercial hub cities such as Sanaa, Taʿizz, Ibb, and even the impregnable mountain city of Shahāra. Despite this geographic dispersal, the closely knit Baniyan community in Yemen was socially cohesive and maintained professional links throughout southern Arabia by way of a wide-reaching system of communication that forecast any political or commercial circumstances that might affect the trade.[6] The Dutch often learned of a faraway plundered caravan or distant tribal unrest through "Baniyan letters."[7] Furthermore, a Baniyan agent in one city never hesitated to rely upon a contact in another city to expedite a trade transaction or facilitate a remote negotiation between a compatriot and a foreign merchant through a formal written recommendation.

Although little is known of their precise responsibilities as brokers for Muslim merchants, European documentation provides details about the roles the Baniyans played as brokers and translators for the Western trading companies. In Mocha, each company hired a Baniyan broker for continuing service, thus assuring loyalty. If needed, extra Baniyan brokers could be hired on a freelance basis—for instance, to be sent as coffee purchasers to Bayt al-Faqīh. The Baniyans served as commercial go-betweens for their European clients by inspecting potential goods for sale, making bids, and arranging delivery of purchased items to them. Essentially, as soon as maritime goods touched Mocha's shores, they were transferred by way of Baniyan agents, who handled all the land-based functions of the trade and its accounting and in many cases obviated the need for direct contact between major merchants. The Baniyans kept all the accounts in the city and were responsible for making sure that payments were delivered according to the three landmark dates of the Nayrūz calendar. They also served as political liaisons to the governor, who would call upon the company's Baniyan broker to complain about or investigate a problem before directly approaching the merchants. The Baniyan broker would be the first to hear a demand for prepayment of the company's seasonal tolls, for example, or to be informed of the governor's complaints about the paucity of the company's annual gifts. Consequently, the role of broker often placed Baniyans in tenuous positions. On many occasions the Baniyan of a European establishment was jailed or fined as indirect punishment of the European sponsor, who would suffer financial loss when his broker was unavailable.

Not all Baniyans in Mocha were directly involved in the international trade, although the most successful ones were.[8] An eighteenth-century observer called them "very rich merchants" but also mentioned "weighers of gold and silver; and indeed all sorts of artificers and mechanicks."[9] Sources make passing mention of Baniyans who earned their livings in service-oriented fields and those who produced and sold everyday crafts and goods for the local market from their small shops in the bazaar.[10] Indeed, the southeastern gate that led directly into the city's *sūq* was called the Baniyan gate, perhaps referring to the high concentration of Baniyan shop owners in that retail sector.

The Baniyan subcommunity in Mocha was well organized, with its own leader, referred to as the *shāhbandar*.[11] Figures for Mocha's Baniyan population in the eighteenth century vary, falling between 200 and 700 people, a fluctuation that reflects their movements to and from Yemen as well as from city to city around Yemen. The Baniyans were always considered temporary residents who never settled down with female family members abroad or married local women. Rare exceptions arose, however, such as the father of the famed poet Ibrāhīm b. Ṣāliḥ al-Hindī (d. 1101/1689–90), a Baniyan living in Sanaa who converted to Islam and established himself permanently in Yemen.[12] As an example of a well-known Baniyan family brokerage team in Mocha, Virachand and his seven sons served all the Europeans in the early eighteenth century.[13] Among other languages, Vira spoke Portuguese, which he used to communicate with many of his European clients.[14] When he died in 1711, his son Pitambar, who was well respected because of his great linguistic skills, took over the European trade.[15] When Pitambar left Mocha in 1716, his brother Virsinsi Trikam assumed responsibility for the Dutch brokerage.

The Baniyans' legal standing in Qāsimī Yemen was analogous to that of the long-settled local Jewish community. From the late seventeenth century, both communities had filled significant economic and professional niches as shop owners, merchants, trade brokers, bankers, and artisans. Like the Jews, the Baniyans maintained the legal status of a *dhimmī*, or protected minority, community upon payment of the poll tax.[16] The Baniyans could not be granted this status under a conventional interpretation of Islamic law, because the *dhimmī* status was reserved for monotheistic communities, or *ahl al-kitāb*. Instead, Imam al-Mutawakkil bestowed this standing upon the Hindu and Jain Baniyans as a gracious act in 1066/1655–66.[17] Beyond the safety of imperial protection, however, the *dhimmī* status entailed restrictions on religious activity and sumptuary dictates that differentiated the Baniyans from the larger Muslim minority while imposing humility and modesty on the group. Some of these restrictions were continually overlooked, whereas others were staunchly enforced. Thus the Baniyans' status was defined by inherent instability.

In practicing their religion in Mocha, the Baniyans conducted devotional activities discretely in the presence of Brahmin priests.[18] There was a Hindu temple within the city wall, but it was not built as a recognizable example of Indian religious architecture.[19] Rather, it consisted of four adjoining houses, with no distinguishing external features, that were set aside for the purpose of worship. A temple decorated with Hindu figural motifs on its exterior walls would not have been tolerated in Mocha or any other city in Yemen at the time.[20] No mention is made of a separate Jain place of worship, because the available sources in Arabic and European languages make little distinction between the two religious communities. It is probably safe to assume that the majority of Mocha's Baniyans were Hindu. The Dutch registers note that the Baniyans publicly celebrated the festivals of Divali and Holi.[21] They were not permitted to cremate their dead, but they were granted permission to bury them in their own cemetery, a mile south of the city. For each interred body they paid a fee, which fluctuated according to the governor's whim.[22]

Because of their central commercial role and the great wealth they amassed, the Baniyans who were associated with the long-distance trade were often financially vulnerable. Dutch sources describe their economic oppression at the hands of Mocha's governor, calling them the "milk cows of the Arab government."[23] Whenever the imam or the governor needed to fill the royal coffers, he called on the Baniyan community to produce large sums of cash as a loan before he approached any of the other merchants. Although the governor always promised to repay these so-called loans with the tolls and duties he would receive in the upcoming trade season, he rarely kept the promise. On rare occasions extreme violence was used against the Baniyans as a means to procure funds.[24] In one instance the governor, Aḥmad Khazindār, called for such brutal treatment that his officers refused to carry out the extreme measures.[25]

Outside of the poll tax and the frequent so-called loans, the Baniyans were required to pay sums to the governor of Mocha or directly to the imam as entry fees when they arrived in Yemen from the Kathiawar Peninsula in large groups seeking work, as well as upon exit. For instance, on April 7, 1720, a boat arrived from Diu, carrying more than 300 Baniyans "who had come to Arabia to make their fortune."[26] Their first stop was the port of Mocha, where they disembarked and paid an immigration fee directly to the governor.[27] Some stayed and settled for a while in Mocha, and the rest left for other Yemeni cities. When they returned home, each Baniyan was obliged to pay another unconditional sum to the governor of Mocha before embarking on the maritime journey.[28] The sums differed yearly, and in one extreme case the governor simply banned a group from leaving by saying that the imam had forbidden it, probably in an effort to retain their poll tax money for the coming year, which would be worth more than their one-time exit fees.[29] Furthermore, the estate of any Baniyan who died in Mocha went directly to the treasury.[30] Because many Baniyans perished in Mocha without any local heirs, their financial legacies constituted another source of income for the governor.

It would be a mistake, however, to consider the Baniyans an outcast community on the basis of records of their social instability and financial abuse in Yemen. Rather, as Ashin Das Gupta explained, their position was a "curious paradox of economic importance and social inferiority."[31] The governors and officials of Mocha acknowledged that the Baniyans had carved out an important niche in the mercantile circuit and played an instrumental role in facilitating the smooth flow of trade and commerce within the city. Although they competed with Muslim merchants for business in Sanaa's marketplace, in Mocha they dominated the brokerage sector without rivals. When Faqīh Aḥmad Khazindār, often cast as a tyrannical figure who treated the Baniyans with unusual harshness, came back to Mocha as governor for the second time in 1730, he worked hard to coax back the Baniyans who had left the city under the cruelty of his predecessor.[32] He recognized that their absence from the port would hurt the season's trade. It would also hinder his ability to remit copious sums to the imam in Sanaa and to garner a significant portion for his own benefit.

The Baniyans played a commanding role in ordering the city's international bulk trade, particularly in the realm of banking. As described in chapter 1, the payment schedule in Mocha operated on the Nayrūz calendar, devised by Baniyans according to maritime seasons of travel rather than the local lunar Islamic calendar. Although the Baniyans' maintenance of their own calendar is unsurprising—the Jews also used a distinct calendar for liturgical and communal purposes—the fact that all the wholesale merchants in the city, including Muslims and Europeans, operated on this Baniyan timetable is striking. Furthermore, among the many coins used for exchange in the city, the Mocha dollar, alternatively called the Baniyan dollar, was the dominant currency, in which wholesale values were tabulated, although never paid. The Baniyans devised this local system of financial reckoning and fixed the value of the Mocha dollar at 21.5 percent below the Spanish riyal.[33] Thus they oversaw systems of both time and fiscal accounting for the wholesale trade in Mocha with local modes of bookkeeping unlike those used in other cities in Qāsimī Yemen.

The Politics of Religious Difference in Qāsimī Yemen

As a final imperial act, on his deathbed in 1676, Imam al-Mutawakkil Ismāʿīl ordered the expulsion of the long-settled Jewish community from Yemen.[34] Three years later his successor, Imam al-Mahdī Aḥmad, followed through on his demand, and the Jews from Sanaa and other Yemeni cities were expelled to the city of Mawzaʿ, in the southern Tihāma in the vicinity of Mocha.[35] It appears that the imam was attempting to secure maritime passage for them off the peninsula to India or Africa, presumably via the port of Mocha. While the community lingered at this "temporary staging post," many members perished from disease and famine in the unhealthful climate of the lowlands.[36] The plan to expel the Jews from Yemen was not carried through, however, and eventually the community returned to homes in Sanaa and other cities.[37]

Although it was ultimately retracted, the imam's attempted expulsion of the Jews reveals the vexed and unstable position of the long-settled religious minorities in Yemen—Jews and Baniyans—during the Qāsimī period. Jews and Baniyans had lived in Yemen for centuries, but their status was scrutinized intensely during this era, when both communities became particularly visible. Inspired by the Sabbatian movement of the 1660s, some Yemeni Jews began to announce the imminent arrival of the messiah, sell off their possessions, and openly prepare for the fall of their Muslim neighbors. Such public acts were seen as a contravention of their protected status and inspired increased resentment and suspicion toward all Jews, which culminated in the Mawzaʿ exile.[38] Meanwhile, the post-Ottoman shifts in the maritime trade (chapter 1), which favored western Indian connections and moved away from the Mediterranean world, heightened the economic importance and public profile of Baniyans on the southern Red Sea coast and, by extension, in the inland cities of Yemen. Sources from the mid-seventeenth century suggest a widespread discomfort with Baniyan religious difference, which was paired with a competitive fear of their rise in the marketplace.[39]

In addition, Bernard Haykel has shown how the manipulation of religious minority status during the Qāsimī era was largely a consequence of clashes between Sunnī-oriented scholars and traditional Zaydī proponents among the religious elites at the imam's court.[40] Although they often enforced strict discriminatory laws against the Jews, such as the forced conversion of Jewish orphans, Zaydī adherents supported the continuing presence of Yemen's Jewish and Baniyan communities because they played key professional and economic roles in society while assuring a constant influx of poll tax revenue that could be spent at the imam's discretion.[41] Sunnī-oriented scholars, whose influence on the imam's legal judgments rose steadily throughout the Qāsimī period, held that such communities should not reside on the Arabian Peninsula, on the basis of their interpretation of one of the Prophet Muḥammad's last commands. The vulnerable religious minorities of Yemen witnessed contradictory performances of acceptance and rejection as part of the debate, which turned on the public representation of sectarian affiliations and larger shifts in doctrinal positions. The devastating Mawzaʿ exile, though ultimately the culmination of a number of contemporary events, must also be cast in light of this sectarian debate.

The Baniyans never witnessed an event as cataclysmic as the attempted Jewish expulsion, but their status was equally tenuous during this time. Many Baniyans, as well as Jews, were massacred or forcibly converted in the late seventeenth century by Sayyid Ibrāhīm al-Maḥaṭwarī, a descendant of a previous imam. But al-Maḥaṭwarī was singled out as a "fanatic," and this event marked a rare moment when the two communities suffered fatal losses on the basis of religious difference alone.[42] In the middle of the eighteenth century, under the influence of the Sunnī-oriented jurist Ibn al-Amīr, Imam al-Mahdī ʿAbbās led a campaign to destroy the Baniyan temple and its devotional images in Mocha.[43] This is the only record of an official act of desecration of Baniyan sacred space in Yemen during the Qāsimī period, and it is notable that it took place in Mocha, where Baniyans practiced their religion fairly openly. And although al-Mahdī was willing to make a public show of destroying Baniyans' religious spaces and objects, he did not support their overall expulsion from Yemen. Rather, as a tacit acknowledgment of their economic centrality, he allowed them to continue to inhabit Qāsimī territory, although he enacted a new law requiring them to wear red turbans as a mode of visual differentiation. It appears that this mid-eighteenth-century sumptuary dictate was enforced, unlike many other codes mandating the dress and behavior of *dhimmī* communities that were quickly abandoned. Sources from the early eighteenth century describe the Baniyans dressed in white gowns with white turbans, whereas sources from the second half of the century, such as Niebuhr and Grandpré, confirm the prominent Baniyan red headgear (fig. 7.1).[44]

The seventeenth and eighteenth centuries constituted an era of great flux among the main religious minority communities of Yemen. Debates over their status emerged as a consequence of the heightened social and economic visibility of both groups during the period, as well as from the internal doctrinal disputes of the ruling elites. As Haykel emphasized, however, regardless of debates over the presence or expulsion of Jews and Baniyans, the Qāsimī imams were never inclined or able to expel either group from Yemen, largely because of their need for poll tax revenue and their dependence upon the professional and economic roles that the two long-standing communities played.

FIG. 7.1 "Courji, a Bannian, chief of the French agents at Mocha." Reproduced from Louis de Grandpré, *A Voyage in the Indian Ocean*, late eighteenth century.

Settlement Patterns

After the Jews returned to their homes from Mawzaʿ in 1680, they experienced severe social dislocation stemming from the loss of community members and property. Although the appointment of a few Jewish notables to government posts such as overseer of the Sanaa mint suggested that their prior social standing had been restored, architectural reminders of the expulsion attempt abounded, particularly in Sanaa. Synagogues had been destroyed or transformed into mosques, such as the Sanaani Mosque of Jalāʾ, which stood as a monument to their period of exile. Their urban status and residential profile had changed incontrovertibly. Before the expulsion, Jews had generally lived within the walled cities of Yemen, close to their Muslim counterparts, in brick-built tower houses conforming to the norm in layout, level of ornamentation, and style, such as the houses represented in figure 7.2.[45] Although there were separate Jewish quarters in intramural Sanaa, it appears that these quarters were not homogeneous or exclusive in religious makeup; rather, they represented areas of heavy community concentration. While the Jews were in Mawzaʿ, new owners took over their empty homes in Sanaa, impelling the group to relocate collectively to a new quarter in the unprotected western part of the city upon their return.[46] This new quarter, called Qāʿ al-Yahūd, constituted a satellite city outside the wall with its own market and limits.[47]

Insecurity about the permanence of their status, together with the immediate need for housing, dictated altered building practices in this new quarter. Unlike the sturdily built, stone and brick tower houses of the old walled city of Sanaa, the new houses were quickly constructed of less permanent and less expensive materials such as unbaked brick, rubble, and packed mud. As featured in the house shown in figure 7.3, external decoration was scant in this modest extramural quarter, and the houses were consistently built low, following the dictate that members of protected minority communities could not reside in houses that towered over those of their Muslim neighbors. This proscription had generally been ignored before the Mawzaʿ exile. Thus the Jews' post-exile status, in Sanaa and other cities, was defined largely by a spatial, visible, physical, and architectural segregation.

The transformed urban status of the Jewish community after the Mawzaʿ exile exemplifies the way religious difference and social inequity may be conceived of and confirmed within the built context through spatial and architectural delineations. The presence of a separate Jewish quarter in Sanaa is neither surprising nor unique in early modern urban history. Numerous examples from the Middle East, as well as from Europe and maritime Asia, show urban segmentation—sometimes voluntary and sometimes enforced—to have been a common measure for separating religious and ethnic groups in traditional cities.[48] Yet despite the resilience of this essentialized image of the historic Arab city, segregated along lines of religious and ethnic difference, scholars have begun to chip away at its underpinnings, suggesting that the relationship between spatial segregation and identity hierarchy is better seen as the result of a complex, evolving process of urbanization than as a standard, fixed mode.[49] Indeed, the case of Qāʿ al-Yahūd demonstrates that Jewish segregation in Sanaa was the result of particular historical circumstances and represents a fairly late innovation in Yemenite urban history.

Studies of other relevant cities raise further questions about the character of the ethnic or religious urban enclave. For instance, in his study of Aleppo, Abraham Marcus suggested that the eighteenth-century names of the city's quarters, which appear to reflect a city segregated along ethnic and religious lines, were often misleading and outdated. In some cases, Jews, Kurds, Persians, or Christians might have occupied a particular quarter in the past, but

FIG. 7.2 View of a residential neighborhood in the walled city, Sanaa, 1996.

FIG. 7.3 House, Qāʿ al-Yahūd, Sanaa, 2000.

by the eighteenth century that quarter had become largely mixed in makeup, despite what its label suggested. In other cases, quarters were named after single groups while other significant cohabiting communities were overlooked. Marcus challenged the idea that the city's early modern shape was broken down into "homogenous units or neat spatial embodiments of social groups" and undermined the transparency of urban toponymy.[50]

From the other side of the Indian Ocean, Heather Sutherland, studying eighteenth-century Makassar (now Ujung Pandang) in Sulawesi, furthered this line of discussion by questioning the notion that a segregated city plan necessarily points to a segmented lifestyle. Under Dutch jurisdiction, this company town appeared to exemplify a strict, ethnically segregated hierarchy. Its fortified residential castle housed VOC officials and symbolized Dutch supremacy in the East Indies, and the city's ethnic quarters were arranged in a continuum based upon loyalty to the VOC. Groups deemed trustworthy, such as Portuguese-speaking Asian Christians, were settled close to the castle, whereas groups considered more capricious, such as the indigenous Makassarese, were transferred farther away. A close reading of local residential registers, however, revealed that these ethnically defined areas, such as the clearly named China Street, were not inhabited exclusively by single groups, despite the intention of official VOC policy to segregate and order the population. Furthermore, the large growth of the mestizo community during this period showed that spatial boundaries were often transgressed and that strong interethnic bonds were formed across neighborhood lines. According to Sutherland, in an increasingly diverse environment, essentialist ideals of untainted European and local identities began to blur and overlap, making "a mockery of the official emphasis on ethnic segregation and Calvinist morality."[51]

These examples from the Ottoman provinces and the far reaches of the Indian Ocean suggest that the practical functions of everyday life may effortlessly override the administrative desire or communal impulse to separate urban communities and undermine the possibility that exclusive urban segregation may function without contestation in a multiethnic and multireligious city.

The Spatial Politics of Difference in Mocha

A perusal of Mocha's city layout (map 5.1) at first suggests a stark religious division delineated by the city wall, like the seventeenth-century split between the walled city of Sanaa and the unwalled Qāʿ al-Yahūd. The Jewish community in Mocha, too, lived in an extramural quarter, located southeast of the city, which was unbounded by walls or any other protection and marked by modest houses. It lacked a separate market but included a place of worship.[52] But the Jews were not the only ones to live outside the wall. The suburb adjacent to the Jewish quarter was described as the Somali quarter.[53] The significant size of the local Somali community may be attributed to immigration resulting from the constant traffic of small shuttle boats from the port of Zaylaʿ, on the African side of the Gulf of Aden, to Mocha, which brought important everyday goods such as butter, oil, sheep, firewood, mats, and water to the city. Traffic on this route increased after Imam al-Mahdī Muḥammad claimed the island as a Qāsimī holding in 1695. Furthermore, as Grandpré mentioned, many Yemeni Arab Muslims lived outside the city wall, to the north in the al-ʿAmūdī quarter and also to the east, outside Bāb al-Shādhilī, an area that was well located because of the abundance of freshwater wells.[54] Although the extramural local Muslim residents of Mocha were most often referred to as Bedouins, modest workers, and coolies, they included other ranks of society, such as the well-respected religious scholar Qāḍī Muḥammad Ṣāliḥ in the 1720s.[55]

In fact, many groups lived outside the city wall, where housing was composed exclusively of modest mud and thatch settlements, unlike the intramural mixture of towering, fortresslike stone and brick houses and clusters of low straw buildings.[56] With conical thatched roofs and packed mud walls, the simple extramural houses were easy and inexpensive to construct using local materials, but not strongly built. Fires were common in the hottest and windiest months of summer and consumed thatch houses quickly, so they were inadequate for storing and protecting valuables. Furthermore, the extramural areas were subject to destruction or looting during a siege. In July 1728, for instance, the troops of Sīdī Aḥmad, the brother of Imam al-Manṣūr Ḥusayn, attacked Mocha in an effort to reclaim it for the imam from his contender Muḥammad b. Isḥāq, who had taken the city. Ismāʿīl b. Muḥammad Isḥāq, the contender's son and representative in Mocha, ordered that the southern, eastern, and northeastern extramural quarters of the city be burned to assure that Aḥmad's troops could not sneak up on the city, concealed by the outside settlements.[57] After the whole area had been burned down, the Dutch evaluated the damage, saying, "The burned houses amounted to 3000, each worth 30 Spanish riyals, so that 90,000 Spanish riyals went up in flames and more than 4000 families were brought into poverty."[58] Although the inhabitants of the extramural quarters, which included the Jews and Somalis, were able to seek temporary shelter inside the walled city, they suffered the loss of their property. This episode demonstrates the tenuous status of the quarters beyond the city wall.

Whereas the Jewish community lived outside the protection of the city wall in mud and thatch houses, the Baniyans of Mocha, who shared the Jews' legal status as a *dhimmī* community, lived inside the wall in lofty, private, stone and brick residences. These immigrant brokers were not relegated to a separate extramural quarter, nor was there a segregated Baniyan quarter within the wall. The Baniyans lived in houses spread around the city in an arbitrary fashion, regardless of their proximity to Muslim religious monuments.[59] Furthermore, Baniyans owned the houses they inhabited, as well as additional properties to rent out for income during the high trade season. That Baniyan ownership of the city's prime real estate was not restricted in scale or location is confirmed by the fact that the Baniyan Mathura owned the prominent Dutch residence, situated along the shore in the northern part of the city, before it was sold to Ḥasan Ḥasūsā, the head *ṣarrāf* of the city, in 1735.[60]

Relying on scanty passing references to Baniyan housing in other Yemeni cities, one can draw the conclusion that Baniyans were not universally accorded this integrated, intramural residential status. Separate Baniyan quarters existed in some cities, examples being Ḥāfat al-Bāniyān in Aden and Ḥārat al-Hunūd in Zabid and ʿAbs.[61] In other cities were found Baniyan trading establishments, such as a Baniyan *khān* in Ibb, Sūq al-Hunūd in al-Shiḥr, and a Baniyan *samsara* in Sanaa that was located to the west of the city, outside the wall in Biʾr al-ʿAzab.[62] In some Yemeni cities, Baniyan merchants may have lived in their *khāns* and *samsaras*, so that their residential status was irrelevant. Clearly, no single or consistent policy regarding Baniyan residence was enforced throughout Qāsimī Yemen. In Mocha, *khāns* and *samsaras* were not used for wholesale trade, so it is no surprise that separate Baniyan trading establishments did not exist there. Because commercial negotiations, storage, and lodging were instead based in houses, everyone who handled overseas trade commodities needed to live inside the wall in order to protect his goods. This practice cut across class lines, so that important Muslim shipowning merchants and their high-profile *nākhūdhas* from Gujarat and the Persian Gulf lived in grand intramural mansions, sharing the safety of the walled space with their Hindu and Jain Baniyan broker counterparts. European merchants also inhabited the intramural space in large stone houses, but they were never considered a *dhimmī* community. Rather, they were treated as temporary, foreign resident merchants whose status was determined by the clauses of their trade agreements.[63]

Extramural urban segregation in Mocha did not operate along religious or ethnic lines alone but was determined according to one's economic worth in the context of overseas trade. The governor protected the merchants who were involved in the international trade, such as the Baniyans, because they provided important services linked to the livelihood of long-distance commerce. If the city was taken by siege—not an unusual occurrence—their houses, rich with commodities stored in ground-floor warehouses, were best protected within the strongly built wall of the city. Inclusion inside the wall was necessary because any financial harm that came to the Baniyan brokers would ripple throughout the city, affecting all the city's merchants and ultimately the imam's treasury revenue.

Additionally, on a functional level, the daily practice of trade required such a residential organization. Many visits between merchants and brokers were conducted in the cooler evenings rather than in the scorching heat of the day, so the Baniyans had to live within the wall in order to orchestrate transactions when the gates were shut at night. Although some Baniyans worked in service fields and as small-scale retailers, their urban status was determined by the qualifications of the most prominent members of the community, which allowed for overall intramural habitation.

The Jews of Mocha, on the other hand, were not engaged in the long-distance trade, although they were central to the production sector of the local economy as artisans and craftspeople. Unlike the Jewish merchants of the medieval Cairo Geniza, who traveled freely as commercial agents from the Mediterranean and India to Aden, Yemeni Jews in this era worked primarily as potters, silversmiths, tailors, jewelry makers, weavers, spinners, and farmers.[64] By the seventeenth century, Jewish international mercantile power had waned in Yemen, even on the coasts.[65] Their major civil responsibility was control of the mint of Sanaa, a privilege accorded to them by Ṣāḥib al-Mawāhib in the late seventeenth century, in the aftermath of their return from Mawzaʿ.[66] Similarly, Somali involvement in the wholesale long-distance trade was limited. Information from the later nineteenth and early twentieth centuries, and comparable data from Aden, shows that in addition to supplying the local market with everyday necessities from the African coast, Somali men and women worked in service-related fields, as domestic servants and water carriers, and in handicrafts, as basket and mat weavers.[67]

In Mocha, a close examination of residential patterns illuminates the uneven politics of intramural and extramural segregation. The Jews, the Somalis, and the local Muslims who maintained separate residential quarters outside the walled city constituted an essential workforce in the city. Regardless, they resided outside the wall in an area that could easily be ravaged by fires and outside attacks. Whereas the Baniyans and the Jews shared the same legal status as *dhimmī* communities and so could be subject to the same residential laws and practices, the Baniyans' urban status in Mocha was determined primarily by their integral place in the brokerage of the overseas trade. Mocha's particular order of trade, which took place in merchants' and brokers' houses, provided a practical rationale for Baniyan intramural residence. Thus the Baniyan residential pattern reveals an economic hierarchy that reinforced the constitutive social hierarchy already present in the city. This social organization, which included the Baniyans and excluded the Jews, was determined by maritime links as an extension of economic class status and occupational convenience. For the Jewish and Somali communities of Mocha, lack of engagement in the maritime trade reaffirmed their social marginalization. For the Baniyan merchants and brokers, their economic role in the overseas trade superseded their *dhimmī* status. Essentially, Mocha's urban residential policies encompassed two types of social orders, one based on the hierarchy of the maritime trade and the other on identity politics, which intersected in discordant ways in the eighteenth century.

Passage through Urban Thresholds

So far I have looked at Mocha's city wall in its defensive capacity and at the way it both effected and confirmed the city's commercial hierarchy. I have cast the intramural area as a space of privilege, safety, and defense, and the extramural space as one of vulnerability and instability. But as Remco Raben has shown for the Dutch colonial port cities of Batavia and Colombo, communities may read major morphological features such as city walls in different ways.[68] For the extramural residents of Mocha, the wall was an obstacle and a tangible borderline. For those who lived within it, the wall was a boundary that could be traversed, and the extramural area was read not only as a marginal space of abjection but also as a potentially meaningful part of the extended urban fabric.

During daylight hours the city gates were open and, although monitored, were relatively porous. Intramural residents exited the wall to procure daily necessities such as firewood and water from wells that provided sweeter supplies than the brackish internal sources. Extramural residents traveled through the city gates to open their shops in the bazaar or to work as domestic servants in the city's large residences. Gatekeepers observed people's passage, and official inspectors examined the goods that left and entered the city to ensure that they were accounted for appropriately. Passage was blocked unconditionally only at night, when the gates were drawn closed, or when a military emergency required that the city be sealed off from its surroundings.[69]

Although the city's main administrative, religious, and residential structures lay inside the wall, a large number of significant tombs were situated outside the wall, constituting a circuit of pilgrimage to local saints.[70] In the eighteenth century, al-Mūsawī mentioned numerous saints who were enshrined in extramural tombs, including descendants of the city's patron saint, al-Shādhilī. Of these extramural shrines, the only one standing today is the tomb of Shaykh Muḥammad b. Saʿīd al-ʿAmūdī (fig. 7.4), who came to Mocha from Wādi Dawʿan in Ḥaḍramawt and was interred to the north of the city before the wall was built.[71] Sayyid Shakr Allāh, also known as al-Jawhar, was buried outside the wall to the northeast of the city center, in a tomb no longer standing.[72] No biographical information exists about the *shaykh*, but it is clear that his legacy was important enough to merit the construction of a new mosque adjoining his tomb in 1727.[73] In addition to these tombs, Muḥammad ʿAbd al-Wahhāb named eighteen extramural mosques, some still standing and others ruined, during the twentieth century, outnumbering the ten he listed inside the wall.[74] Numerous burial grounds were also situated outside the wall, such as the one found to the north of the city near the Tomb of al-ʿAmūdī.[75] It is not surprising that many people desired a burial near the tomb of this revered saint, because popular beliefs deemed such holy men capable of bestowing *baraka*, or blessing, in death as well as in life.

Communal prayer on feast days such as ʿĪd al-Fiṭr, marking the close of the month of Ramaḍān, and ʿĪd al-Aḍḥā, the celebration at the end of the pilgrimage season, was conducted in a large, open-air, designated space called the *muṣallā*, located north of the city wall and east of al-ʿAmūdī's tomb (map 5.1).[76] As Islamic practice dictated, all the pious male members of the community gathered to pray together on these important days, which necessitated a large, unrestricted extramural area like the *muṣallā*. No structural information remains about the now-ruined *muṣallā* in Mocha, but

FIG. 7.4 Tomb of al-ʿAmūdī, Mocha, 2000.

clearly it was not elaborate.[77] A later description, from the early nineteenth century, provides details, calling it "a large square enclosure near the North Gate, where a great part of the male population of the city was assembled, all dressed in their best manner . . . seated in rows on the ground."[78] Local residents who remember praying in the *muṣallā* during the ʿĪd in the mid-twentieth century add that it was paved with small pebbles and marked by a *miḥrāb*, or prayer niche indicating the direction of Mecca, that rose two meters high next to a domed, raised area for the prayer leader.[79]

During these feast days the governor, with his officials, his army, and the local notables, inscribed the entire city under his authority through elaborate ceremonies of entry and exit. Dressed splendidly, they made a grand procession on horseback, carrying banners and flags, before exiting by one of the city gates.[80] After completing prayer in the *muṣallā*, they rode around the exterior of the city, sparring and jousting. They returned through another gate, to the accompaniment of cannon fire.[81] The procession passed by the European residences, where the governor and his party expected to be greeted with shots from the company sentries. Finally, they proceeded to the governor's house, where their celebration continued indoors. This ceremonial tour around the city, conducted on each of several days for both ʿĪd al-Fiṭr and ʿĪd al-Aḍḥā, represented the governor's control over the entire city. His choice of movement through all the gates, not just through Bāb al-Shādhilī, the largest, or Bāb al-ʿAmūdī, the gate nearest the *muṣallā*, emphasized his free and fluid passage. By moving seamlessly across urban thresholds that were normally monitored and controlled, the governor demonstrated his authority over the city and marked out his military command and administrative ownership of Mocha's landscape.

Certain notable arrivals to Mocha were accepted with extraordinary pomp and ceremony, particularly at the two major gates, Bāb al-Shādhilī and Bāb al-Sāḥil, the Sea Gate. The arrivals of ships in Mocha's harbor after lengthy voyages were long-awaited moments for both those on land and those aboard. The most lavish displays were prepared for the great *nākhūdhas* of Gujarat. It was expected that the notables of the city would greet the officials of each major commercial ship at the Sea Gate, with an impressive display of soldiers, horses, musicians, and banners. After being escorted to the governor's palace, the overseas merchants and sea captains were received with coffee and the burning of incense, and the governor adorned each of them with a *khilʿa*, or robe of honor. Similarly, extravagant ceremony marked ships' departures back out to sea. Their major officers visited the governor before leaving and then were led out of the city under flags, banners, and the beating of drums to board their vessels.

Somewhat less lavish ceremonies were held to receive honored guests who came in from the eastern side of the city, along the land route. For example, when the governor Amīr Rizq returned to Mocha after a trip to the highlands in 1720, he was greeted warmly with shots fired from the bastions around the city and from ships in the harbor.[82] Messengers sent by the imam to Mocha carrying important letters arrived at Bāb al-Shādhilī, such as the one who was cordially welcomed outside the gate by the governor with his garrison in January 1725.[83] Because messengers from the imam's court entered the city through this gate, the governor Khazindār expressly assigned his most trustworthy servants as its gatekeepers, so that he could have letters brought to him directly, without interception.[84] The significance of Bāb al-Shādhilī as an official site of reception, as well as the city gate associated with Mocha's patron saint, is underscored by the fact that Europeans were often denied passage through it and were forced to use the smaller gates of the city, particularly Bāb al-ʿAmūdī.[85] The entry of an important notable or merchant into the city by way of the Sea Gate or Bāb al-Shādhilī was a delicate and important affair, highlighting the significance of urban thresholds as sites of official approval or rejection.

The Baniyan Sanctuary

Mocha's extramural tombs, mosques, cemeteries, and *muṣallā* were clearly inscribed along a sacred Muslim topography, a network of sites of visitation and veneration for Mocha's residents, including those who resided inside the wall. The extramural areas were tied into the fabric of the intramural city when the governor represented his control over the entirety of the urban sphere through elaborate performances of ingress and egress during the ʿĪd. City thresholds served as the sites of official reception of visitors and arriving merchants, where Mocha's military and the governor's finest displays were mobilized to represent local authority and the imam's approval. These movements, spatial practices, and ceremonies of reception constituted a major part of public urban activity, and they contribute to an understanding of the meaning of city space for its distinct communities, an understanding beyond the fixed logic of settlement patterns and the permanence of built features.

Daily records from the city reveal how Baniyans, who had the privilege of living within the wall, often escaped to the extramural space as a place where they could resist financial demands from the city's officials. They were continually forced to yield to the governor's demands for so-called loans, advance payment of tolls, and compulsory gifts of annual tribute above the normal, expected amounts. Sometimes this much-abused community opposed such egregious demands. On Wednesday, September 21, 1729, the Dutch daily entry recorded: "People heard that the Baniyans have closed their houses and stores and in great numbers they have fled to the grave of an Arab saint (located just outside of this city as a free place where no one can use violence or remove them from) to escape the brutal treatment of the second of this city [Muḥyī al-Dīn al-ʿArāsī], who sent soldiers to their houses continually to force them to fulfill the demand."[86] This "free place" was mentioned frequently as a sanctuary to which the Baniyans would flee in order to gain the leverage to subvert an unreasonable financial demand.[87] The sources do not mention exactly which tomb they used, but undoubtedly it was one of the major tombs outside the wall that visitors frequented as popular sites of veneration.[88] It is unsurprising that the Baniyans would occupy the tomb of a Muslim saint in order to find sanctuary, because it was assumed that no blood could be spilled at a sacred site and that safe haven would be granted there regardless of one's religious identity.[89] The site indeed protected them, and they often spent many days there patiently waiting out a demand while the city's trade languished without them. That the Baniyans could use their self-imposed exile outside the city wall to bring trade in the city to a standstill underscores the significant economic and professional role they played in the Mocha trade network.

The Baniyans' rebellious movement from inside to outside subversively transformed the spatial order of the city by reversing the official control over urban thresholds that the governor and his gatekeepers and inspectors normally exercised. In one instance when the Baniyans refused a demand for a loan, the governor immediately alerted all the gatekeepers around the city to let no Baniyan pass through, for fear that they would escape to the immunity of the extramural tomb. Not only did the act of occupying the saint's tomb confer safe status upon the Baniyans, but also their performance of exiting the city wall allowed them to overturn the governor's mechanisms of authority along the city's limits.

On at least one rare occasion, the safe haven offered by this saint's tomb was overridden. The governor broke the standing rule in the city and ordered that his soldiers remove some Baniyans from the tomb against their will. Observers recorded the event with shock as a first-time occurrence: "With violence, the governor [Faqīh Zayd Ṣāliḥ al-Shāmī] had some soldiers remove the previously mentioned Baniyans, who were from Bayt al-Faqīh, from the holy grave outside and place them under house arrest. This was a violation of the free place and caused a great upheaval among the Baniyans. This has never happened before, but the governor did not care a bit."[90]

More often city officials negotiated to coax the Baniyans back into the city, often by lowering the amount of the demand or postponing its payment. Flight to this tomb, therefore, was a negotiating tool for the Baniyans, who had no organized mode of representation in Yemeni cities. Although in another rare instance some Surati Muslims escaped to the tomb when the governor demanded an unreasonable sum of money from them, other groups seldom used the tomb as a place of refuge, probably because they could seek help from high-ranking persons of their own community in case of need.[91] The Baniyans had no means of intervention in the city other than withholding their services from Mocha's major merchants.

That the Baniyans perceived extramural Mocha as a space of agency and autonomy is further demonstrated by their practice of exiting the city gates to celebrate their main religious festival, Divali.[92] This time held special meaning for the merchant communities of Gujarat, both Hindu and Jain, because it marked the beginning of the new year and accordingly a turnover of the Nayrūz calendar.[93] In the Hindu tradition, Divali calls for veneration of the goddess of wealth, Lakshmi, an appropriate devotional concentration for this financially savvy group. Known as the festival of lights, Divali was celebrated in Mocha by the lighting of candles throughout the Baniyans' establishments. Outside the city wall Baniyans set off fireworks, illuminating the entire city.[94] On rare occasions they were prohibited from lighting their fireworks, not because of religious intolerance but because during seasons when fires had ravaged the city the governor feared that unnecessary sparks would exacerbate the risk in the extramural quarters of mud and thatch.[95]

The Baniyans of Mocha lived as a protected merchant community inside the city wall, in their strongly built private homes and with the privilege of their intramural temple. But intramural Mocha, where they were subject to the governor's economic oppression, did not always signify safety and protection. Their modest and discrete temple was sacked on at least one occasion at the order of Imam al-Mahdī ʿAbbās, and its devotional images were destroyed. In contrast, the extramural space of the city, although unprotected from outside marauders, was a space of autonomy with its site of sanctuary, which the Baniyans sometimes used to challenge authority and subvert a local demand. Flight outside the wall offered political agency, religious freedom, and asylum. By overturning control of the city's thresholds and occupying a Muslim shrine in an act of resistance, the Baniyans revealed the economic underpinnings of the governor's control of the city and laid bare their social and financial centrality, which was often obscured by acts of oppression at the hands of the governor and his officials. These transformations of the social order of the city, however, were temporary.

The Baniyans could always be coaxed back inside, and inevitably the governor pressed them for money again.

The eighteenth-century city of Mocha presents a complex overlay of hierarchical orders and reveals an unequal residential status for *dhimmī* communities at a moment when religious identity in Yemen was being highly politicized at court. Religious difference was only one axis along which spatial segregation was articulated throughout the city. Association with the maritime trade was an equally important feature of community identity in this coastal city. The Baniyans were accorded an integrated and intramural residential status because of their prominent role in Mocha's overseas trade. Yet rather than seeing the intramural city only as a space of protection and safety, one must also frame it as a site of control and surveillance over the Baniyan community. The extramural area, while signifying exclusion and segregation through its Somali and Jewish residential quarters, may be considered a multidimensional space that provided refuge, sanctuary, and religious autonomy for the Baniyans. Their actions transgressed the spatial norms determined by the city wall and destabilized a fixed relationship between intramural and extramural Mocha. The exclusionary politics of inside and outside were deeply interwoven with the economic hierarchy of the trade, and these politics could be both confirmed and contested by spatial practices and ceremonial acts in the eighteenth-century city.

Conclusion: The End of the Mocha Era

The stories of many Indian Ocean port cities conform to the familiar narrative of humble beginning, illustrious peak, and eventual collapse. Although the ruins of Mocha's once monumental buildings and traces of its jetty, now submerged, testify to the end point of its story, I have tried to avoid the predictable unraveling of urban prominence by plotting change along geographical and spatial vectors rather than sketching a chronological rise and fall. Yet it seems necessary to conclude with a few words about Mocha's last gasps as a major international port of the Qāsimī dynasty.

In 1196/1783, Imam al-Manṣūr ʿAlī b. al-Mahdī ʿAbbās appointed Sayyid Ibrāhīm b. ʿAbd Allāh al-Jurmūzī as governor of Mocha.[1] The governorship was appropriately accorded to al-Jurmūzī after he had brought Rayma, the agricultural area previously under his authority, to profitability during a time of great drought and hardship. It was said that he borrowed 13,000 riyals from the wazir ʿAlī al-Shāmī to stimulate the region economically and the next year returned to his lender a profit more than five times the initial sum. His appointment in Mocha was therefore both a gift to a successful governor and a strategic choice hinging on the hope that al-Jurmūzī would multiply the port revenues just as he had done those in Rayma. Al-Jurmūzī succeeded, bringing 380,000 riyals to the royal treasury from Mocha during his two years as governor.[2] His appointment, though short-lived, represents the continuation of the close ties between coast and capital seen in the movement of officials around Qāsimī Yemen in the late seventeenth and early eighteenth centuries (chapter 3). Like Sayyid Zayd Jaḥḥāf, al-Jurmūzī was a member of a notable, learned Zaydī family from the highlands who worked to bring the dispersed regions of Qāsimī Yemen together under the umbrella of the imamate. He did so by facilitating the smooth flow of revenue from Yemen's agricultural lands and its Red Sea ports to the imam's seat.

Although Ibrāhīm al-Jurmūzī represents the ideal administrator during this era of tight connections between sea and center, he was the last of his generation. Sultan Ḥasan, whom Imam al-Manṣūr ʿAlī appointed governor of Mocha after al-Jurmūzī's dismissal, exemplifies the breakdown of the imperial order that defined the Mocha trade network. Sultan Ḥasan, who was said to be the former slave of a wazir, aspired to autonomy when great instability and tribal unrest plagued the end of Imam al-Manṣūr's rule.[3] Although he dared not declare independence from the imamate, he brazenly withheld revenue from the capital, built up a formidable army, and strengthened the fortifications of the city, signaling that secession was on his mind.[4] When Aḥmad, the imam's son, assumed the role of wazir in 1223/1808 and essentially claimed the imamate without yet taking the title, Sultan Ḥasan refused to pay tribute to the new leader.[5] As a symbol of his status, he built a huge palace on Mocha's main square (fig. C.1), replacing the previous governor's house, which dated from the seventeenth century and must by then have been dilapidated.[6] Although Sultan Ḥasan's decadent three-story palace, with multiple *rawshans* and ornate plaster detail on its exterior, no longer stands, it may be considered a harbinger of the port's imminent decline.

Although Sultan Ḥasan eventually ceded to the new imam, al-Mutawakkil Aḥmad, after the death of his father, al-Manṣūr ʿAlī, in 1124/1809, his bold break with the court is indicative of the political and economic shifts that eventually severed the ports from Sanaa. His break was also fueled by other major disruptions that destabilized the centrality of the Qāsimī imamate, such as ongoing tribal conflicts, the looming influence of the growing Wahhabi movement, and the quickly expanding campaign of the independent Sharīf Ḥamūd b. Muḥammad Abū Mismār (d. 1233/1818) in the Tihāma. The disintegration of the political and economic authority that underpinned Qāsimī power provided an opening for the Ottomans to return for a second period of occupation and for the British to take Aden, two events that launched Mocha's slow and predictable demise.[7]

Writers of books about urban subjects often try to bestow upon their cities a sense of uniqueness by isolating them from the rural world and

FIG. C.1 The palace of Sultan Ḥasan (now destroyed), Mocha. Photograph by Hermann Burchardt, 1909.

highlighting their preeminence and distinction from other urban sites. Mocha, however, refuses the standard frame of urban history; it demands to be viewed not in isolation but at the core of its inland and overseas trade network. For Mocha one must emphasize the relevance of connected sites in a land-based network encompassing an agricultural hinterland, inland market centers, and distant highland capitals. One must consider the city's maritime port counterparts and its surrounding extramural quarters. All these elements contributed to Mocha's social, commercial, and political structure, its architectural and urban shape, and its historical significance. The city's connections were constitutive of its identity and built shape, rather than external to them.

With its elite composed of governors sent from the imam's capital, shipowning merchants, and *nākhūdhas* who served as representatives of

Gujarati entrepreneurs, Mocha hosted many outsiders who made the city their temporary home. "Outsiders" included even several long-settled religious minority communities—Baniyans, who lived inside the city walls, and Jews and Somalis, who lived outside them. Geographical connections and long-distance communication can be traced through the movement of people who traveled both inland and maritime routes, including the imam's wazirs, the governors of Mocha, high-profile *nākhūdhas*, profit-seeking merchants, expatriated brokers, and mobile religious scholars. Although the imams of Yemen have always been cast as cut off from the outside world, it is evident that the Qāsimīs were deeply engaged in the international sphere, albeit through the intercession of their coastal governors and cosmopolitan *nākhūdhas*. Inevitably, the long-distance trade had an effect on the landed Zaydī notable class of the interior, and its economic rewards appeared in lavish buildings and expensive manuscripts in the center of the Qāsimī realm.

Art and architectural historians have traced the circulation of visual motifs in exchange networks surrounding the Indian Ocean and the Mediterranean. The underlying assumption is that the eye plays a key role in confirming the saturation of cultural contact, whether by identifying shared decorative motifs or by recognizing the duplication of architectural floor plans. I believe we must probe beyond the replication of visual or built idioms in order to ask how architecture mediates the experiences and the practices of trade. In Mocha, commercial needs and economic impulses played important roles in determining the functional uses of public and private structures and their relationships to one another. I have read the city's architectural structures not as built hosts of formal features that displayed international influence or cosmopolitan design, but rather as practical spaces used by merchants for the everyday needs of their trade. Turning away from the visually identifiable elements of architectural form, I have looked at the vectors of movement through city space, the modes of organizing house space for commercial purposes, and the malleable order of authority that was defined along the city wall and its gates.

The space of the city and its buildings played an instrumental role in negotiating the experience of trade and long-distance travel for merchants who came not just from overseas but also from inland Qāsimī Yemen. Mocha's urban shape and spatial organization, stemming from its past as a lowland town organized around a saint's tomb and its illustrious position as a major Ottoman port, allowed for a transition from the world of the interior into the world of the maritime, and from the sea to the mountains. Urban structures and landmarks served as mediating built elements and spatial tools of translation. Towering merchants' houses with recognizable external decorative features—projecting wooden windows, elaborate carved arches and bands in gypsum—confirmed the economic reliability of their inhabitants while providing convenient places to conduct business away from the public eye. In essence, the shape of the city and the architectural properties of its buildings allowed for a commercial engagement that assumed cultural, geographic, and linguistic multiplicity and provided guests from afar with recognizable modes of handling trade transactions in an urban space that was at once familiar and foreign.

By highlighting Mocha's sites of commercial practice, I want to encourage a rethinking of the role of often-overlooked examples of non-monumental architecture, particularly commercial and domestic buildings. The houses of Mocha served as the sites for trade in the absence of public caravanserais, which have generally been understood as ubiquitous structures of wholesale trade in the Arab world. Furthermore, the model of Mocha's commercialized house allows one to question the nature of the Arab house as the uniformly private and protected domain of the family. On another level, domestic architecture in Yemen has been circumscribed within the paradigm of vernacular architecture, which entails a localized sense of style, craftsmanship, and materials. Mocha's domestic architecture, however, was closely related to its functional counterparts extending all the way down the African Swahili coast and across the Arabian Sea. Local modes of building and iconic regional house types may therefore be understood as much more globally oriented than they have previously been cast.

In the case of coastal Yemen, it is important to look beyond the dominant models for understanding Arab urbanism and architecture, most of which derive from assumptions based on well-known Mediterranean prototypes. In Mocha, one may not find the classic Arab courtyard house with its inward-facing orientation, nestled away in distinctly private quarters. But although Mocha's city layout and commercial structure are atypical of Arab Mediterranean examples, I do not wish to categorize the city under another regional rubric, such as that of the Red Sea or the Indian Ocean. Rather, I want to highlight the cross-regional and temporal context within which these features emerged. Mocha's particular site, as a port city in communication with the Yemeni interior and the Indian Ocean, and its moment, in the early modern era between two Ottoman occupations, provide the context for its urban form and architecture. Wider regional patterns may be drawn from its example, but its geographic and temporal specificity are of key significance here.

Although I have relied heavily on textual sources, the textual record has its limitations. Moving forward in understanding Mocha's cultural profile and the details of its economic activity requires the contribution of archaeologists, who can open up the material record for historians, art historians, and anthropologists. In seventeenth- and eighteenth-century Mocha, many houses collapsed structurally before they were abandoned. The daily records of the city tell frequently of the fall of a seemingly sound house because of heavy seasonal winds or everyday wear and tear. One can assume that the contents of the rooms and warehouses of many of Mocha's merchants' homes would be reasonably intact if they were excavated today. Like the excavation of the "sheikh's house" of thirteenth-century Quṣayr al-Qadīm on Egypt's Red Sea coast, which yielded remarkable documents about the city's trade and accounting, an excavation of Mocha would undoubtedly produce private records of negotiations and open a new window into the use of commercial space and the local dimensions of material culture among the city's merchant class.[8] Lying under mounds of sand and rubble in a ruined historic port city, each merchant's house is a potential archive awaiting future investigation.

APPENDIX A. THE IMAMS OF QĀSIMĪ YEMEN AND THE GOVERNORS OF MOCHA

The Qāsimī Imams through the Early Nineteenth Century

1006/1598 to 1029/1620	Al-Manṣūr Qāsim b. Muḥammad
1029/1620 to 1054/1644	Al-Mu'ayyad Muḥammad b. al-Manṣūr Qāsim
1054/1644 to 1087/1676	Al-Mutawakkil Ismā'īl b. al-Manṣūr Qāsim
1087/1676 to 1092/1681	Al-Mahdī Aḥmad b. Ḥasan b. al-Manṣūr Qāsim
1092/1681 to 1097/1686	Al-Mu'ayyad Muḥammad b. al-Mutawakkil Ismā'īl
1097/1686 to 1130/1718	Al-Mahdī Muḥammad b. al-Mahdī Aḥmad (also known as Ṣāḥib al-Mawāhib)
1130/1718 to 1139/1727	Al-Mutawakkil Qāsim b. Ḥusayn b. al-Mahdī Aḥmad
1139/1727 to 1161/1748	Al-Manṣūr Ḥusayn b. al-Mutawakkil Qāsim
1161/1748 to 1189/1775	Al-Mahdī 'Abbās b. al-Manṣūr Ḥusayn
1189/1775 to 1224/1809	Al-Manṣūr 'Alī b. al-Mahdī 'Abbās
1224/1809 to 1231/1816	Al-Mutawakkil Aḥmad b. al-Manṣūr 'Alī

The Governors of Mocha from the Mid-seventeenth through the Mid-eighteenth Century

Dates set in italics are those given in the most precise reference found, not the definite date of appointment to or removal from a position. All dates and chronological information were derived from al-Wazīr, *Tārīkh al-Yaman*, Abū Ṭālib, *Tārīkh al-Yaman*, the Dag Registers of the corresponding years, and selected entries from Zabāra, *Nashr al-ʿarf.*

? to 1063/1652–53	Saʿīd b. Rayḥān
1063/1652–53	Muḥammad b. Aḥmad b. Amīr al-Muʾminīn Ḥasan b. ʿAlī b. Dāwūd b. al-Imām (d. 1063/1652–53)
1066/1655–56 to 1080/1669–70	Sayyid Zayd b. ʿAlī Jaḥḥāf (d. 10 Rabīʿ al-awwal 1108/1696)
1080/1669–70 to 1095–96/1683	Sayyid Ḥasan b. Muṭahhar al-Jurmūzī (b. 1044/1634–35, d.1100/1688–89)
1097/1685–86	Zayd b. al-Mutawakkil
1105/1693–94	Faqīh Ḥasan al-Ānisī
1114/1702 to 1123/1712	Shaykh Sāliḥ b. ʿAlī al-Ḥuraybī (d. 1136/1723)
1715 to 1718	Sayyid Ḥasan b. Ṣāliḥ
1718 to February 1721	Amīr Rizq Allāh (d. Feb. 18, 1721)
February 1721 to February 1724	Faqīh Aḥmad b. Yaḥyā Khazindār (d. 1157/1744–45)
February 1724 to March 1727	Sīdī ʿAlī b. Amīr Rizq Allāh
March 1727 to December 1727	Shaykh ʿAmr b. Muḥsin al-Mughallas
December 1727 to September 1728	Sayyid Qāsim Amīr al-Dīn
September 1728 to 1730	Faqīh Zayd Ṣāliḥ al-Shāmī
1730 to 1737	Faqīh Aḥmad b. Yaḥyā Khazindār (d. 1157/1744–5)
1733 to 1734	Faqīh ʿAbd Allāh b. Aḥmad al-Khazindār (deputy governor for his father)
August 1737 to 1738	Shaykh Muḥyī al-Dīn b. Jābir al-ʿArāsī
1153/1740–41	Saʿd b. Saʿīd al-Majzabī
1748 to 1753	Sulaymān al-Manṣūr

APPENDIX B. ARCHIVAL AND MUSEUM SOURCES CONSULTED

1. The National Archives, The Hague, Netherlands

The National Archives (formally the General State Archives, or Algemeen Rijksarchief) in the Hague holds the most comprehensive collection of documents left by the merchants and administrators of the VOC. The most important group of documents is the Dag Registers, written by Dutch merchants and officials who held posts at the VOC trading establishment in Mocha. These logbooks contain daily entries made by resident observers and serve as important records of everyday life. The Dag Registers were copied and sent back to officials in Batavia to be inspected by administrators there. They were then copied again and sent to the home offices in the Netherlands. The Dutch officials also wrote periodic reports on missions to Mocha before the establishment of the permanent, year-round factory, and they sent home comprehensive letters regarding the trade and the political situation of the host country. In the archives, many different types of documents are bound together, especially documents pertaining to the same establishment, so the same reference number may appear for multiple documents. I list the documents I consulted in the following three sections.

Daily Reports from Seasonal Missions to Mocha

Because most pages include multiple-date entries and some are unpaginated, in the endnotes I refer to the daily reports from seasonal missions to

Mocha by date and VOC reference number rather than page number. The daily reports I used were the following:

VOC 1434 (microfilm 1053)	May–September 1685, pp. 513–99
VOC 1660 (microfilm 4236)	May–September 1701, pp. 771–810; Report by Dirck Clercq and Cornelius Snoeck, Signed September 22, 1701
VOC 1714	March–September 1704, pp. 126–88; Report by Joan Josua Ketelaar and Slaacq van der Hoeve to Pieter de Vos
VOC 9115 (Zeeland kamer)	July 16, 1705–September 13, 1706; Report by Joan Josua Ketelaar and Joan van der Needen on the Oostersteijn to Mocha
VOC 1784 (microfilm 2478)	September 1, 1708–August 31, 1709, pp. 1862–2226

Dag Registers

All the regular Dag Registers for Mocha open on July sixteenth and close on July fifteenth of the next year. Because many Dag Registers are unpaginated and most pages include multiple-date entries, in the endnotes I refer to the registers by date rather than page number, along with the VOC reference number. The name of the *kamer*, or regional home office, to which the register belonged is given in parentheses in the following list.

VOC 9116 (Zeeland kamer)	1719–20
VOC 9117 (Zeeland kamer)	1722–23
VOC 9118 (Zeeland kamer)	1723–24
VOC 9119 (Zeeland kamer)	1724–25
VOC 9120 (Zeeland kamer)	1725–26
VOC 9121 (Zeeland kamer)	1726–27
VOC 9122 (Zeeland kamer)	1727–28
VOC 9123 (Zeeland kamer)	1728–29
VOC 2202 (Amsterdam kamer)	1729–30

VOC 2252 (Amsterdam kamer)	1730–31, first register, pp. 201–417
VOC 2252 (Amsterdam kamer)	1731–32, second register, pp. 161–275
VOC 2356 (Amsterdam kamer)	1733–34, first register, pp. 95–133
VOC 2356 (Amsterdam kamer)	1734–35, second register, pp. 106–82
VOC 2415 (Amsterdam kamer)	1735–36, pp. 205–316
VOC 2447 (Amsterdam kamer)	1736–37, first register, pp. 118–271
VOC 2447 (Amsterdam kamer)	1737–38, second register, pp. 98–182
VOC 9113 (Zeeland kamer)	November 19, 1739–August 23, 1740

Reports and Logs

The merchants who visited Mocha on exploratory missions during the late seventeenth and early eighteenth centuries, before the VOC establishment was permanently opened, wrote most of the reports and logs in the following list. For the reports, I refer to the documents by VOC number and page number, when available.

VOC 1406	Report on a season of trade in Mocha by Hubert Cloecq and Aert Spender to Jacques de Bricquoy, dated September 20, 1683, pp. 1106–21
VOC 1406	Report on the city of Mocha by Hubert Cloecq and Aert Spender to Jacques de Bricquoy, dated September 20, 1683, pp. 1121–26
Van Hoorn Van Riebeck Papers 12	Description of the city of Mocha, from Gerrit Huigelbosch to Joan van Hoorn, dated March 24, 1701
VOC 1843	Report about the 1712 Mocha trade season by Christiaan van Vrijbergen to Abraham van Riebeck, dated August 20, 1713, pp. 32–59
VOC 1964	Report by Abraham Pantzer, dated August 19, 1719, pp. 74–120

2. British Library, London

The India Office Records of the British Library holds a large number of varied documents concerning Mocha. The most voluminous are the factory records left by the officials of the company who held posts at the trading establishment in the city, most of which date to the early eighteenth century and consist of letters, trading notes, and financial summaries. The factory records I used were the ones catalogued as G/17/1–4. Each volume consists of multiple parts; in the endnotes I refer to them by folio number and date. Two travel diaries concerning Mocha from this collection were also useful: "Observations on a voyage to Moka in 1800: Presented by G. Dominicus with remarks on the weather," IOR Mss Eur E2, and "Miscellaneous diary no. 323 of 1819–21, Captain William Bruce's Diary of the happenings in the Gulf of Aden and Mokha," IOR neg 11689.

3. Personal Library of Muḥammad ʿAbd al-Wahhāb, Mocha, Yemen

Muḥammad ʿAbd al-Wahhāb, "Iklīl al-Mukhāʾ," unpublished manuscript, 1988.

4. Ethnologisches Museum, Staatliche Museen zu Berlin, Stiftung Preußischer Kulturbesitz

The German traveler Hermann Burchardt visited Mocha in 1909 and left some of the most important visual records of the city. Of his photographs, a small number were published in a 1926 monograph edited by Eugen Mittwoch, which includes the travel notes left by Burchardt's Yemeni travel companion. Six plates of Mocha appear in the monograph (lower plate 22 and lower plate 23, both from Radāʿ, were incorrectly identified as Mocha), three of which are featured in this book (figs. 4.1, 5.4, and C.1). Aside from those six published images, many other images from Burchardt's visit to Mocha are held in the collection of the Ethnologisches Museum in Berlin. Four of those unpublished images appear in this book (figs. 5.1, 5.6, 5.8, and 6.14). It is curious that the images published in the 1926 volume are not held in the museum's collection today. The present location of those negatives has yet to be discovered.

5. Musée Bartholdi, Colmar, France

The French artist Auguste Bartholdi, who was the first photographer in Yemen, took six early photographs of Mocha. His photographs and drawings are held in the collection of the Musée Bartholdi in Colmar, France. They were reproduced in the exhibition catalog *Au Yémen en 1856: Photographies et dessins d'Auguste Bartholdi* (Colmar, 1994).

6. Peabody Essex Museum, Salem, Massachusetts

The Department of Maritime Arts and History and the Phillips Library at the Peabody Essex Museum hold textual and pictorial documents relating to the nineteenth-century American presence in Mocha. These are the "Caroline" Journal, 1821, Log 656 1821C, Phillips Library; "Engraving, Mocha, Arabia Harbor," negative number 31,262, accession number M18340; and "View of Mocha from the North," negative number 31,261, accession number M18855.

7. Royal Geographical Society, London

Rupert Kirk visited Mocha in 1832. His vivid watercolors of the port, its defenses, and its environs are held in the collection of the Royal Geographical Society in London.

NOTES

Introduction

1 It has been suggested that Mocha was ancient Mouza, but that theory has not been accepted widely, and archaeologists are still attempting to pinpoint the past location of Mouza.

2 Regarding the commercial history and urban shape of Aden, see Roxani Eleni Margariti, "Like the Place of Congregation on Judgment Day: Maritime Trade and Urban Organization in Medieval Aden (ca. 1083–1229)" (Ph.D. diss., Princeton University, 2002), and Margariti, *Aden and the Indian Ocean Trade: 150 Years in the Life of a Medieval Arabian Port* (Chapel Hill: University of North Carolina Press, 2007).

3 Limited amounts of coffee were exported from Ethiopia and Eritrea in the sixteenth century, before coffee cultivation in Yemen was effectively harnessed. After coffee cultivation was fully expanded in Yemen, small amounts of East African beans were still shipped to Mocha for resale in the seventeenth and eighteenth centuries. Beginning in 1712, the Dutch shipped small amounts of coffee from Java in addition to purchasing Yemeni coffee. By 1724 the quantity of Javan beans shipped to Europe exceeded the quantity of Yemeni beans that the Dutch purchased and shipped from Mocha. D. Bulbeck et al., compilers, *Southeast Asian Exports since the 14th Century: Cloves, Pepper, Coffee, and Sugar* (Singapore: Institute of Southeast Asian Studies, 1998), 144.

4 Samuel Lachmann, "The Ottoman Copper Coins Struck at Mocha," *Spink Numismatic Circular* 51 (1993): 44; R. B. Serjeant, "The Yemeni Coast in 1005/1597: An Anonymous Note on the Flyleaf of Ibn al-Mujāwir's *Tārīkh al-Mustabṣir*," *Arabian Studies* 7 (1985): 187–91.

5 ʿAbd Allāh b. ʿAlī al-Wazīr, *Tārīkh al-Yaman khilāl al-qarn al-ḥādī ʿashar al-hijrī, al-sābiʿ ʿashar al-mīlādī*, ed. Muḥammad ʿAbd al-Raḥīm Jāzim (Sanaa: Markaz al-Dirāsāt wa al-Buḥūth al-Yamanī, 1985), 173, 250.

6 K. DeGryse and J. Parmentier, "Maritime Aspects of the Ostend Trade to Mocha, India and China (1715–1732)," in *Ships, Sailors and Spices: East India Companies and Their Shipping in the 16th, 17th and 18th Century*, eds. J. R. Bruijn and F. S. Gaastra (Amsterdam: NEHA, 1993), 139–76; Eric Macro, "The First Americans at Mocha," *Geographical Journal* 130, no. 1 (March 1964): 183–84; Howard A. Reed, "Yankees at the Sultan's Port: The First Americans and Early Trade with Smyrna and Mocha," in *Contributions à l'histoire économique et sociale de l'empire ottoman*, eds. O. L. Barkan, J.-L. Bacqué-Grammont, and P. Dumont (Leuven, Belgium: Editions Peeters, 1983), 353–83.

7 May 6, 1706, VOC 9115.

8 A detailed account of the event from the French perspective appears in Pierre François Guyot Desfontaines, *Relation de l'expédition de Moka en l'année 1737 sous les ordres de M. de la Garde-Jazier, de Saint-Malo* (Paris, 1739).

9 John Baldry, "The Early History of the Yemeni Port of al-Ḥudaydah," *Arabian Studies* 7 (1985): 42.

10 R. J. Gavin, *Aden under British Rule* (London: Hurst, 1975), 55.

11 Abraham Marcus, *The Middle East on the Eve of Modernity: Aleppo in the Eighteenth Century* (New York: Columbia University Press, 1989); James Grehan, *Everyday Life and Consumer Culture in Eighteenth-Century Damascus* (Seattle: University of Washington Press, 2007); Nelly Hanna, *Making Big Money in 1600: The Life and Times of Ismaʿil Abu Taqiyya, Egyptian Merchant* (Syracuse, N.Y.: Syracuse University Press, 1998); André Raymond, *Grandes villes arabes à l'époque ottomane* (Paris: Sindbad, 1985); J. Hanssen, T. Philipp, and S. Weber, eds., *The Empire in the City: Arab Provincial Capitals in the Late Ottoman Empire* (Würzburg: Ergon Verlag, 2002).

12 On the Islamic city, see Janet Abu-Lughod, "The Islamic City: Historic Myth, Islamic Essence, and Contemporary Relevance," *International Journal of Middle East Studies* 19 (1987): 155–76, and Masashi Haneda and Toru Miura, eds., *Islamic Urban Studies: Historical Review and Perspectives* (New York: Kegan Paul, 1994). On the Arab city, see Nezar Alsayyad, *Cities and Caliphs: On the Genesis of Arab Muslim Urbanism* (Westport, Conn.: Greenwood Press, 1991), and André Raymond, "Islamic City, Arab City: Orientalist Myths and Recent Views," *British Journal of Middle Eastern Studies* 21, no. 1 (1994): 3–18.

13 Rhoads Murphey, "Traditionalism and Colonialism: Changing Urban Roles in Asia," *Journal of Asian Studies* 29, no. 1 (1969): 67–84. Later volumes that privilege the colonial port city include Frank Broeze, ed., *Brides of the Sea: Port Cities of Asia from the 16th—20th Centuries* (Honolulu: University of Hawaii Press, 1989); Broeze, ed., *Gateways of Asia: Port Cities of Asia in the 13th–20th Centuries* (London: Kegan Paul, 1997); Indu Banga, ed., *Ports and Hinterlands in India, 1700–1950*

(New Delhi: Manohar, 1992); and Dilip Basu, ed., *The Rise and Growth of the Colonial Port Cities in Asia* (Lanham, Md.: University Press of America, 1985).

14 Rhoads Murphey, "On the Evolution of the Port City," in *Brides of the Sea*, 234; Remco Raben, "Batavia and Colombo: The Ethnic and Spatial Order of Two Colonial Cities" (thesis, Rijksuniversiteit, Leiden, Netherlands, 1996), 1; Jeremy Taylor, "The Bund: Littoral Space of Empire in the Treaty Ports of East Asia," *Social History* 27, no. 2 (May 2002): 127.

15 One could even argue that the rubric of colonial port city has subsumed that of colonial city. Robert Ross and Gerald J. Telkamp, "Introduction," in *Colonial Cities: Essays on Urbanism in a Colonial Context*, eds. R. Ross and G. Telkamp (Boston: Martinus Nijhoff, 1985), 2.

16 Murphey, "Traditionalism and Colonialism," 83.

17 Deborah Howard, *Venice and the East: The Impact of the Islamic World on Venetian Architecture* (New Haven, Conn.: Yale University Press, 2000), 2.

18 On the question of influence in cross-cultural art historical studies, see Oleg Grabar's review of a number of relevant studies. Oleg Grabar, "Review of *Venice's Mediterranean Colonies: Architecture and Urbanism*, by Maria Georgopoulou; *Venice and the East: The Impact of the Islamic World on Venetian Architecture*, by Deborah Howard; *Global Interests: Renaissance Art between East and West*, by Lisa Jardine and Jerry Brotton; and *Bazaar to Piazza: Islamic Trade and Italian Art*, by Rosamund Mack," *Art Bulletin* 85, no. 1 (2003): 189–92.

19 Ruth Barnes, "The Painted Decoration: an Influence from Indian Textiles?" in Selma Al-Radi, *The ʿAmiriya in Radaʿ: The History and Restoration of a Sixteenth-Century Madrasa in the Yemen* (Oxford: Oxford University Press, 1997): 139–48.

20 Jerry Brotton, *Trading Territories: Mapping the Early Modern World* (London: Reaktion Books, 1997), 119–150; Howard, *Venice and the East*; Amin Jaffer and Anna Jackson, eds., *Encounters: The Meeting of Asia and Europe, 1500–1800* (London: V & A Publications, 2004).

21 Brotton, *Trading Territories*, 28.

22 Howard, *Venice and the East*.

23 Grabar, "Review," 191.

24 See Barnes, "Painted Decoration"; Paul Bonnenfant, "La marque de l'Inde à Zabîd," *Chroniques Yéménites* 8 (2000) (http://cy.revues.org/document7.html); Elizabeth Lambourn, "Carving and Recarving: Three Rasulid Gravestones Revisited," *New Arabian Studies* 6 (2001): 10–30; Ronald Lewcock, "Architectural Connections between Africa and Parts of the Indian Ocean Littoral," *Art and Archaeology Research Papers* (April 1976): 13–23; Venetia Porter, "The Rasulids in Dhofar in the VIIth–VIIIth/XIIIth–XIVth Centuries: Three Rasulid Tombstones from Ẓafār," *Journal of the Royal Asiatic Society* 1 (1988): 32–37; and V. S. Pramar, "Discovery of Links between Ancient Gujarat and Abyssinia," *Marg* 36, no. 1 (1984): 22–32.

25 Notable exceptions include Aḥmad al-Nuʿmī, *Ḥawliyyāt al-Nuʿmī al-tihāmiyya min tārīkh al-Yaman al-ḥadīth*, ed. Ḥusayn b. ʿAbd Allāh al-ʿAmrī (Damascus: Dār al-Fikr, 1987); Ismāʿīl b. Muḥammad al-Wushalī, *Dhayl nashr al-thanāʾ al-ḥasan al-munabbiʾ bi-baʿḍ ḥawādith al-zaman min gharāʾib al-wāqiʿa fī al-Yaman*, ed. Muḥammad b. M. al-Shuʿaybī (Sanaa: Maṭābiʿa al-Yaman al-ʿAṣriyya, 1982); and ʿAbd al-Raḥmān b. Aḥmad al-Bahkalī, *Imams, notables et bédouins du Yémen au XVIIIe siècle, ou, Quintessence de l'or du règne de Chérif Muḥammad b. Aḥmad: Chronique de ʿAbd al-Raḥmān b. Ḥasan al-Bahkalī* (Cairo: Institut Français d'Archéologie Orientale du Caire, 1992).

26 Although the Dutch left the most copious records during this period, they were not the most prominent traders in the city. Both the English and the French surpassed them in trade volume. The Dutch records, however, cannot be matched in their level of detail or fine state of preservation. They serve as important documents of contemporary city life but not of commercial dominance. R. J. Barendse, *The Arabian Seas, 1640–1700* (Leiden: Research School of Asian, African, and Amerindian Studies, 1998), 8.

27 A great deal of urban folklore exists about the city's past, but little of it is topographically or historically accurate. For instance, in a local weekly paper, a journalist stated that Mocha had 360 mosques but now only 8 remained, obviously a gross exaggeration. Muḥammad ʿAbduh Sufyān, "Al-Mukhā māḍin muzdahir wa ḥāḍir mundathir," *Taʿizz*, March 1, 2000, 6. However, ʿAbduh ʿAlī Muḥammad, of ʿAbd al-Qādir al-Khayyāṭ quarter, and the *ustā*, or master builder, Nājī Muḥammad Sayf were rich sources of information about Mocha's history and monuments.

28 The version of the Iklīl that the ʿAbd al-Wahhāb family holds today, written in the author's hand, is not the original but a copy made after the original was taken by an official who promised to publish it. The manuscript was never published, and the official, who is simply referred to as Jabr b. Jabr, never returned with the original copy. Residents told me that Jabr b. Jabr died in 2000. Personal communication, ʿĀdil ʿAbd al-Wahhāb, Mocha, Yemen, March 2000. Dirar Abdel-Daim, in his short article on Mocha, referred to it as a "manuscript that recounts Mokha's history." Dirar Abdel-Daim, "Mokha: The City of the Past and Future," in *Development and Urban Metamorphosis: Yemen at the Crossroads*, vol. 1: *Yemen at the Crossroads*, ed. Ahmet Evin, Proceedings of seminar eight in the series "Transformations in the Islamic World, Sanaʿa, May 25–30, 1983" (Singapore, 1983), 85.

29 I owe a great deal to Muḥammad ʿAbd al-Wahhāb and his grandson ʿĀdil, who shared parts of the unpublished manuscript with me and gave me much information that could not be obtained from any other source. I translated and annotated the topographical information from the manuscript in Appendix C in Nancy Um, "A Red Sea Society in Yemen: Architecture, Urban Form, and

Cultural Dynamics in the Eighteenth-Century Port City of al-Mukhā" (Ph.D. diss., University of California, Los Angeles, 2001).

30 Kenneth McPherson, *The Indian Ocean: A History of People and the Sea* (Oxford: Oxford University Press, 1993), 154.

31 Sugata Bose, *A Hundred Horizons: The Indian Ocean in the Age of Global Empire* (Cambridge, Mass.: Harvard University Press, 2006); K. N. Chaudhuri, *Trade and Civilisation in the Indian Ocean: An Economic History from the Rise of Islam to 1750* (Cambridge: Cambridge University Press, 1985); K. N. Chaudhuri, *Asia before Europe: Economy and Civilisation of the Indian Ocean from the Rise of Islam to 1750* (Cambridge: Cambridge University Press, 1990); McPherson, *Indian Ocean*.

1 The Mocha Trade Network

1 Patricia Risso, *Merchants and Faith: Muslim Commerce and Culture in the Indian Ocean* (Boulder, Colo.: Westview Press, 1995), 1. This disjuncture stands in stark contrast to the way maritime Mediterranean history has been relatively well integrated into the study of the western Islamic world in regard to Spain, North Africa, the Arab eastern Mediterranean, and Anatolia. Studies of Ottoman affairs in the Indian Ocean by Palmira Brummett and Giancarlo Casale, however, counter this larger trend. Palmira Brummett, *Ottoman Seapower and Levantine Diplomacy in the Age of Discovery* (Albany, N.Y.: SUNY Press, 1994); Giancarlo Casale, "The Ottoman 'Discovery' of the Indian Ocean in the Sixteenth Century," in *Seascapes: Maritime Histories, Littoral Cultures, and Transoceanic Exchanges*, eds. J. H. Bentley, R. Bridenthal, K. Wigen (Honolulu: University of Hawaii Press, 2007), 87–104.

2 This imbalance can be accounted for partially by the fact that the last ruling imams of Yemen, of the Ḥamīd al-Dīn line, were known for their harsh, autocratic policies, which remain vivid in the contemporary national memory. The Yemen Arab Republic was founded on their expulsion in 1962. Hence, most post-Revolution trends have leaned away from "imamic" history. Recently, new efforts have been made to edit Zaydī manuscripts, and related studies have emerged. Bernard Haykel, "A Zaydi Revival?" *Yemen Update* 36 (1995): 20–21.

3 As an example of the erasure of the Qāsimīs from Indian Ocean history, see Glamann's chapter on coffee trade. He erroneously claims that the Ottoman pasha was still in charge of Mocha in the late seventeenth and eighteenth centuries. Kristof Glamann, *Dutch Asiatic Trade, 1620–1740* (Copenhagen: Danish Science Press, 1958), 188.

4 Salih Özbaran, "A Turkish Report on the Red Sea and the Portuguese in the Indian Ocean," in *The Ottoman Response to European Expansion: Studies on Ottoman-Portuguese Relations in the Indian Ocean and Ottoman Administration in the Arab Lands during the Sixteenth Century* (Istanbul: Isis Press, 1994), 103–4.

5 Salih Özbaran, "The Ottomans in East Africa: A Tribute to Cengiz Orhonlu," in *The Ottoman Response to European Expansion*, 193.

6 Michel Tuchscherer, "Trade and Port Cities in the Red Sea–Gulf of Aden Region in the Sixteenth and Seventeenth Century," in *Modernity and Culture: From the Mediterranean to the Indian Ocean*, eds. L. T. Fawaz and C. A. Bayly (New York: Columbia University Press, 2002), 34.

7 Ibid., 33.

8 High-profile Cairene contemporaries of Abū Ṭāqiyya's also benefited from the profits of the Red Sea trade. An example is the merchant Aḥmad al-Ruwiʿī, whose son was based in Mocha. Hanna, *Making Big Money*, 17, 30.

9 Tuchscherer, "Trade and Port Cities in the Red Sea," 39. Accordingly, the trade of western India shifted away from the Southeast Asian spice market and toward the Red Sea during this period. Ashin Das Gupta, *Indian Merchants and the Decline of Surat, c. 1700–1750* (Wiesbaden, Germany: Franz Steiner Verlag, 1979; Delhi: Manohar, 1994), 5, n. 1, 70.

10 André Raymond discussed the Jidda gap first in 1973 and again in 2002. Michel Tuchscherer elaborated on it in 1993 and 2002. Raymond, *Artisans et commerçants au Caire au XVIIIe siècle* (Damascus: Institut Français de Damas, 1973), 1: 117; Raymond, "A Divided Sea: The Cairo Coffee Trade in the Red Sea Area during the Seventeenth and the Eighteenth Centuries," in Fawaz and Bayly, *Modernity and Culture*, 46–57; Tuchscherer, "Le commerce en Mer Rouge aux alentours de 1700: Flux, espaces, et temps," in *Circulation des monnaies, des marchandises et des biens*, eds. Rika Gyselen and Michael Alram (Bures-sur-Yvette: Groupe pour l'Étude de la Civilisation du Moyen-Orient, 1993), 170–71; Tuchscherer, "Trade and Port Cities in the Red Sea."

11 William Facey confirms that geographic and climatic factors also played a large role in defining the maritime segmentation of the Red Sea and the centrality within it of Jidda, which is strategically located at the crux where the winds shift regionally. Before the age of steamship travel, it was easy to navigate from Bāb al-Mandab to Jidda, but the prevailing winds made the trip from Jidda's latitude to points farther north more challenging. Indian Ocean merchants traveling on large vessels preferred to stop at Jidda in order to avoid a treacherous journey through the northern waters, leaving the task of transshipment to smaller vessels whose pilots were familiar with the particularities of Red Sea navigation. William Facey, "The Red Sea: The Wind Regime and Location of Ports," in *Trade and Travel in the Red Sea Region: Proceedings of Red Sea Project I, Held in the British Museum, October 2002*, eds. P. Lunde and A. Porter, BAR Series 1269 (2004), 7–18.

12 Bernard Haykel, *Revival and Reform in Islam: The Legacy of Muhammad al-Shawkānī* (Cambridge: Cambridge University Press, 2003), 35; E. van Donzel, *A Yemenite Embassy to Ethiopia, 1647–1649* (Stuttgart: Franz Steiner Verlag, 1986), 30–31.

13 R. B. Serjeant, "The Post-Medieval and Modern History of Ṣanʿāʾ and the Yemen, ca 953–1382/1515–1962, in *Ṣanʿāʾ: An Arabian Islamic City*, eds. R. B. Serjeant and R. Lewcock (London: World of Islam Trust, 1983), 80.

14 Haykel, *Revival and Reform*, 117.

15 Serjeant, "Post-Medieval and Modern History," 85.

16 Haykel, *Revival and Reform*, 17.

17 R. B. Serjeant, "Omani Naval Activities off the Southern Arabian Coast in the Late 11th/17th Century, from Yemeni Chronicles," in *Customary and Shariʿah Law in Arabian Society* (Hampshire, Great Britain: Variorum, 1991), 77.

18 Haykel, *Revival and Reform*, 56.

19 *Ghurāb* means "raven" or "a sword's blade" in Arabic. English sources referred to the boat as the "grab," and the Dutch used *goerab*.

20 Ellison B. Findly, "The Capture of Maryam-uz-Zamani's Ship: Mughal Women and European Traders," *Journal of the American Oriental Society* 108, no. 2 (1988): 227–38.

21 The best survey of the different types of cloth that appeared at Mocha in an earlier period is C. G. Brouwer, *Al-Mukhā: The Transoceanic Trade of a Yemeni Staple Town as Mapped by Merchants of the VOC, 1614–1640: Coffee, Spices and Textiles* (Amsterdam: D'Fluyte Rarob, 2006), 231–256.

22 This range of porcelains is evidenced in the archaeological finds from a 1993–95 survey. Claire Hardy-Guilbert and Axelle Rougeulle, "Ports islamiques du Yémen: Prospections archéologiques sur les côtes yéménites (1993–1995)," *Archéologie Islamique* 7 (1997): 156.

23 Tranke is an English term (the Dutch use *trank*) for which no equivalent has been found in Persian or Arabic, but it is known as a local vessel of the Persian Gulf. Henry Yule and A. C. Burnell, *Hobson-Jobson: A Glossary of Colloquial Anglo-Indian Words and Phrases, and of Kindred Terms, Etymological, Historical, Geographical and Discursive* (London: Murray, 1903), 937.

24 December 31, 1727, VOC 9122.

25 Thabit Abdullah, *Merchants, Mamluks, and Murder: The Political Economy of Trade in Eighteenth-Century Basra* (Albany, N.Y.: SUNY Press, 2001), 41.

26 December 28, 1729, January 8, 1730, VOC 2252.

27 Both G. R. Tibbetts and Roxani Margariti discuss the *jalba* as a Red Sea vessel noted as early as the twelfth century by Ibn Jubayr. G. R. Tibbetts, *Arab Navigation in the Indian Ocean before the Coming of the Portuguese, Being a Translation of* Kitāb al-Fawāʾid fī uṣūl al-baḥr wa'l qawāʾid *of Aḥmad b. Mājid al-Najdī* (London: Royal Asiatic Society of Great Britain and Ireland, 1981), 47; Margariti, "Maritime Trade," 248; Margariti, *Aden*, 154.

28 Serjeant, "Post-Medieval and Modern History," 83.

29 Tibbetts, *Arab Navigation*, 361–62.

30 Daniel Varisco has written extensively on the use of the Nayrūz calendar in a thirteenth-century Rasulid almanac, which appears to be the first written record of the calendar's use in Yemen. The Nayrūz calendar lacks a leap year, so it was reformed periodically to match the appropriate season. For this reason it is almost impossible to translate Nayrūz dates into Julian dates in any systematic fashion. Daniel Martin Varisco, *Medieval Agriculture and Islamic Science: The Almanac of a Yemeni Sultan* (Seattle: University of Washington Press, 1994), 73–74.

31 Ashin Das Gupta, "Gujarati Merchants and the Red Sea Trade, 1700–1725," in *The Age of Partnership: Europeans in Asia before Dominion*, eds. B. B. King and M. N. Pearson (Honolulu: University of Hawaii Press, 1979), 132–33.

32 VOC 1843, 46.

33 Nicholas Lowick, "The Mint of Ṣanʿāʾ: A Historical Outline," in Serjeant and Lewcock, *Ṣanʿāʾ*, 307.

34 As examples, see one struck by al-Mahdī Aḥmad, dated 1091/1679–80, and another struck by al-Mutawakkil Qāsim, dated 1137/1724–25. Samuel Lachmann, "The Zaidī Imām al-Mahdī Aḥmad b. al-Ḥasan, 1087–1092H/1676–1681," *Numismatic Circular* (June 1988): 143; Robert E. Darley-Doran, "Examples of Islamic Coinage from Yemen," in *Yemen: 3000 Years of Art and Civilisation in Arabia Felix*, ed. W. Daum (Frankfurt: Umschau Verlag, 1988), 202.

35 Raymond, *Artisans*, 1: 17.

36 Prutky claimed that the Spanish riyal was worth around 70 or 80 *komassis* in the mid-eighteenth century but at times was exchanged for as few as 15 or 20 *komassis*. *Prutky's Travels in Other Countries*, trans. and ed. J. H. Arrowsmith-Brown (London: Hakluyt Society, 1991), 374.

37 Ibid., 374–75; Carsten Niebuhr, *Description de l'Arabie: Faites sur des observations propres et des avis recueillis dans les lieux mêmes*, trans. F. L. Mourier (Amsterdam: S. J. Baalde, 1774), 191.

2 The Yemeni Coffee Network

1 Haykel, *Revival and Reform*, 16. Export figures are from Michel Tuchscherer, "Coffee in the Red Sea Area from the Sixteenth to the Nineteenth Century," in *The Global Coffee Economy in Africa, Asia, and Latin America, 1500–1989*, eds. W. G. Clarence-Smith and S. Topik (Cambridge: Cambridge University Press, 2003), 55.

2 Carsten Niebuhr, *Travels through Arabia and Other Countries in the East*, trans. R. Heron (Beirut: Librairie du Liban, 1968 [1792]), 2: 88.

3 Tuchscherer, "Coffee in the Red Sea Area," 50.

4 C. G. Brouwer, "Al-Mukhā as a Coffee Port in the Early Decades of the Seventeenth Century according to Dutch Sources," in *Le commerce du café avant l'ère*

des plantations coloniales: Espaces, réseaux, sociétés (XVe–XIXe siècle), ed. Michel Tuchscherer, *Cahier des Annales Islamologiques* 20 (2001): 271–90. Brouwer then treated the debate again in a more recent expanded study. Brouwer, *Transoceanic Trade*, 31–60.

5 Brouwer made the important distinction between the Indian Ocean sources, which stress Mocha's multipurpose status as a port, and the "monographic studies" of Mocha, which focus on coffee. Brouwer, "Al-Mukhā as a Coffee Port," 271–74.

6 Ralph S. Hattox, *Coffee and Coffeehouses: The Origins of a Social Beverage in the Medieval Near East* (Seattle: University of Washington Press, 1985), 25. A later article challenged the claims of the Ṣufi role in the later spread of the drink. Éric Geoffroy, "La diffusion du café au Proche-Orient arabe par l'intermédiaire des soufis: mythe et réalité," in Tuchscherer, *Commerce du café*, 7–14.

7 It appears, however, that coffee beans were used earlier for medicinal purposes in Ethiopia, but not for making the beverage.

8 A notable linguistic exception is Amharic, in which the term *buna* is used to refer to bean and beverage and provides the etymological basis for the Arabic *bunn*.

9 Michel Tuchscherer, "Commerce et production du café en mer Rouge au XVIe siècle," in Tuchscherer, *Commerce du café*, 85; Mutsuo Kawatoko, "Coffee Trade in the al-Ṭūr Port, South Sinai," in Tuchscherer, *Commerce du café*, 54.

10 VOC 1784, 112. During the first Ottoman occupation of Yemen, black brewed coffee was consumed, as is attested by Pieter van den Broecke, who referred to *qahwa* as a black liquid in 1616. It appears that *qishr* took the place of brewed coffee after the Ottomans were expelled. Pieter van den Broecke, *Korte historiael ende Journaelsche Aenteyckeninghe van al 't geen merckwaerdigh voorgevallen is, in de langdurighe Reysen, soo nae Cabo Verde, Angola, & c. als insodernheyd van Oost-Indien, beneffens de beschryving en afbeeldigh van verscheyden Steden op de Custe van Indien, Persien, Arabien, en aen 't Roode Meyr* (Amsterdam: Herman Jansz Brouwer, 1634), 52.

11 Jean de La Roque, *Voyage to Arabia the Happy by way of the Eastern Ocean, and the Streights of the Red-Sea: Perform'd by the French for the first time, A.D. 1708, 1709, 1710* (London: G. Straham: 1726 [1716]), 40.

12 Tuchscherer, "Coffee in the Red Sea Area," 52.

13 Ibid. Ethiopian production of export coffee was not harnessed until the nineteenth century, although small quantities of wild Ethiopian coffee did appear in Mocha's market before then. Merid Aregay, "The Early History of Ethiopia's Coffee Trade and the Rise of Shawa," *Journal of African History* 29 (1988): 19–25; Charles G. H. Schaefer, "Coffee Unobserved: Consumption and Commoditization of Coffee in Ethiopia before the Eighteenth Century," in Tuchscherer, *Commerce du café*, 24.

14 Steven Topik, "Integration of the World Coffee Market," in Clarence-Smith and Topik, *Global Coffee Economy*, 28.

15 In particular, the Dutch merchants mentioned beans from al-ʿUdayn, Ḥarāz, and Ḥayma. When they heard of political unrest or tribal conflict in the highlands, they were aware of whether the place was in a coffee-producing region or not, because any political disturbance could disrupt the flow of coffee beans to the lowland market.

16 Brouwer, *Transoceanic Trade*, 41.

17 Tuchscherer, "Coffee in the Red Sea Area," 54.

18 Brouwer, *Transoceanic Trade*, 41.

19 R. B. Serjeant, "Yemeni Merchants, 13th–16th Centuries," in *Marchands et hommes d'affaires asiatiques dans l'Océan Indien et la Mer de Chine, 13e–20e siècles*, eds. D. Lombard and J. Aubin (Paris: Éditions de l'École des Hautes Études en Sciences Sociales, 1988), 70–71; R. B. Serjeant and Ismāʿīl al-Akwaʿ, "The Statute of Ṣanʿāʾ (*Qānūn Ṣanʿāʾ*)," in Serjeant and R. Lewcock, *Ṣanʿāʾ*, 180.

20 La Roque, *Voyage to Arabia*, 98.

21 Ibid.

22 Notably, land-based transport to the Ḥijāz was limited during this period. Tuchscherer, "Commerce en mer rouge," 174–75.

23 VOC 1964, 112.

24 VOC 1714, 151–52.

25 On rare occasions European merchants tried to procure beans in Mocha, such as during the 1719–20 trade season, when a temporary ban was placed on European purchases at Bayt al-Faqīh (VOC 9116). The French purchased coffee beans from a merchant who obtained them directly from growers in 1726–27 (VOC 9121), and the English made limited purchases in the 1728–29 trade season (VOC 9123).

26 Peter Boxhall, "The Diary of a Mocha Coffee Agent," *Arabian Studies* 1 (1974): 108; December 23, 1719, VOC 9116.

27 Desfontaines, *Relation*, viii–ix.

28 La Roque, *Voyage to Arabia*, 98.

29 Robert Laulan, "Comment, en 1737, le drapeau français flotta ṣur Moka," *Terre, Air, Mer: Géographie* 57 (April 1932): 283; Eric Macro, *Bibliography on Yemen and Notes on Mocha* (Coral Gables, Fla.: University of Miami Press, 1960), 37; Macro, "Topography of Mocha," *Proceedings of the Seminar for Arabian Studies* 10 (1980): 62.

30 Numerous scholars have noted the role of al-Ḥudayda and al-Luḥayya in the coffee trade. See, for example, Baldry, "Early History," 44–46; Boxhall, "Diary," 102, 112; Tuchscherer, "Trade and Port Cities in the Red Sea," 40.

31 For sources on al-Ḥudayda and its history, see Baldry, "Early History," 37–52; Aḥmad ʿUthmān Muṭayyir, *Al-durra al-farīda fī tārīkh madīnat al-Ḥudayda* (Al-Ḥudayda: Dār al-Miṣbāḥ li al-Ṭibāʿa, 1984).

32 Hans Becker, Volker Höhfeld, and Horst Kopp, eds., *Kaffee aus Arabien* (Wiesbaden: Franz Steiner Verlag, 1979), 24.

33 Merchants in Cairo and Jidda exaggerated the amount of European coffee capital that arrived in Yemen in order to raise the market price for their *bunn* once it reached Cairo. These strategic inflations caused an unfounded sense of hysteria about and overestimation of the European effect on that market. Raymond, *Artisans*, 1: 138–39, 150.

34 Becker, Höhfeld, and Kopp, *Kaffee*, 23–24.

35 Raymond, "Divided Sea," 46–47.

36 C. van Arendonk and K. N. Chaudhuri, "Ḳahwa," in *The Encyclopedia of Islam* (Leiden, E. J. Brill, 1978), 4: 454.

37 Baldry, "Early History," 45.

38 Patricia Risso, *Oman and Muscat: An Early Modern History* (London: Croom Helm, 1986), 77.

39 All citations come from VOC 9116. These excerpts cannot amplify the comparative statistical data on coffee shipping, because the lack of exact figures for the commercial activity of Arab, Turkish, and Persian merchants is misleading and incommensurate with the precise data available for the European trade.

40 All the weights have been converted into Dutch pounds from original figures in local weight units such as bales and *bahars*. The Bayt al-Faqīh *bahar* is calculated at 735 pounds, and the Mocha *bahar* at 405 pounds, following Glamann's guide. When the documents do not specify whether the weight in *bahars* was calculated in Bayt al-Faqīh or Mocha *bahars*, Bayt al-Faqīh *bahars* are used as the default. Glamann, *Dutch-Asiatic Trade*, 303–6.

41 The English began minor shipping from al-Ḥudayda in the 1720s. July 25, 1722, VOC 9117; August 12, 1723, VOC 9118.

42 For an example of a northern fleet ship dated about 1750, see the excavation of the Sadana Island shipwreck, off the coast of Egypt, which was carrying Chinese porcelain, copper vessels (probably from the Gulf), clay vessels, Yemeni coffee, aromatics, and spices. Cheryl Haldane, "An Ottoman Period Shipwreck off Egypt's Red Sea Coast," in *Dirāsāt fī tārīkh Miṣr al-iqtiṣādī wa al-ijtimāʿī fī al-ʿaṣr al-ʿuthmānī*, eds. Daniel Crecelius, Ḥamza ʿAbd al-ʿAzīz Badr, and Muḥammad Ḥusām al-Dīn Ismāʿīl (Cairo: Dār al-Āfāq al-ʿArabiyya, 1997), 23–38.

43 Raymond, "Divided Sea," 54.

44 As the Safavid historian Rudi Matthee has shown, much of the Muscat coffee was intended for Iran but was shipped first via this Omani port rather than directly to Bandar ʿAbbās, because of Muscat's advantageous toll rate. Rudi Matthee, "Coffee in Safavid Iran: Commerce and Consumption," *Journal of the Economic and Social History of the Orient* 37 (1994): 16.

45 December 13 and 14, 1727, VOC 9122.

46 For instance, in 1728 merchants on two ships from India chose to dock at al-Luḥayya instead of Mocha because they believed they had been overtaxed by the governor, Shaykh ʿAmr, in the previous trade season. March 24, 1728, VOC 9122.

47 However, as Patricia Risso and Thabit Abdullah have described, Persian Gulf merchants shipped coffee from Mocha more consistently in the second half of the eighteenth century. Risso, *Oman and Muscat*, 77–78; Abdullah, *Merchants*, 65.

48 Ashin Das Gupta, "A Note on Out-Station Factories: Mocha Factory," in *The World of the Indian Ocean Merchant 1500–1800: Collected Essays of Ashin Das Gupta*, ed. Uma Das Gupta (New Delhi: Oxford University Press, 2001), 457.

49 Alain Stella, *The Book of Coffee*, trans. Louise Guiney (Paris: Flammarion, 1996), 24.

3 A Littoral Society in Yemen

1 M. N. Pearson, "Littoral Society: The Case for the Coast," *The Great Circle* 7 (1985): 1.

2 Engseng Ho, *The Graves of Tarim: Genealogy and Mobility across the Indian Ocean* (Berkeley: University of California Press, 2006).

3 Husayn b. ʿAbdullah al-ʿAmri, *The Yemen in the 18th and 19th Centuries: A Political and Intellectual History* (London: Ithaca Press, 1985), 30.

4 Das Gupta, "Gujarati Merchants," 138.

5 Haykel, *Revival and Reform*, 75.

6 Ibid., 56.

7 Al-ʿAmri, *The Yemen*, 29–30.

8 Ibid., 24.

9 Ibid., 30.

10 In the Dutch sources the post is referred to as *mierbaar* (*amīr al-baḥr*) or *strand-voogd* (shore guard).

11 La Roque, *Voyage to Arabia*, 104.

12 December 9 and 12, 1727, VOC 9122.

13 Al-Shawkānī specified that this was an upward move by saying, "Rafa'ahu 'anhā [the post in al-Luḥayya] li al-kitāba fī bandar al-Mukhā." Muḥammad b. ʿAlī al-Shawkānī, *Al-badr al-ṭāliʿ bi-maḥāsin man baʿd al-qarn al-sābiʿ* (Beirut: Dār al-Maʿrifa, n.d.), 2: 183.

14 September 12, 1731, VOC 2252.

15 The Dutch used *nakib* or *hoofd van baab cheddelies poort*. November 1, 1737, VOC 2447; March 25, 1737, VOC 2447. The English referred to the tax collector posted at this gate as the "meggaba" or *majbā*.

16 Ḥasan Ḥasūsā does not merit an entry in the biographical dictionaries, but al-ʿAmri called him by the title *qāḍī*. Al-ʿAmri, *The Yemen*, 26. He also appears in an

episode described by Abū Ṭālib. Ḥusām al-Dīn Muḥsin al-Ḥasan (Abū Ṭālib), *Tārīkh al-Yaman fī ʿaṣr al-istiqlāl ʿan al-ḥukm al-ʿuthmānī al-awwal*, ed. ʿAbd Allāh Muḥammad al-Ḥibshī (Sanaa: Al-Mufaddal Offset Printers, 1990), 476.

17 The Dutch called this representative the *konings koopman*, or the king's merchant. January 8, 1723, VOC 9117.

18 The *muḥtasib* was referred to in Dutch as the *sjouws* [*chaush*] *of opsiender van de bazaar*, "sergeant or the inspector of the bazaar." January 14, 1737, VOC 2447; September 8, 1734, VOC 2356.

19 The Dutch called the *qāḍī cazee* and *regter*, or judge.

20 Muḥammad Zabāra, *Nashr al-ʿarf li-nubalāʾ al-Yaman baʿd al-alf* (Sanaa: Markaz al-Dirāsāt wa al-Buḥūth al-Yamanī, 1985), 2: 222; Ismāʿīl b. ʿAlī al-Akwaʿ, *Hijar al-ʿilm wa maʿāqila fī al-Yaman* (Beirut: Dar al-Fikr al-Muʿāṣir, 1995), 1: 414.

21 John O. Voll, "Linking Groups in the Networks of Eighteenth-Century Revivalist Scholars: The Mizjaji Family in Yemen," in *Eighteenth-Century Renewal and Reform in Islam*, eds. N. Levtzion and J. O. Voll (Syracuse, N.Y.: Syracuse University Press, 1987), 69–92.

22 Al-Shawkānī, *Al-badr al-ṭāliʿ*, 2: 82.

23 Haykel, *Revival and Reform*, 42.

24 Al-Shawkānī, *Al-badr al-ṭāliʿ*, 1: 293.

25 Al-ʿAmri, *The Yemen*, 30.

26 Zabāra, *Nashr al-ʿarf*, 2: 654.

27 The eighteenth-century Dutch sources use the title *de gouverneur* or *steedevoogd*. Nineteenth-century British sources generally use the title *dawla* or *dola*.

28 George Viscount Valentia, *Voyages and Travels to India, Ceylon, the Red Sea, Abyssinia, and Egypt* (London, 1809), 2: 353.

29 Das Gupta, "Gujarati Merchants," 139.

30 Muqarrab Khan is a good example of a Mughal governor-merchant of Surat in the early seventeenth century. Syed Ali Nadeem Rezavi, "An Aristocratic Surgeon of Mughal India: Muqarrab Khan," in *Medieval India 1: Researches in the History of India, 1200–1750*, ed. Irfan Habib (Delhi: Oxford University Press, 1992), 154–67.

31 The second of the city has been documented only in Dutch sources, which do not indicate what the Arabic title was for this position. Although the second served immediately below the governor, in many cases when the governor was called to the imam's court, his son was placed in charge, rather than the second. Also, the son of the governor consistently received official presents from merchants and visitors. IOR G/17/1, pt. 1, ff. 12–13.

32 Catherine Asher, "Mughal Sub-Imperial Patronage: The Architecture of Raja Man Singh," in *The Powers of Art: Patronage in Indian Culture*, ed. B. S. Miller (Delhi: Oxford University Press, 1992), 183–201; Yasser Tabbaa, *Constructions of Power and Piety in Medieval Aleppo* (University Park: Pennsylvania State University Press, 1997), 27–52.

33 Al-Mutawakkil's mother was the daughter of Shams al-Dīn al-Ḥasan ʿIzz al-Dīn Jaḥḥāf. Zabāra, *Nashr al-ʿarf*, 1: 29.

34 Muḥammad Amīn al-Muḥibbī, *Khulāṣat al-athar fī aʿyān al-qarn al-ḥādī ʿashar* (Cairo: Maṭbaʿa al-Wahbiyya, 1284/1867–68), 3: 128; Muḥammad Amīn al-Muḥibbī, *Nafḥāt Rayḥāna wa rashḥat ṭilāʾ al-ḥāna*, ed. ʿAbd al-Fattāḥ Muḥammad al-Ḥulw (Cairo: Dār Iḥyāʾ al-Kutub al-ʿArabiyya, 1388/1968), 3: 410–11.

35 Zabāra, *Nashr al-ʿarf*, 1: 654–55; Abū Ṭālib, *Tārīkh al-Yaman*, 118.

36 Al-Wazīr, *Tārīkh al-Yaman*, 173; Abū Ṭālib, *Tārīkh al-Yaman*, 84; R. B. Serjeant, *The Portuguese Off the South Arabian Coast: Ḥaḍramī Chronicles* (Oxford: Clarendon Press, 1963), 120.

37 Al-Wazīr, *Tārīkh al-Yaman*, 173.

38 Unfortunately, a dispute arose between Jaḥḥāf's troops and those of the sultan, and the sultan was unable to complete the pilgrimage that year. Al-Wazīr, *Tārīkh al-Yaman*, 250. R. D. McChesney confirms that other Central Asian pilgrims chose the Mocha route to Mecca in the sixteenth and seventeenth centuries. McChesney, "The Central Asian Hajj-Pilgrimage in the Time of the Early Modern Empires," in *Safavid Iran and Her Neighbors*, ed. Michael Mazzaoui (Salt Lake City: University of Utah Press, 2003), 129–56.

39 These events were described at length by Serjeant, who relied on an unedited manuscript by al-Jurmūzī, as well as varied European accounts. Serjeant, *The Portuguese*. Since then the al-Jurmūzī manuscript has been edited and published. Al-Muṭahhar b. Muḥammad al-Jurmūzī, *Tuḥfat al-asmāʿ wa al-abṣār bi-mā fī al-sīra al-mutawakkiliyya min gharāʾib al-akhbār: sīrat al-Imām al-Mutawakkil ʿalā Allāh Ismāʿīl b. al-Qāsim, 1019–87*, ed. ʿAbd al-Hakīm ʿAbd al-Majīd al-Hajrī (Amman: Muʾassasat al-Imām Zayd b. ʿAlī al-Thaqāfiyya, 2002), 2: 948–55.

40 Al-Wazīr, *Tārīkh al-Yaman*, 251, 252, 261.

41 Zabāra, *Nashr al-ʿarf*, 1: 659.

42 Abū Ṭālib, *Tārīkh al-Yaman*, 74, n. 2. A variation from a secondary manuscript has been chosen for this translation. I thank Fatimah Muhaidat for translating this and the following passage.

43 Ibid., 74–75.

44 Ibid., 75. However, al-Akwaʿ noted that the imam stayed there occasionally. Al-Akwaʿ, *Hijar al-ʿilm*, 1: 423, n. 3.

45 Here I draw from Jerry Brotton's discussion of early modern maps of the Indian Ocean as "transactional" images that mediated cross-cultural encounters, defining, representing, emerging from, and facilitating economic exchange. Brotton, *Trading Territories*, 128.

46 Zabāra, *Nashr al-ʿarf*, 1: 659.

47 Local residents recounted the story when I visited in June 2002, and two inscriptions in black paint on the eastern side of the mosque confirmed the information.

48 Zabāra, *Nashr al-ʿarf*, 1: 659.

49 Ibid.

50 The mosque's construction is often attributed to Imam al-Mutawakkil Ismāʿīl but was indeed the patronage of his brother Ḥasan. Bruce Paluck and Rayya Saggar, *The al-Ḥasan bin al-Qāsim Mosque Complex: An Architectural and Historical Overview of a Seventeenth Century Mosque in Ḍūrān, Yemen* (Sanaa: American Institute for Yemeni Studies and Centre Français d'Archéologie et de Sciences Sociales de Sanaa, 2002), 15.

51 The walls of the tomb still stand, but the *madrasa* has been reduced to an indistinguishable pile of rubble. Here I rely on Paluck and Saggar's reconstructed plan, figure 1.

52 Al-Jurmūzī, *Tuḥfat al-asmāʿ*, 2: 619; Abū Ṭālib, *Tārīkh al-Yaman*, 25.

53 Al-Wazīr, *Tārīkh al-Yaman*, 345.

54 Zabāra, *Nashr al-ʿarf*, 1: 660.

55 The Dutch rendered his name "Seeg Sale Horrebie." Jean de la Roque used "Cheikh Saleh El Harreby." La Roque, *Voyage to Arabia*, 77.

56 Before al-Mahdī Muḥammad became known as Ṣāḥib al-Mawāhib, he was referred to as Ṣāḥib al-Manṣūra. Muḥammad b. Aḥmad al-Ḥajrī, *Majmūʿ buldān wa qabāʾil al-Yaman*, ed. Ismāʿīl b. ʿAlī al-Akwaʿ (Sanaa: Dār al-Ḥikma al-Yamaniyya, 1996), 2: 240; Abū Ṭālib, *Tārīkh al-Yaman*, 129.

57 Zabāra, *Nashr al-ʿarf*, 1:772.

58 Abū Ṭālib, *Tārīkh al-Yaman*, 266. According to the historian Luṭf Allāh b. Aḥmad Jaḥḥāf, al-Mahdī made his son Ibrāhīm wazir first and then was obliged to make the older al-Ḥuraybī wazir as well. Zabāra, *Nashr al-ʿarf*, 1: 775–76.

59 Al-Mūsawī gives the date 1702 as the earliest mention of his presence at the port, which would amend Das Gupta's date of 1704 from the Dutch sources. Das Gupta, "Gujarati Merchants," 139. We know that at least some of his family was settled with him because his young child died and was buried at the port on May 3, 1709. VOC 1784.

60 Key sources include the VOC documents, the narrative of the first French forays into the Mocha trade in 1709, 1710, and 1711, written by Jean de la Roque, the history of Abū Ṭālib, and excerpts of the unedited manuscript by Luṭf Allāh b. Aḥmad Jaḥḥāf, *Tārīkh Jaḥḥāf*, which is in the Manuscript Library of the Great Mosque of Sanaa and is quoted at length in Zabāra, *Nashr al-ʿarf*. Al-Ḥuraybī was also discussed in Ashin Das Gupta's 1979 article about the officials and merchants of Mocha from the Dutch sources and in Michel Tuchscherer's article about the Red Sea trade from the French sources. However, neither cross-referenced the corresponding Arabic material. Das Gupta, "Gujarati Merchants"; Tuchscherer, "Commerce en Mer Rouge."

61 La Roque, *Voyage to Arabia*, 84.

62 Das Gupta, "Gujarati Merchants," 139.

63 February 28, March 4 and 10, 1706, VOC 9115.

64 Das Gupta, *Decline of Surat*, 158; VOC 1606, 182.

65 October 16, 1708, and May 15, 1709, VOC 1784; Das Gupta, *Decline of Surat*, 158.

66 The ship was originally called the *Overwinnaar*. The French started out at a price of 30,000 Spanish riyals for the vessel, but al-Ḥuraybī offered 8,000. The French counteroffered with a final price of 12,000 Spanish riyals, but without any weaponry. Al-Ḥuraybī did not accept. June 14, 1708, VOC 1784.

67 Abū Ṭālib, *Tārīkh al-Yaman*, 297; VOC 1660, 784. Abū Ṭālib refers to the ambassador as "al-ʾīljī," or the infidel, indicating that the Zaydīs felt no shared Shīʿī connection to the Safavids.

68 VOC 1714, 159, 165; July 3, 1709, VOC 1784. Das Gupta called Nūr al-Ḥaqq "the censor of public morals at Ahmedabad." Das Gupta, *Decline of Surat*, 128.

69 According to the Dutch, the *sharīf* came from al-Mawāhib to check on al-Ḥuraybī and eventually left to perform the pilgrimage. December 30, 1708, and March 28, 1709, VOC 1784. In the French account this *sharīf* was an exile from Mecca who had taken refuge in Mocha under the imam's protection. La Roque, *Voyage to Arabia*, 110–11.

70 January 16, 1706, VOC 9115.

71 VOC 1714, 134; December 19, 1705, VOC 9115.

72 Zabāra, *Nashr al-ʿarf*, 1:771–72.

73 La Roque, *Voyage to Arabia*, 130.

74 VOC 1714, 176.

75 Das Gupta called Muḥsin al-Ḥubayshī "Faqi Musa," derived from the early Dutch sources, which used "Facqui Moesson." Das Gupta, "Gujarati Merchants." The first historical mention of al-Ḥubayshī dates from 1112/1700–1701, and he is later identified as a wazir in 1115/1703–4. Abū Ṭālib, *Tārīkh al-Yaman*, 292, 307.

76 Abū Ṭālib's hatred for al-Ḥuraybī was due in part to the fact that he was closely linked to the family of the previous wazir, Aḥmad al-Rājiḥ, who was dismissed in order for al-Ḥuraybī to assume his position. Abū Ṭālib, *Tārīkh al-Yaman*, 265, 266, 296.

77 Ibid., 310.

78 Ibid., 292; Zabāra, *Nashr al-ʿarf*, 1: 772.

79 Zabāra, *Nashr al-ʿarf*, 2: 383.

80 The Dutch attributed the fall of al-Ḥubayshī to an incident involving a merchant named ʿAlī Wazīr, whom al-Ḥuraybī had banished. ʿAlī Wazīr's participation is absent in the Arabic sources. July 24, 1709, VOC 1784; Das Gupta, "Gujarati Merchants," 140–41.

81 Abū Ṭālib, *Tārīkh al-Yaman*, 327–28; Zabāra, *Nashr al-ʿarf*, 1: 775.

82 Zabāra, *Nashr al-ʿarf*, 1: 775.

83 July 24, 1709, VOC 1784; Zabāra, *Nashr al-ʿarf*, 1: 775.

84 August 29, 1709, VOC 1784.

85 Zabāra, *Nashr al-ʿarf,* 1: 777.

86 Abū Ṭālib, *Tārīkh al-Yaman,* 415.

87 Zabāra, *Nashr al-ʿarf,* 1: 778.

88 Umberto Scerrato, Giovanna Ventrone, and Paolo Cuneo, "Yemen: Archaeological Activities in the Yemen Arab Republic, 1985," *East and West* 35, no. 4 (1985): 395. Some information about Masjid al-Mashraʿ is also provided in Francine Stone, ed., *Studies on the Tihāmah: The Report of the Tihāmah Expedition 1982 and Related Papers* (Essex, UK: Longman, 1985), 55.

89 ʿAbbās b. ʿAlī al-Mūsawī al-Makkī, *Nuzhat al-jalīs wa munyat al-adīb al-anīs,* ed. Muḥammad Mahdī Khurasān (Al-Najaf, Iraq: al-Maṭbaʿa al-Ḥaydāriyya, 1967), 2: 252–53.

90 Khazindār was referred to indistinguishably as "Facqui Hamet ibne Heija" by the Dutch and "Fuckee Hamed" by the English. His biographical entry in Zabāra, *Nashr al-ʿarf,* confirms that he was the often-mentioned governor, as does a copy of the French treaty of 1737, which identifies him as "Faqi Ahmad, fils de hyahya Kazendar." Desfontaines, *Relation,* 90.

91 Zabāra, *Nashr al-ʿarf,* 2: 300.

92 Ibid., 1: 304. Serjeant, however, suggested that members of the family lived in Yemen in pre-Ottoman times. Serjeant and al-Akwaʿ, "The Statute," n. 5.

93 I rely on the dates of his appointments given in the Dag Registers, because they document his actual presence at the port. The order of events described in his biographical entry by Zabāra concurs with the Dag Registers, but the dates diverge. Zabāra says he returned to Sanaa from Mocha in 1132/1719–20, not 1724. Al-Mūsawī referred to Khazindār as wazir in his long string of superlatives regarding the governor, but I found no other evidence that he was named wazir. Al-Mūsawī, *Nuzhat al-jalīs,* 2: 253.

94 A house in Sanaa, Bayt Faqīh Aḥmad Khazindār, was still known by his name in the mid-twentieth century. Muḥammad b. Aḥmad al-Ḥajrī, *Masājid Ṣanʿāʾ ʿāmiruha wa muwaffīha* (Sanaa: Maktabat al-Yaman al-Kubrā, 1361/1942–43, reprint 1398/1977–78), 53.

95 January 20, 1724, VOC 9118.

96 IOR G/17/1, pt. 1, ff. 299.

97 Serjeant and al-Akwaʿ, "The Statute," 179, n. 5, translation from Zabāra, who quoted from Jaḥḥāf.

98 This is called Document A by Serjeant and al-Akwaʿ.

99 Serjeant and al-Akwaʿ, "The Statute," 182.

100 In Dutch, "Mochase Nero" and the "Dwingeland."

101 All excerpts from 1722 are from VOC 9122.

102 September 9, 1723, VOC 9118.

103 Muḥammad Ḥajj is mentioned many times in the Dag Registers, but without specification, so it is impossible to determine where he was from. September 10, 1723, VOC 9118.

104 October 17, 1722, VOC 9117.

105 August 13, 1723, VOC 9118.

106 August 7, 1725, VOC 9120. The relationship between al-Ḥubayshī and Khazindār deteriorated again the next year, when they were both jailed because of their bad relations. August 31, 1726, VOC 9121; Zabāra, *Nashr al-ʿarf*, 2: 377 (after Jaḥḥāf).

107 A detailed account of the bombardment from the French perspective is described in Desfontaines, *Relation de l'expédition de Moka*. Other accounts of the story are available in both the Arabic and Dutch sources. Abū Ṭālib, *Tārīkh al-Yaman*, 470–71; Zabāra, *Nashr al-ʿarf*, 1: 303; VOC 2447, First Mocha Register, 1736–37, and Second Mocha Register, 1737–38.

108 Al-Mūsawī, *Nuzhat al-jalīs*, 2: 253.

109 Ibid. Al-Mūsawī mentioned only two forts, which Niebuhr included in his 1763 map. Carsten Niebuhr, *Reisebeschreibung nach Arabien und den umliegenden Ländern* (Graz, Austria: Akademische Druck-u. Verlagsanstalt, 1968 [1774]), 1: fig. 72. The Dutch, on the other hand, identified three forts under construction in 1730. September 25, 1730, VOC 2252.

110 This tower is the current home of the local *muwaṣṣalāt*, or communications center.

111 Al-Mūsawī, *Nuzhat al-jalīs*, 2: 263; Zabāra, *Nashr al-ʿarf*, 3: 168 (largely excerpted from al-Mūsawī).

112 In 1727, when the forces of Amīr Aḥmad b. al-Mutawakkil from Taʿizz surrounded the walls of Mocha to claim the town from Āl Isḥāq, the lack of intramural wells was one of the biggest sources of stress on the city. Eventually, because of hunger and thirst, the intramural city surrendered to Aḥmad. Khazindār tried unsuccessfully to dig an intramural well in 1731. October 15, 1731, VOC 2252.

113 Zabāra, *Nashr al-ʿarf*, 1: 300.

114 Ibid.

115 Jan Just Witkam, "Manuscripts and Manuscripts: Qurʾān Fragments from Ḍawrān (Yemen)," *Manuscripts of the Middle East* 4 (1989): 159, pl. 12.

116 Of the thirty-four examples that Witkam published, the majority are multiple-volume and measure the size of the al-Qarābī example, which suggests that this was a common format.

117 Marco Salati, "A Shiite in Mecca: The Strange Case of Mecca-born Syrian and Persian Sayyid Muḥammad Ḥaydar (d. 1139/1727)," in *The Twelver Shia in Modern Times: Religious Culture and Political History*, eds. R. Brunner and W. Ende (Leiden: E. J. Brill, 2001), 4. Unfortunately, I was unable to consult Salati's longer study

on al-Mūsawī *Nuzhat al-jalīs*. Marco Salati, *I viaggi in Oriente di sayyid ʿAbbās b. ʿAlī al-Makkī, letterato e cortigiano (1718–1729)* (Padua, 1995).

118 Muḥammad Mahdī Khurasān, "Introduction," in al-Mūsawī al-Makkī, *Nuzhat al-jalīs*, 1: 12; Zabāra, *Nashr al-ʿarf*, 3: 28.

119 Khurasān, "Introduction," 14.

120 Key examples of mobile religious scholars are Murtaḍā al-Zabīdī, the famed author of the dictionary *Tāj al-ʿArūs*, and the Ḥadramī *sayyids* who moved to India to take important local positions. Stefan Reichmuth, "Murtaḍā az-Zabīdī (d. 1791) in Biographical and Autobiographical Accounts: Glimpses of Islamic Scholarship in the 18th Century," *Die Welt des Islams* 39: 1 (1999): 64–102; Omar Khalidi, "Sayyids of Hadhramaut in Early Modern India," *Asian Journal of Social Science* 32, no. 3 (2004): 329–52.

121 Zabāra, *Nashr al-ʿarf*, 1: 302.

122 A notable exception was the appointment of Sayyid Ibrāhīm al-Jurmūzī to the post in 1196/1782. Al-ʿAmri, *The Yemen*, 30; Muḥammad Zabāra, *Nayl al-waṭar min tarājim rijāl al-Yaman fī al-qarn al-thālith ʿashar* (Sanaa: Markaz al-Dirāsāt wa al-Abḥath al-Yamanī, n.d.), 1: 16–17.

123 Haykel, *Revival and Reform*, 54. Amīr Ulmās ʿAbd al-Rahmān was governor of Bayt al-Faqīh with authority over the whole Tihāma coastal region, from Mocha to Wādi Mawr in the north, in the 1730s and 1740s. Sulaymān al-Manṣūr was appointed governor of Mocha in the mid-eighteenth century. Both were slave *amīrs* who received high-level appointments from the imam. Tuchscherer, *Imams, notables et bédouins*, 69–70.

4 Merchants and Nākhūdhas

1 Gabriele Vom Bruck, *Islam, Memory, and Morality: Ruling Families in Transition* (New York: Palgrave Macmillan, 2005), 165–66.

2 Hanna, *Making Big Money*; Raymond, *Artisans*, 2: 399–415; Raymond, "Une famille de grands negociants en café au Caire dans la première moitié du XVIIIe siècle: Les Sharāybī," in Tuchscherer, *Commerce du café*, 111–24.

3 Raymond, "Une famille," 114, 116.

4 Daniel Schroeter, *Merchants of Essaouira: Urban Society and Imperialism in Southwestern Morocco, 1844–1886* (New York: Cambridge University Press, 1988), 23.

5 Raymond, *Artisans*, 2: 373–415.

6 S. D. Goitein, *A Mediterranean Society: The Jewish Communities of the World as Portrayed in the Documents of the Cairo Geniza* (Berkeley: University of California Press, 1983), 2: 155.

7 M. N. Pearson, *Merchants and Rulers in Gujarat: The Response to the Portuguese in the Sixteenth Century* (Berkeley: University of California Press, 1976).

8 Philip D. Curtin, *Cross-Cultural Trade in World History* (Cambridge: Cambridge University Press, 1984).

9 Occasionally a Baniyan shipowner or a *nākhūdha*, the owner's agent, is mentioned in passing in the European records, but these men do not represent the greater part of Baniyans in Mocha, who eschewed direct involvement in maritime affairs.

10 M. N. Pearson, "Brokers in Western Indian Port Cities: Their Role in Servicing Foreign Merchants," *Modern Asian Studies* 22, no. 3 (1988): 457.

11 Although European merchants depended heavily on their brokers for linguistic and commercial intercession around the Indian Ocean rim, the practice of brokerage has age-old roots in Yemen and other Indian Ocean regions and was not innovated in response to the cross-cultural requirements of European trade. Das Gupta, *Decline of Surat*, 84; Serjeant, "Yemeni Merchants," 76–77.

12 Ashin Das Gupta, "Indian Merchants and Trade in the Indian Ocean, c. 1500–1750," in Das Gupta, *World of the Indian Ocean Merchant*, 69.

13 Ibid., 68.

14 May 30, 1685, VOC 1434; May 16, 1701, VOC 1660.

15 Das Gupta, *Decline of Surat*, 22.

16 Ibid., 30. Another historian erroneously claimed that he was an Ismāʿīlī Bohra based on his title *mullā*. Balkrishna Gokhale, *Surat in the Seventeenth Century: A Study in Urban History of Pre-modern India* (London: Curzon Press, 1978), 127.

17 The Dutch sources from Mocha referred to ʿAbd al-Ghafūr's ships and his house by his name until 1727, nine years after his death, when Muḥammad ʿAlī showed up in Mocha to establish himself as the heir to the family business.

18 Ashin Das Gupta, "The Merchants of Surat, 1700–1750," in *Elites in South Asia*, eds. E. Leach and S. N. Mukherjee (Cambridge: Cambridge University Press, 1970), 208.

19 Das Gupta, *Decline of Surat*, 30.

20 Das Gupta called him "Mulla Abdulla Hai."

21 Das Gupta, "Merchants of Surat," 206.

22 March 21, 1729, VOC 9123.

23 June 22, 1724, VOC 9118.

24 Das Gupta, *Decline of Surat*, 212.

25 Ibid., 197–240.

26 Ashin Das Gupta, "The Maritime Merchant and Indian History," in Das Gupta, *World of the Indian Ocean Merchant*, 24.

27 March 30, 1727, VOC 9121.

28 Das Gupta, *Decline of Surat*, 30.

29 Ibid., 208–9.

30 The existing date on the minaret is difficult to read and lacks a numeral. Archibald Walls, who surveyed the city in 1980, surmised that the worn-away date

could be read as 1295/1898, which commemorates the minaret's later reconstruction. Archibald G. Walls, *Preservation of Monuments and Sites: Architectural Survey of Mocha* (Paris: UNESCO, 1981), 8.

31 Al-Mūsawī, *Nuzhat al-jalīs*, 2: 261.

32 Walls, *Preservation*, 8.

33 Al-Mūsawī, *Nuzhat al-jalīs*, 2: 262.

34 Ibid.

35 The Mosque of Shaykh Jawhar is listed in ʿAbd al-Wahhāb's list of Mocha's mosques but noted as "Only its remains are left." Muḥammad ʿAbd al-Wahhāb, "Iklīl al-Mukhāʾ" (unpublished manuscript, 1988, personal library of Muḥammad ʿAbd al-Wahhāb, Mocha, Yemen), 19.

36 Abdullah, *Merchants*, 96–97.

37 Aḥmad Chalabī was the chief heir to Muḥammad Ṣāliḥ's legacy, but ʿUthmān is mentioned in regard to the Red Sea trade the most often.

38 August 15, 1729, VOC 2202; May 13, 1730, VOC 2202; July 20, 1730, VOC 2252.

39 Faaeza Jasdanwalla, "The Sidi Kingdom of Janjira," in *African Elites in India: Habshi Amarat*, eds. K. Robbins and J. McLeod (Ahmedabad: Mapin Publishing, 2006), 180–81.

40 Dutch sources use "Cassum Tourbettij bin Tahir." English sources use "Cosum Turbaty" and "Cossim Turbetty." In his 1981 article, Baldry specified "Turbally," which seems to have been derived from a transcription error that occurs in some of the British sources. John Baldry, "The English East India Company's Settlement at al-Mukhā, 1719–1739," *The Arab Gulf* (University of Basra) 13, no. 2 (1981): 24. In terms of his background, the Dutch referred to him as an Arab merchant and sometimes a Turkish merchant. It is possible that al-Turbatī's family was of Turkish descent, like Aḥmad Khazindār's, but by the eighteenth century he and his family were integrated into Yemeni society, irrespective of their possible Turkish origin.

41 Das Gupta, "Gujarati Merchants," 140, n. 40.

42 May 20, 1704, VOC 1714, 144; December 23, 1705, VOC 9115.

43 September 20, 1723, VOC 9118.

44 VOC 1964, 19.

45 He rented a house to a Dutch skipper and bookkeeper in February 1725. February 14, 1725, VOC 9119.

46 January 18 and May 20, 1720, VOC 9116.

47 Das Gupta, "Gujarati Merchants," n. 47.

48 IOR G/17/1, pt. 11, ff. 134–37. Al-Mūsawī calls him Shaykh ʿAlī al-Turbatī. Al-Mūsawī, *Nuzhat al-jalīs*, 2: 266.

49 January 18, 1723, VOC 9117; Das Gupta, *Decline of Surat*, 165. The Meccan traveler and short-term resident of Mocha al-Mūsawī met both brothers during his

stay in the city, although he did not mention their father. Al-Mūsawī, *Nuzhat al-jalīs*, 2: 266.

50 Unfortunately, Zayd Muṣṭafā went bankrupt and fled Mocha for Surat sometime before 1719. VOC 1843, 52; VOC 1964, 110.

51 In 1727, Qāsim al-Turbatī owed 9,360 Rijksdaalders to the VOC. January 29, 1727, VOC 9121.

52 November 5, 1723, VOC 9118; April 20, 1735, VOC 2356.

53 IOR G/17/1, pt. 1, ff. 301, dated March 15, 1724.

54 IOR G/17/1, pt. 3, ff. 425–30.

55 January 19, 1726, VOC 9120.

56 IOR G/17/1, pt. 3, ff. 394.

57 November 17, 1722, VOC 9117; September 25, 1725, VOC 9120.

58 July 15, 1738, VOC 2447.

59 Zabāra, *Nashr al-ʿarf*, 2: 726.

60 Ibid.

61 Ibid., 727; R. B. Serjeant, "The Hindu, Bāniyān Merchants and Traders," in Serjeant and Lewcock, *Ṣanʿāʾ*, 434–35.

62 Zabāra, *Nashr al-ʿarf*, 2: 725–26.

63 Ibid., 725.

64 Ibid., 728.

65 Vom Bruck, *Islam, Memory, and Morality*, 166.

66 These ships were referred to as *ghurābs*, and their names were the *Imamshahi* and "Nu al-Jaydi" (perhaps *al-Nūr al-Zaydī*) or *Ḥaydarī*. In 1704 the senior helmsman of the second ship was a certain Pieter Jacobszoon from Flanders. In some years only one ship was sent. VOC 1714, 182; December 21, 1705, VOC 9115; Das Gupta, *Decline of Surat*, 131.

67 The imam's ships also traveled under the protection of the Dutch convoy, as the Mughal fleet did, in the early eighteenth century.

68 Venetia Porter, "The Ports of Yemen and the Indian Ocean Trade during the Tahirid Period (1454–1517)," in *Studies on Arabia in Honour of Professor G. Rex Smith*, eds. G. R. Smith, J. F. Healey, and V. Porter (New York: Oxford University Press, 2002), 184; Serjeant, "Yemeni Merchants," 67.

69 Tibbetts, *Arab Navigation*, 2.

70 Margariti, "Maritime Trade," 219, 226; Margariti, *Aden*, 143.

71 George F. Hourani, *Arab Seafaring in the Indian Ocean in Ancient and Early Medieval Times*, rev. by J. Carswell (Princeton, N.J.: Princeton University Press, 1951, reprint 1995), 112–13; Das Gupta, "Gujarati Merchants," 126; C. G. Brouwer, *Al-Mukhā: Profile of a Yemeni Seaport as Sketched by Servants of the Dutch East India Company (VOC), 1614–1640* (Amsterdam: D'Fluyte Rarob, 1997), 316.

72 Das Gupta, "Gujarati Merchants," 125.

73 Ibid., 143.

74 Brouwer, *Profile*, 314.

75 In the Dutch sources he appears as "Amier Resiek" and is referred to as the "admiral of the imam's ships."

76 The generic nature of his title indicates that he may have been a former slave.

77 VOC 1964, 84.

78 Ibid.

79 Das Gupta, *Decline of Surat*, 162.

80 May 20, 1705, VOC 9115.

81 VOC 1843, 39.

82 May 27, 1706, VOC 9115; May 21, 1709, VOC 1784.

83 VOC 1964, 90; November 9, 1722, VOC 9117.

84 VOC 1964, 88.

85 In 1720 the Dutch wrote that the governor was very sick for lack of alcohol, awaiting the arrival of European ships in the coming weeks. January 10–12, 1720, VOC 9116.

86 John Baldry noted the large quantities of alcohol requested by the English East India Company in Mocha in 1720. Although he did not cite the governor's needs, it is possible that Amīr Rizq was partially responsible for those high figures. Baldry, "English East India Company's Settlement," 19–20.

87 May 19, 1720, VOC 9116.

88 March 19, 1723, VOC 9117; August 14, VOC 9119.

89 July 24, 1725, VOC 9120.

90 July 29, 1725, VOC 9120.

91 IOR G/17/1, pt. 1, ff. 299–300.

92 March 4, 1727, VOC 9121.

5 The Urban Form and Orientation of Mocha

1 Margariti noted the same spatial configuration for medieval Aden. Margariti, *Aden*, 102.

2 Macro, "Topography of Mocha," 56–57.

3 La Roque, *Voyage to Arabia*, 85.

4 Brouwer, *Profile*, 207.

5 Willem Floor, *The Persian Gulf: A Political and Economic History of Five Port Cities, 1500–1730* (Washington, D.C.: Mage Publishers, 2006), 251, 497.

6 VOC 1843, 48. Their presence in the market of Sanaa is mentioned in a mid-eighteenth-century Yemeni text, and there is still a Lotia quarter in Muscat, Oman. ʿAlī b. ʿAbdullāh b. al-Qāsim, *City of Divine and Earthly Joys: The Description of Ṣanʿāʾ*, trans. Tim Mackintosh-Smith, ed. ʿAbdullāh b. Muḥammad al-Ḥibshī (Ardmore, Penn.: American Institute for Yemeni Studies, 2001), 26, n. 132. Calvin Allen claimed that they were Hindus from Sind who had converted to

Islam. Calvin Allen, "The Indian Merchant Community of Masqaṭ," *Bulletin of the School of Oriental and African Studies* 44 (1981): 49.

7 Eugen Mittwoch, ed., *Aus dem Jemen: Hermann Burchardts Letzte Reise Durch Südarabien* (Leipzig: F. A. Brockhaus, 1926), 30.

8 In 2000 a square concrete support was added to reinforce its deteriorated base.

9 Eric Macro and C. G. Brouwer have both published alternative proposed maps of the early modern city. Macro, "Topography of Mocha," 65; Brouwer, *Profile*, 143. For my reconstruction, I privileged the eighteenth-century maps of Jacques Bellin, de la Garde Jazier, and Carsten Niebuhr. I also drew heavily on the textual descriptions of European merchants and travelers, the Meccan resident of Mocha al-Mūsawī, and the twentieth-century account of Muḥammad ʿAbd al-Wahhāb.

10 Anthony D. King, *Urbanism, Colonialism, and the World-Economy: Cultural and Spatial Foundations of the World Urban System* (London: Routledge, 1990), 1.

11 Niebuhr, *Travels*, 1: 397–98.

12 Versions of the local legend are also summed up in Abdel-Daim, "Mokha," 81; E. van Donzel, "Al-Mukhā," in *The Encyclopedia of Islam: New Edition* (Leiden: E. J. Brill, 1993), 7: 513; Macro, *Bibliography on Yemen*, 32; and Joseph B. Osgood, *Notes of Travel or Recollections of Majunga, Zanzibar, Muscat, Aden, Mocha and other Eastern Ports* (Freeport, N.Y.: Books for Libraries Press, 1972), 164–65.

13 Brouwer, *Profile*, 25–40.

14 Al-Mūsawī, *Nuzhat al-jalīs*, 2: 261. Al-Burayhī corroborates the date, but al-Sharjī says he died in 821/1418–19. ʿAbd al-Wahhāb b. ʿAbd al-Raḥmān al-Burayhī, *Ṭabaqāt ṣulaḥāʾ al-Yaman al-maʿrūf bi-tārīkh al-Burayhī*, ed. ʿAbd Allāh M. al-Ḥibshī (Sanaa: Maktabat al-Irshād, 1983), 267; Abī al-ʿAbbās Aḥmad al-Sharjī, *Ṭabaqāt al-khawāṣṣ ahl al-ṣidq wa al-ikhlāṣ*, ed. ʿAbd Allāh M. al-Ḥibshī (Sanaa: al-Dār al-Yamaniyya, 1986), 233.

15 Geoffroy, "Diffusion du café," 7–15. Ralph Hattox's volume is the accepted source in English on the origins of coffee consumption and prohibitions against it, but Hattox overlooked all the biographical information in Arabic on Mocha's al-Shādhilī. Hattox, *Coffee and Coffeehouses*, 12–26.

16 Brouwer, *Profile*, 40. The major debate regarding pre-fifteenth-century Mocha centers on the city of Mouza, noted in the famous *Periplus of the Erythrean Sea*. Some scholars contend that this city was actually Mocha or its neighbor to the east, Mawzaʿ. No conclusive evidence has been presented. Al-Mūsawī claimed that Mocha was first settled by Persians who were sent out of Jidda, a reference to the sixth-century Sasanians. Al-Mūsawī, *Nuzhat al-jalīs*, 2: 252.

17 Al-Sharjī, *Ṭabaqāt al-khawāṣṣ*, 233.

18 Brouwer, *Profile*, 129; Yaḥyā b. al-Ḥusayn, *Ghāyat al-amānī fī akhbār al-quṭr al-Yamānī*, ed. Saʿīd ʿAbd al-Fattāḥ ʿĀshūr (Cairo, 1968), 2: 828.

19 Louis de Grandpré, *A Voyage in the Indian Ocean and to Bengal, 1789–90; An Account of the Sechelles Islands and Trincomale; A Voyage to the Red Sea, Mocha, Yemen*, trans. from French (London, 1803; reprint, New Delhi, 1995), 2: 163–64. Bellin labels the market for perishables "Marché aux Herbes" on his map.

20 Muḥammad ʿAbd al-Wahhāb called Mocha's inland retail market al-Sūq al-Bālī, or the old market.

21 VOC 1406; Grandpré, *Voyage in the Indian Ocean*, 2: 164.

22 Brouwer described coffee shops for the early seventeenth century. Brouwer, *Profile*, 140–41.

23 VOC 1406.

24 Henry Dufton, *Narrative of a Journey through Abyssinia* (Westport, Conn.: Negro Universities Press, 1970), 239; "Observations on a voyage to Moka in 1800: Presented by G. Dominicus with remarks on the weather," IOR MSS Eur E2, British Library, London.

25 Niebuhr, who was usually accurate concerning topography, erroneously claimed that al-Shādhilī's tomb was located outside the city. He was probably referring to the al-Shādhilī wells, which lay outside Bāb al-Shādhilī. Niebuhr, *Travels*, 1: 399.

26 Al-Mūsawī, *Nuzhat al-jalīs*, 2: 261.

27 These builders were of a famous tribe, Ḥumayr al-Akbar b. Sabʾā al-Akbar b. Yashjīb b. Yaʿrab b. Qaḥṭān. That builders came from another city suggests that monumental building was uncommon in Mocha at the time. Al-Mūsawī, *Nuzhat al-jalīs*, 2: 261.

28 Ibid.; al-Burayhī, *Ṭabaqāt ṣulaḥāʾ al-Yaman*, 267. Some later sources say that ʿAbd al-Raʾūf was buried at the fort named after him on the southern island. This does not seem to be the case.

29 Brouwer, *Profile*, 34.

30 Archibald Walls's structural analysis of the contemporary building supports the two phases of construction described by al-Mūsawī. Walls, *Preservation*, 18.

31 Al-Mūsawī, *Nuzhat al-jalīs*, 2: 261.

32 Barbara Finster, "An Outline of the History of Islamic Religious Architecture in Yemen," *Muqarnas* 9 (1992): 142–43.

33 ʿAbd al-Ṣamad b. Ismāʿīl al-Mawzaʿī, *Al-iḥsān fī dukhūl mamlakat al-Yaman*, ed. ʿAbd Allāh Muḥammad al-Ḥibshī (Sanaa: Manshūrat al-Madīna, 1986), 110.

34 Walls, *Preservation*, 15.

35 Al-Mūsawī, *Nuzhat al-jalīs*, 2: 261. On the basis of stylistic rather than textual evidence, Walls and Vassallo disagree with the late-sixteenth-century or early-seventeenth-century date for the mosque and favor Rasulid patronage in the fifteenth century. Walls, *Preservation*, 14; Giovanna Ventrone Vassallo, "The Al-Farāwī Mosque in Yemen," *Proceedings of the Seminar for Arabian Studies* 24 (1994): 213.

36 Al-Mūsawī, *Nuzhat al-jalīs*, 2: 262.

37 Al-Mūsawī states that the "Banū al-Nāʾiba" built it but gives no date. Ibid., 2: 253.

38 Al-Wushalī, *Dhayl nashr al-thanāʾ*, 107; John Baldry, "The Turkish-Italian War in the Yemen, 1911–12," *Arabian Studies* 3 (1976): 56.

39 From his visit in 1980, Walls noted that its foundations were still evident. Walls, *Preservation*, 2. In 2000 only a pile of rubble that used to be the minaret remained. Personal communication, ʿĀdil ʿAbd al-Wahhāb, Mocha, Yemen, March 2000.

40 After the Great Mosque's destruction, the wooden columns were taken from it and used for the modern eastern enlargement of the Mosque of al-Shādhilī. Some of the unused columns were still being stored in the Tomb of al-Shādhilī in May 2000, where Walls mentioned seeing them in 1980. Walls, *Preservation*, 15.

41 Muḥammad ʿAbd al-Wahhāb calls it "the cemetery of al-Shādhilī and the Great Mosque." ʿAbd al-Wahhāb, "Iklīl," 19.

42 In 1731 the Dutch observed how the governor tried to dig new wells near the Great Mosque but instead dug up bones. One can assume that he dug too close to the burial ground between the Great Mosque and the al-Shādhilī monuments. October 15, 1731, VOC 2252.

43 Personal communication, ʿĀdil ʿAbd al-Wahhāb, Mocha, Yemen, June 2000. On the basis of architectural form and style, Walls dated the Tomb of al-Ṣiddīq to the period of the Tomb of al-Shādhilī, either preceding it or closely following it. Walls, *Preservation*, 18.

44 Edmond Combes and Maurice Tamisier, *Voyage en Abyssinie, dans les pays des Galla, de Choa et d'Ifat: Précédé d'une excursion dans l'Arabie-Heureuse, et accompagnés d'une carte des diverse contrées* (Paris: Louis Desessart, 1838), 71.

45 I thank ʿĀdil ʿAbd al-Wahhāb for identifying this unassuming structure for me in March 2000.

46 Al-Muḥibbī, *Khulāṣat al-athar*, 1: 500.

47 Two generations ago the ʿAbd al-Wahhāb family moved from Ḥārat al-Shādhilī to the extramural al-Mughaynī quarter. Personal communication, ʿĀdil ʿAbd al-Wahhāb, Mocha, Yemen, June 2000.

48 John Nankivell, "Tihāmah Architecture: An Architectural Artist's View," in *Studies on the Tihāmah: The Report of the Tihāmah Expedition 1982 and Related Papers*, ed. Francine Stone (Essex, UK: Longman, 1985), 57.

49 Brouwer, *Profile*, 136.

50 Van Hoorn van Riebeck Papers 12.

51 Dutch daily records of fires can help in reconstructing the distribution of settlements within the city walls on a general level. For instance, on November 6, 1723, the Dutch noted a fire that started in an unspecified area of the city. It

raged for 30 to 45 minutes, and 25 houses burned down, 3 or 4 of which were of stone. This type of account helps one to imagine a quarter in the city where a majority of mud and thatch dwellings dominated, with a few stone houses interspersed. See Appendix B in my 2001 dissertation, where I examined the records of fires in the city to get a sense of the distribution of building types. Um, "A Red Sea Society in Yemen," 349–52.

52 Van den Broecke, *Korte historiael*, 51.

53 Lachmann, "The Ottoman Copper Coins Struck at Mocha," 44. No trace or description of this mint remains, only the coins.

54 Serjeant, "The Yemeni Coast," 187–91.

55 Floor, *The Persian Gulf*, 356–57, 437.

56 The French sources refer to *la place*, and the Dutch sources to *het pleijn*.

57 La Roque, *Voyage to Arabia*, 91.

58 Grandpré, *Voyage in the Indian Ocean*, 2: 145–46. Carsten Niebuhr's drawing of a military exhibition in the city of al-Luḥayya is illustrative of such displays. Niebuhr, *Description*, plate 16.

59 La Roque, *Voyage to Arabia*, 121–22.

60 March 20, 1727, VOC 9121.

61 Grandpré, *Voyage in the Indian Ocean*, 2: 146. La Garde-Jazier's map identifies two structures, located near each other, related to the function of customs. Both are labeled *douanes*. I have identified the main building (corresponding to number 3 on his map) as the customs house and the other as the *wikāla*. I believe the contemporary existing structure in the city (in ruins) marks the location of that early customs house, although it has undergone several stages of restoration and rebuilding over time.

62 Brouwer, *Profile*, 133.

63 Al-Mūsawī, *Nuzhat al-jalīs*, 2: 253.

64 Grandpré, *Voyage in the Indian Ocean*, 2: 146.

65 In the twentieth century an inland structure replaced it.

66 He arrived shackled on May 11, 1724 (VOC 9118) and was released on April 17, 1725 (VOC 9119). He is simply called "Mhamet bin Hassan." For the Arabic version of the same events, see Zabāra, *Nashr al-ʿarf*, 3: 140.

67 July 1, 1725, VOC 9120.

68 Ḥajjī ʿAbd al-Ḥaqq al-Sharaybī, a local benefactor, has supported the rebuilding of the mosque, attached to the existing minaret. The builders were completing work in June 2000.

69 The word *ṣandal* means "boat," and the mosque sits at the point where small lighter boats came on shore. Observers describe the yearly *ziyāra* held for a saint named Shaykh al-Ṣandal, but other than his name (with no *nisba*), no biographical information about him survives. Apparently his legacy declined in importance for city residents after the early nineteenth century, when the

structure was destroyed (probably in Türkçe Bilmez's razing of the southern part of the city in 1833). Many contemporary residents do not recognize that a saint was ever buried there.

70 The Dutch called it *de facaula off s'jmans pakhuijs*. February 1, 1735, VOC 2356.

71 Brouwer, *Profile*, 129.

72 Grandpré, *Voyage in the Indian Ocean*, 2: 133; La Roque, *Voyage to Arabia*, 91; Al-Mūsawī, *Nuzhat al-jalīs*, 2: 252.

73 Van Hoorn van Riebeck Papers 12.

74 Al-Mūsawī, *Nuzhat al-jalīs*, 2: 252–53.

75 August 17, 1719, VOC 9116; July 19, 1728, VOC 9123; October 25, 1726, VOC 9121.

76 Al-Mūsawī, *Nuzhat al-jalīs*, 2: 253.

77 Al-Mūsawī mistakenly called it Bāb al-ʿAlmūdhī. Ibid.

78 Walls called both the gate and the mosque "al-Sandal." Arabic sources confirm the name al-Ṣandal, with a *ṣād*. ʿAbd al-Wahhāb, "Iklīl," 18; Abū Ṭālib, *Tārīkh al-Yaman*, 456; Anonymous, *Ḥawliyyāt Yamāniyya: al-Yaman fī al-qarn al-tāsiʿ ʿashar al-milādī*, ed. ʿAbd Allāh Muḥammad al-Ḥibshī (Sanaa: Dār al-Ḥikma al-Yamāniyya, 1991), 63. Hardy-Guilbert and Rougeulle follow Walls's variation. Furthermore, they say that Bāb al-Ṣandal was also called "Porte de Malte." This appears to be an erroneous conflation with the Mālṭa Fort, east of the gate. Hardy-Guilbert and Rougeulle, "Ports islamiques," 151.

79 Grandpré, *Voyage in the Indian Ocean*, 2: 135.

80 Al-Mūsawī, *Nuzhat al-jalīs*, 2: 253.

81 Grandpré, *Voyage in the Indian Ocean*, 2: 139.

82 Al-Mūsawī, *Nuzhat al-jalīs*, 2: 253. It was named and noted as early as 1081/1670–71 in the Arabic sources. Al-Wazīr, *Tārīkh al-Yaman*, 268. Brouwer also mentioned it as part of the early-seventeenth-century landscape. Brouwer, *Profile*, 129.

83 Al-Mūsawī, *Nuzhat al-jalīs*, 2: 253.

84 The two promontories are completely submerged today, but the foundations of the two forts can be seen in aerial photographs.

85 A great deal of confusion surrounds the name of the southern fort. Because it was named for the son of al-Shādhilī, the proper name would be Qalʿat ʿAbd al-Raʾūf. Desfontaines called it "Le Fort Abdelrout," a possible transcription error. Niebuhr's map and accompanying account also show a misreading, calling it "Kalla Abdurrab." An Arabic biographer called the same fort Qalʿat ʿAbd al-Ghafūr, an interesting error because he mistakenly transposed the name of one of the most important merchants in the city with the name of the fort in the entry for Aḥmad Khazindār. Zabāra, *Nashr al-ʿarf*, 2: 303. Macro followed Niebuhr's error. Macro, *Bibliography on Yemen*, 51.

86 Desfontaines, *Relation*, 53–54.

87 September 5, 1737, VOC 2447.

88 Brouwer, *Profile*, 143–44.

89 Salvatore Aponte, *La vita segreta dell'Arabia Felice* (Milan: A. Mondadori, 1936), fig. 10.

90 Donatella Calabi, *The Market and the City: Square, Street, and Architecture in Early Modern Europe*, trans. Marlene Klein (Burlington, Vt.: Ashgate, 2004), 40–94.

91 Suzanne Preston Blier, *The Anatomy of Architecture: Ontology and Metaphor in Batammaliba Architectural Expression* (Cambridge: Cambridge University Press, 1987), 37.

92 Ibid., 57.

93 M. N. Pearson, *Pilgrimage to Mecca: The Indian Experience, 1500–1800* (Princeton, N. J.: Markus Weiner, 1996), 108.

94 Calabi, *The Market and the City*, xxiii, 92.

6 Trading Spaces

1 Mohamed Scharabi, *Der Bazar: Das traditionelle Stadtzentrum in Nahen Osten und seine Handelseinrightungen* (Tübingen, 1985). Although Scharabi gives the Turkish and Persian equivalents of terms in each case, I refer only to the relevant Arabic terms. Aside from Scharabi's encyclopedic study, most studies of Arab commercial architecture focus on Cairo. Nelly Hanna, *An Urban History of Bulaq in the Mamluk and Ottoman Periods*, Supplement to *Annales Islamologiques* 3 (1983); Sylvie Denoix, Jean-Charles Depaule, and Michel Tuchscherer, eds., *Le Khān al-Khalīlī et ses environs: Un centre commercial et artisanal au Caire du XIIIe au XXe siècle*, 2 vols. (Cairo: Institut Français d'Archéologie Orientale du Caire, 1999).

2 *Samsara* is used along with *khān* in Yemen. The *samsara*, however, functions sometimes like the urban *khān*, with lodging cells above, and in other cases like the *qayṣariyya*, as a specialized market structure without lodging. *Samsara*, from the word *samsar*, or broker, appears to be a relatively new term, perhaps coming into use during the first Ottoman occupation. Ronald Lewcock, "The Buildings of the Sūq/Market," in Serjeant and Lewcock, *Ṣanʿāʾ*, 277.

3 Olivia Remie Constable discusses the differences between urban and nonurban *khāns* in regard to the Mamluk Mediterranean. Olivia Remie Constable, *Housing the Stranger in the Mediterranean World: Lodging, Trade and Travel in Late Antiquity and the Middle Ages* (Cambridge: Cambridge University Press, 2003), 252–59.

4 The exact date for Samsarat al-Naḥḥās is unknown, but Lewcock surmised that it was later than Samsarat al-Majja, which was built in the seventeenth century and was said to have been linked to the endowment of the Aḥmad b. al-Qāsim Mosque in al-Rawḍa. Lewcock, "Buildings of the Sūq/Market," 283. Samsarat al-Naḥḥās was recently restored and is used as a marketplace catering to tourists.

5 Raymond, *Grandes villes*, 261.

6 Lewcock, "Buildings of the Sūq/Market," 280, 282–83.

7 Goitein, *A Mediterranean Society*, 1: 61, 350.

8 Margariti, "Maritime Trade," 156, 160–61, 321-22; Margariti, *Aden*, 103.

9 Margariti, "Maritime Trade," 163; Margariti, *Aden*, 103–4.

10 Drawing on a different pool of documents for the same period in Quṣayr, a port on the Egyptian coast of the Red Sea, Li Guo confirms the absence of the *funduq*, or urban *khān*. The warehouse, or *shūna*, is prominently mentioned, as well as houses. Li Guo, *Commerce, Culture and Community in a Red Sea Port in the Thirteenth Century: The Arabic Documents from Quseir* (Leiden: E. J. Brill, 2004). Constable also describes a widening of housing options for European merchants in fifteenth-century Syria to include private homes. She attributes this change to shifts in larger regional trading patterns. Constable, *Housing the Stranger*, 293.

11 Constable, *Housing the Stranger*, 1.

12 Howard, *Venice and the East*, 120.

13 Although her larger framework is extremely useful, I diverge from Constable, who identified the *khān* and the *wikāla* as rival institutions to the *funduq*, with the first two types eventually replacing the last in the eastern Mediterranean. Instead, I classify all three institutions under the rubric of the urban *khān*, which overrides these particularities.

14 Margariti, "Maritime Trade," 160.

15 Brouwer, *Profile*, 140.

16 Volker Höhfeld also noted this prominent absence. Höhfeld, "Die gegenwärtige Situation Mochas als Kleinstadt," in Becker, Höhfeld, and Kopp, *Kaffee Aus Arabien*, 26.

17 The *wikāla* was established as a *waqf* to the Prophet's tomb in Madīna. Al-Mūsawī, *Nuzhat al-jalīs*, 2: 253.

18 The caravanserai was first mentioned in 1683 in a Dutch report that describes merchants using it. This report is the only one that characterizes the *wikāla* as commercial. VOC 1406.

19 Grandpré, *Voyage in the Indian Ocean*, 2: 146.

20 The caravanserai was not the only place where pilgrims stayed in the city. In the early nineteenth century an anonymous American observer noted how the newly arrived pilgrims in the city had built up a small provisional settlement out of reed mats along the city walls. The same source describes Malay pilgrims taking shelter in the Mosque of al-Ṣandal, in the southern part of the city. Anonymous, "Caroline" Journal, 1821, Phillips Library, Peabody Essex Museum, Salem, Massachusetts, Log 656 1821C.

21 Al-Mūsawī, *Nuzhat al-jalīs*, 2: 263.

22 *Prutky's Travels*, 363–64.

23 Ibid., 373.

24 In regard to medieval Aden, Margariti described the building named Dār al-Ṭawīla, which was located next to the customs house and was probably dedi-

cated to the functions of the royal trade. Dār al-Ṭawīla predated Mocha's royal *wikāla* by several centuries, indicating that a precedent existed for an imperial trading establishment in a Yemeni port city. Margariti, "Maritime Trade," 154; Margariti, *Aden*, 99.

25 Lewcock, "Buildings of the Sūq /Market," 277.

26 The scribe wrote *mikhāya*. Mittwoch, *Aus dem Jemen*, 28.

27 September 13, 1727, VOC 9122.

28 Abū Ṭālib, *Tārīkh al-Yaman*, 301.

29 Similarly, there was no *qayṣariyya* or any other dedicated retail structure.

30 December 22, 1737, VOC 2447; February 10, 1738, VOC 2247.

31 Niebuhr, *Travels*, 1: 319–21.

32 As the source recounts, after the French bombardment of the city, a French captain was killed "at the door of a store in Mocha" ("fī bāb dukkān bi al-Mukhā"). Zabāra, *Nashr al-ʿarf*, 1: 304. The Dutch specified that the French captain Monsieur "Rickekomme" was slain in front of the French house. June 30, 1737, VOC 2447.

33 All the entries from 1705–6 are from VOC 9115.

34 March 23, 1725, VOC 9119.

35 As a rule, the majority of ship's crew members remained on the boat in port while the *nākhūdhas* and major merchants stayed on shore.

36 January 8, 1706, VOC 9115.

37 January 18, 1723, VOC 9117.

38 La Roque, *Voyage to Arabia*, 72.

39 April 16 and 19, 1705, VOC 9115.

40 IOR G/17/1, pt. 1, ff. 66.

41 The house was later immortalized in the mislabeled painting *Marchand de chevaux au Caire*, by Jean-Léon Gerôme. *Au Yémen en 1856: Photographies et dessins d'Auguste Bartholdi* (Colmar, France: Musée Bartholdi, 1994), 85.

42 The term *mashrabiyya* is common in Egypt, but the Persian term *rawshan* is used to refer to these projecting windows throughout the lower Red Sea.

43 Grandpré, *Voyage in the Indian Ocean*, 2: 165.

44 Mahā al-Ḥabshī drew the plans of the surveyed houses, and Krista Lewis assisted in the project. Um, "A Red Sea Society," 360–76.

45 The contract of sale says that the house was purchased for 200 French riyals (Maria Theresa thalers) on 23 Safar 1350, or July 10, 1931. I thank the al-Maḥfadī family for allowing me to draw plans of their house and to photograph it, for helping with my research, and for welcoming me whenever I visited Mocha.

46 According to the residents, they applied this coat of concrete on the exterior of the house as well as on the third floor in 1986 in order to repair cracks and support weakened surfaces.

47 Gabriele Vom Bruck, "A House Turned Inside Out: Inhabiting Space in a Yemeni City," *Journal of Material Culture* 2, no. 2 (1997): 151.

48 Bayt al-Maḥfaḍī's roof level was completely reconstructed in the early twentieth century, but in the past it likely held a rooftop pavilion, now replaced by the built *majlis* that stands there today.

49 Anne Meneley, *Tournaments of Value: Sociability and Hierarchy in a Yemeni Town* (Toronto: University of Toronto Press, 1996); La Roque, *Voyage to Arabia*, 86.

50 The al-Maḥfaḍī family has boarded up the passageway between the southwestern room shown in figure 6.11 and the main storage area.

51 A dual entry system is a standard solution for dealing with mixed traffic and family privacy in other Arab house types as well, such as in Baghdad, but without the comparable commercial aspects. John Warren and Ihsan Fethi, *Traditional Houses in Baghdad* (Horsham, UK: Coach Publishing House, 1982), 52, 55.

52 Occasionally Dutch merchants brought their families to Mocha to reside with them, as in the case of the Colombus family, whose young son died in Mocha. April 28, 1706, VOC 9115.

53 The Scottish merchant and captain Alexander Hamilton invited a merchant who had not paid his debt to the upper stories of his house and threatened to throw him from the top of the house to force him to disperse the funds. Alexander Hamilton, *A New Account of the East Indies* (London, 1930), 35–36.

54 Grandpré, *Voyage in the Indian Ocean*, 2: 169–71.

55 The plan of Bayt al-Maḥfaḍī shows only the modern door swings, but many of the now open door frames had separate doors with locks, as were found in two other examples of historic houses, Bayt al-Miʿyād and the Idāra building.

56 July 12, 1730, VOC 2202.

57 December 11, 1731, VOC 2252.

58 I thank al-Muqaddam Aḥmad Qāʾid Ṣalāh, the *mudīr* of the municipality, who graciously allowed me to draw plans of and photograph this government building in 2000.

59 Eric Macro, *Yemen and the Western World* (London: C. Hurst, 1968), 63; Baldry, "The Turkish-Italian War," 51.

60 J. Ch. Depaule, S. Noweir, J. F. Mounier, Ph. Panerai, and M. Zakariyya, *Actualité de l'habitat ancien au Caire: Le Rabʿ Qizlar* (Cairo: Centre d'Études et de Documentation Économiques, Juridiques et Sociales, 1985); André Raymond, "The Rabʿ: A Type of Collective Housing in Cairo during the Ottoman Period," in *Architecture as Symbol and Self-identity* (Philadelphia: Aga Khan Awards, 1980), 55–62.

61 Raymond, "The Rabʿ," 57.

62 The houses in the city of Rosetta reveal another unique response in domestic architectural plan and form to intense commercial activity in an early modern Egyptian riverine port city. A. Lézine and A.-R. Abdul Tawab, "Introduction à l'étude des maisons anciennes de Rosette," *Annales Islamologiques* 10 (1972): 149–205.

63 Constable, *Housing the Stranger*, 64.

64 Paul Bonnenfant, "La maison dans la péninsule Arabique," in *L'habitat traditionnel dans les pays musulmans autour de la Mediterranée*, ed. Jean-Claude Garçin (Cairo, 1991), 3: 715–99, 932–39.

65 Derek Matthews, "The Red Sea Style," *Kush* 1, no. 1 (1953): 60.

66 Stone, *Studies on the Tihāmah*, 58, pl. 6.10.

67 Paul Bonnenfant and Jeanne-Marie Gentilleau, "Une maison de commerçant-armateur sur la mer Rouge: Bayt ʿAbd al-Udūd à al-Luḥayyah (Yémen)," in *Les villes dans l'empire ottoman: Activités et sociétés*, ed. Daniel Panzac (Paris: CNRS Editions, 1994), 2: 144–49.

68 Jean-Pierre Greenlaw, *The Coral Buildings of Suakin* (Boston: published privately 1976; London: Kegan Paul, 1995), 17.

69 Matthews, "Red Sea Style," 63.

70 Greenlaw, *Coral Buildings*, 38–40.

71 Ibid., 76. Matthews described the *wikāla* as a typical urban *khān* with two stories of storerooms and lodging and referred to it as "the last building to be erected in Suakin in the Red Sea style; it is a monument to the decline of the port." Matthews, "Red Sea Style," 62.

72 Bonnenfant, "La maison," 774; Geoffroy King, *Traditional Architecture of Saudi Arabia* (London: I. B. Tauris, 1998), 44.

73 Mohamed El Amrousi has argued that the *rawshans* in Jidda are not local to the city's architecture but are the result of nineteenth-century restoration that strove to circumscribe the city in pan-Arab terms. Mohamed El Amrousi, "Beyond Muslim Space: Jeddah, Muscat, Aden and Port Said" (Ph.D. diss., University of California, Los Angeles, 2001), 90.

74 Bonnenfant, "La maison," 774.

75 King, *Traditional Architecture*, 41, 44.

76 Ibid., 30.

77 V. S. Pramar, "A Study of Some Indo-Muslim Towns in Gujarat," *Environmental Design: Journal of the Islamic Environmental Design Research Centre* 0 (1984): 28–31.

78 V. S. Pramar, *Haveli: Wooden Houses and Mansions of Gujarat* (Middletown, N.J.: Grantha, 1989), 86.

79 Bonnenfant, "La marque de l'Inde."

80 Santhi Kavuri-Bauer coined the phrase "spatial logic of trade" and allowed me to use it in this chapter as well as in my 2003 article. Um, "Spatial Negotiations," 187.

81 This local sponsorship dominated the city before the Egyptian occupation of 1865, after which the traditional trade structure of the region broke down. Jonathan Miran, "Facing the Land, Facing the Sea: Commercial Transformation and Urban Dynamics in the Red Sea Port of Massawa, 1840s–1990s" (Ph.D. diss., Michigan State University, 2004), 144, 177.

82 Horton gives a summary review of the most prominent sources in Arabic, Chinese, and European languages. Mark Horton, "Swahili Architecture, Space and Social Structure," in *Architecture and Order: Approaches to Social Space*, eds. M. P. Pearson and C. Richards (London: Routledge, 1994), 164–67.

83 Thomas Gensheimer, "Cross-Cultural Currents: Swahili Urbanism in the Late Middle Ages," in *Hybrid Urbanism: On the Identity Discourse and the Built Environment*, ed. Nezar AlSayyad (Westport, Conn.: Praeger, 2001), 37.

84 Horton, "Swahili Architecture," 166.

85 Ibid.

86 Paul Bonnenfant, *Zabid au Yémen: Archéologie du vivant* (Aix-en-Provence, France: Edisud, 2004), 179.

87 Curtin, *Cross-Cultural Trade*, 1.

7 On the Politics of Inside and Out

1 Serjeant's study of the Baniyan community in Yemen may be considered an authoritative compilation of many of the oft-cited sources on the Baniyans, mainly the Arabic sources. Rather than resummarizing that material here, I add information about the Baniyans of Mocha from the Dag Registers. R. B. Serjeant, "Bāniyān Merchants," 432–45.

2 Lakshmi Subramanian, *Indigenous Capital and Imperial Expansion: Bombay, Surat and the West Coast* (Delhi: Oxford University Press, 1996), 123.

3 Irfan Habib, "Merchant Communities in Pre-colonial India," in *The Rise of Merchant Empires: Long-Distance Trade in the Early Modern World, 1350–1750*, ed. James D. Tracy (Cambridge: Cambridge University Press, 1990), 380.

4 In one case they are referred to as *kafarat al-rājbūt*, or "the Rajput infidels." Zabāra, *Nayl al-Waṭr*, 1: 229.

5 Serjeant, "Bāniyān Merchants," 432.

6 The same regional cohesiveness was maintained between Baniyans in India as well. Habib, "Merchant Communities," 391.

7 January 6, 1731, VOC 2252.

8 Bonnenfant emphasized the diversification of Baniyan trades in Zabid. Bonnenfant, "La marque de l'Inde."

9 La Roque, *Voyage to Arabia*, 123–24.

10 Baniyan washers, barbers, and cuppers are mentioned. Niebuhr, *Description*, 115; March 5, 1728, VOC 9122; December 1, 1731, VOC 2252.

11 February 1, 1737, VOC 2447; August 28, 1728, VOC 9123. The term *shāhbandar* was used across the maritime Indian Ocean, but its meaning was not fixed. In the context of Southeast Asia, Anthony Reid described the *syahbandar* as the leader of a foreign merchant community and its liaison to the local government. Reid, *Southeast Asia in the Age of Commerce, 1450–1650* (New Haven, Conn.:

Yale University Press, 1993), 2: 120. In Ottoman Cairo, the *shāhbandar al-tujjār* was the head of the merchant's guild of Cairo, not a leader of a foreign group. Hanna, *Making Big Money*, 36–39. The role of the *shāhbandar* of the Baniyans in Mocha resembled the Indian Ocean understanding of the position more closely than that of Mediterranean Egypt.

12 Zabāra, *Nashr al-ʿarf*, 1: 29–30.

13 He was known as "Wiera" in Dutch sources, "Bira" in Jean de la Roque's account of early French expeditions, and "Vera" by the English.

14 La Roque, *Voyage to Arabia*, 71.

15 Das Gupta, "Gujarati Merchants," 134.

16 Serjeant noted that the total annual poll tax for the Baniyans in the mid-eighteenth century was equivalent to that paid by the Jewish community, even though the latter's population was much larger. Serjeant, "Bāniyān Merchants," 434.

17 The Qāsimīs were not the first or only Muslim rulers to recognize that conferring the *dhimmī* status on Hindus could be beneficial. The sixteenth-century Mughal emperor Akbar was known for making this controversial judgment in India.

18 September 26, 1724, VOC 9119.

19 March 4, 1728, VOC 9122. Das Gupta described how the governor demanded 20,000 Spanish riyals from the Baniyans in order to keep their temples and called it a breakdown of tolerance. That was not the case. Rather, it was the temporary overlord, Ismāʿīl b. Muḥammad b. Isḥāq, and not the governor, who called on the Baniyans to pay this sum during his short period of control of the city. The demand was eventually negotiated and the temple was not affected. Hence it reflects no change in overall status for the Baniyans. Das Gupta, "Gujarati Merchants," n. 17.

20 The only other Yemeni city in which a Hindu place of worship is mentioned is nineteenth-century Aden, before the British conquest of the port. Serjeant, "Bāniyān Merchants," 435.

21 March 7, 1724, VOC 9118.

22 The burial fee fluctuated between ten and twenty Mocha dollars in the eighteenth and nineteenth centuries. One time, however, the Baniyans were unable to bury a body because the governor demanded an exorbitant 500 Spanish riyals for the permission. Van Hoorn Van Riebeck Papers 12; "Observations on a Voyage to Moka in 1800, with remarks on the weather," IOR Mss Eur E2, British Library, London; March 23, 1732, VOC 2252.

23 February 2, 1729, VOC 9123.

24 January 21, 1731, VOC 2252; November 7, 1736, VOC 2447.

25 December 18, 1730, VOC 2252.

26 April 7, 1720, VOC 9116.

27 March 30, 1735, VOC 2356.
28 August 26, 1737, VOC 2447.
29 August 23, 1734, VOC 2356.
30 Zabāra, *Nashr al-ʿarf*, 1: 767.
31 Das Gupta, "Gujarati Merchants," 132.
32 February 11, 1730, VOC 2202.
33 Das Gupta, "Gujarati Merchants," 133.
34 Haykel, *Revival and Reform*, 117.
35 Ibid., 120–21.
36 Ibid., 118. During this time Mocha residents used Mawzaʿ as a vacation spot to escape the brackish water and the intolerable heat and wind of the coast. The record of Jewish exile casts the town in a very different light.
37 The most commonly held opinion regarding their eventual return to Sanaa and the highlands was that the imam realized they were indispensable as craftspeople and required their labor in Sanaa. Ester Muchawsky-Schnapper, *The Yemenites: Two Thousand Years of Jewish Culture* (Jerusalem: Israel Museum), 15; A. Shivtiel, Wilfred Lockwood, and R. B. Serjeant, "The Jews of Ṣanʿāʾ," in Serjeant and Lewcock, *Ṣanʿāʾ*, 392. Haykel counters, citing al-Jirāfī, who wrote that the imam was unable to find a safe place to send them to and so allowed their return. Haykel, *Revival and Reform*, 120.
38 Yosef Tobi, *The Jews of Yemen: Studies in Their History and Culture* (Leiden: E. J. Brill, 1999), 80.
39 Serjeant, "Bāniyān Merchants," 432–33.
40 Haykel, *Revival and Reform*, 121.
41 The imam and the other *sayyids* were not allowed access to the *zakat*, the obligatory charitable tax, but the imam could use the *jizya*, or poll tax, for personal purposes.
42 Serjeant, "Bāniyān Merchants," 433.
43 Zabāra, *Nashr al-ʿarf*, 3: 41.
44 Serjeant, "Bāniyān Merchants," 434; La Roque, *Voyage to Arabia*, 71, 125; Niebuhr, *Description*, 59.
45 The pre-expulsion intramural Jewish Sanaani quarters shifted around the city and cannot be pinpointed today. Shivtiel, Lockwood, and Serjeant, "The Jews of Ṣanʿāʾ," 391. Scholars have taken numerous positions regarding the uniqueness of Jewish house forms in Yemen. Rathjens and Muchawsky-Schnapper both argued that the Jewish Sanaani courtyard house derived from Mediterranean models and cited pre-expulsion intramural examples. Carl Rathjens, *Jewish Domestic Architecture in San'a, Yemen* (Jerusalem: Israel Oriental Society, 1957), 65; Muchawsky-Schnapper, *The Yemenites*, 28–29. Lewcock and Serjeant rejected the idea of Mediterranean influence as well as the uniqueness of

Jewish housing before the expulsion. Lewcock and Serjeant, "The Houses of Ṣanʿāʾ," in Serjeant and Lewcock, *Ṣanʿāʾ*, 499.

46 This western area had been a site of development during the first Ottoman period as an extended suburb for country houses of the elite. The whole area was walled in the early nineteenth century. Horst Kopp and Eugen Wirth, *Sanaa: Développement et organisation de l'espace d'une ville arabe*, trans. B. Blukacz-Louisfert and F. Blukacz (Aix-en-Provence: Institut de Recherches et d'Études sur le Monde Arabe et Musulman, 1994), 25.

47 Many Jewish craftsmen and traders still worked in the walled city of Sanaa, although their residences were external. Lewcock and Serjeant, "Houses of Ṣanʿāʾ," 496.

48 Donatella Calabi, "The Jews and the City in the Mediterranean Area," in *Mediterranean Urban Culture, 1400–1700*, ed. A. Cowan (Exeter: University of Exeter Press, 2000), 56–58; Raben, "Batavia and Colombo," 161–96.

49 Abu-Lughod, "The Islamic City," 164–67; Raymond, "Islamic City, Arab City," 14–16; T. H. Greenshields, "'Quarters' and Ethnicity," in *The Changing Middle Eastern City*, eds. G. H. Blake and R. I. Lawless (London: Croom Helm, 1980), 120–40.

50 Marcus, *Aleppo*, 317.

51 Heather Sutherland, "Eastern Emporium and Company Town: Trade and Society in Eighteenth-Century Makassar," in Broeze, *Brides of the Sea*, 121.

52 March 11, 1705, VOC 9115. Brouwer, on the basis of van den Broecke's early observations, held that a Jewish place of worship did not exist in the early seventeenth century. It might have been built in the late seventeenth century after the Jewish expulsion in Mawzaʿ increased the population on the coast, or perhaps an ordinary house was used for the purpose, escaping van den Broecke's notice, as was the case in other Yemeni cities. Today no remains of this synagogue exist. Brouwer, *Profile*, 229.

53 Mocha's Somali community must be distinguished from the *akhdām*, a socially marginalized group in Yemen that is often assigned ambiguous African origins, although the *akhdām* were also characteristically excluded by extramural status. Paul Bonnenfant, "Les descendants des akhdâm à Zabid: Pauvreté, dépendance et exclusion," in *Dynamiques de la pauvreté en Afrique du Nord et au Moyen Orient*, eds. B. Destremau, A. Deboulet, and F. Ireton (Paris: Karthala, 2004), 193–216; Franck Mermier, *Le cheikh de la nuit, Sanaa: Organization des souks et société citadine* (Paris: Sindbad Actes Sud, 1997), 91–93.

54 Grandpré, *Voyage in the Indian Ocean*, 2: 134; Höhfeld, "Die gegenwärtige Situation," 27.

55 Al-Mūsawī, *Nuzhat al-jalīs*, 2: 263.

56 Some prominent merchants in the city, including Baniyans and Europeans, owned houses far outside the city limits along the southern coast, where there

was a lush date palm grove. Some of these garden houses were built of stone and brick, unlike the mud and thatch ones in the immediate suburbs. Grandpré, *Voyage in the Indian Ocean*, 2: 211–14; Rupert Kirk's drawing, "Country House of Sheikh Tybe, 1832," x228/021678, Royal Geographical Society, London.

57 July 30, 1728, VOC 9123.

58 August 1, 1728, VOC 9123.

59 On one occasion, the governor Khazindār called on the Baniyans to move from their houses, which were located near mosques that had become blackened from the smoke of their chimneys. They quickly paid him off, however, and he dropped his demand. November 9, 1730, VOC 2252.

60 The Dutch surmised that Ḥasan Ḥasūsā was purchasing the house in his name but on behalf of the governor, Khazindār, to whom Mathura owed 5,000 to 6,000 Spanish riyals. The governor could not own houses in his name because the royal treasury would seize any such property were he to leave his post in the city.

61 Serjeant, "Bāniyān Merchants," 432; Bonnenfant, "La marque de l'Inde."

62 Serjeant, "Bāniyān Merchants," 434.

63 This distinction in policies toward local, settled *dhimmī* Christians and temporary European merchant communities has also been noted for Egypt in an earlier period. Constable, *Housing the Stranger*, 115–16.

64 S. D. Goitein, "From the Mediterranean to India: Documents on the Trade to India, South Arabia, and East Africa from the Eleventh and Twelfth Centuries," *Speculum: A Journal of Mediaeval Studies* 29 (April 1954): 181–97; Tobi, *Jews of Yemen*, 40–41.

65 Shivtiel, Lockwood, and Serjeant, "Jews of Ṣanʿāʾ," 394. Some members of the Jewish community of Radāʿ were involved in the India trade, but they were a small minority of Jewish overseas merchants in this era. Tobi, *Jews of Yemen*, 125.

66 Haykel, *Revival and Reform*, 149.

67 Osgood, *Notes of Travel*, 192–94; Edward A. Alpers, "The Somali Community at Aden in the Nineteenth Century," *Northeast African Studies* 8, nos. 2–3 (1986): 145, 152.

68 Raben, "Batavia and Colombo," 39.

69 Visitors described a small, secret door that could be used for passage during the night. Dufton, *Journey through Abyssinia*, 237; Grandpré, *Voyage in the Indian Ocean*, 2: 213.

70 La Roque, *Voyage to Arabia*, 110.

71 Al-Mūsawī, *Nuzhat al-jalīs*, 2: 262; William Revett, "Appendix B: William Revett's Narrative of Events at Aden, His Voyage to Mocha, etc," in *The Journal of John Jourdain, 1608–17, Describing His Experiences in Arabia, India, and the Malay Archipelago*, ed. William Foster (Cambridge: Hakluyt Society, 1905), 356. Today a modern mosque stands to the east of it.

72 Personal communication, ʿĀdil ʿAbd al-Wahhāb, Mocha, Yemen, March 1, 2000.

73 Al-Mūsawī, *Nuzhat al-jalīs*, 2: 262.

74 ʿAbd al-Wahhāb, "Iklīl," 19.

75 The two intramural cemeteries that ʿAbd al-Wahhāb mentions are al-Ṣandal cemetery and the cemetery of al-Shādhilī and the Great Mosque. He names ten more outside the city wall. Um, "A Red Sea Society," 357–58. The European cemetery was a small, marked-off square area to the northeast of the tomb of al-ʿAmūdī, presumably separated from but near the Muslim burials, about twenty-five meters east of the present round tower. The Jewish burial ground was also located north of the city, and according to ʿAbd al-Wahhāb, may have been the same place as the Christian cemetery. Personal communication, ʿAbduh ʿAlī Muḥammad and Nājī Muḥammad Sayf, Mocha, Yemen, March 1, 2000; ʿAbd al-Wahhāb, "Iklīl," 19.

76 ʿAbd al-Wahhāb called this space Muṣallā al-ʿĪd, al-Jabbāna. In addition to its use on ʿĪd al-Fiṭr and ʿĪd al-Aḍḥā, it was used for the *istisqā*ʾ, or prayer for rain during a drought. ʿAbd al-Wahhāb, "Iklīl," 19; July 21 and 22, 1723, VOC 9118.

77 The Dag Register describes it as an "open, but marked place on the field." September 21, 1722, VOC 9117.

78 "Caroline" Journal, June 21, 1821, Peabody Essex Museum, Log 656 1821C.

79 Personal communication, ʿAbduh ʿAlī Muḥammad and Nājī Muḥammad Sayf, Mocha, Yemen, March 1, 2000.

80 This ceremonial procession outside the city mirrored the imam's urban procession in Sanaa but had specific spatial dimensions related to the built form of Mocha. June 16, 1728, VOC 9120. Haykel documented the rise of ceremonial pomp at the court of the eighteenth-century imams. Haykel, *Revival and Reform*, 51–52.

81 April 2, 1706, VOC 9115.

82 May 18, 1720, VOC 9116.

83 January 8, 1725, VOC 9119.

84 November 14, 1731, VOC 2252.

85 May 22, 1724, VOC 9118; Grandpré, *Voyage in the Indian Ocean*, 2: 134.

86 September 21, 1729, VOC 2202.

87 The Dag Registers record the existence of these "free places" in other cities in Yemen, including Sanaa and Bayt al-Faqīh. In mid-eighteenth-century Sanaa, the free place was the newly built Tomb of Imam al-Mutawakkil Qāsim, west of the city. In 1729 the Baniyans of Sanaa fled to that tomb to avoid paying a loan of 6,000 Spanish riyals to Imam al-Manṣūr Ḥusayn, after having just paid him 10,000 Spanish riyals for a previous loan. October 1, 1729, VOC 2202.

88 Das Gupta mistakenly called it "a mosque outside the town walls." Das Gupta, "Gujarati Merchants," 143.

89 An oft-quoted witness of the British invasion of Aden mentioned the Baniyans and Jews of the city fleeing to a mosque with a truce flag flying over it in order to seek sanctuary and confirm their neutrality. Serjeant, "Bāniyān Merchants," 435.

90 December 10, 1729, VOC 2202.

91 November 13, 1727, VOC 9122.

92 The Dutch sources often refer to the festival as Baniyan New Year or simply "Noruz." October 9, 1723, VOC 9118.

93 P. Thomas, *Festivals and Holidays of India* (Bombay: Taraporevala Sons, 1971), 4.

94 October 9, 1723, VOC 9118; September 26, 1724, VOC 9119.

95 November 8, 1722, VOC 9117.

Conclusion: The End of the Mocha Era

1 Zabāra, *Nayl al-Waṭar*, 1: 16.

2 Ibid., 1: 17. Ḥasan al-ʿUlufī was named wazir in 1784, and he "treacherously dismissed" al-Jurmūzī. Al-ʿAmri, *The Yemen*, 30.

3 Valentia, *Voyages and Travels to India*, 2: 353.

4 Al-ʿAmri, *The Yemen*, 66; Henry Salt, *A Voyage to Abyssinia* (London: Cass, 1814, reprint 1967), 126.

5 Al-ʿAmri, *The Yemen*, 63–64.

6 Salt, *Voyage to Abyssinia*, 126.

7 Paul Dresch, *A History of Modern Yemen* (Cambridge: Cambridge University Press, 2000), 4.

8 Guo, *Commerce, Culture, and Community*, 1–28.

GLOSSARY

alphandigo. The customs house, a term used by the Dutch, from a Portuguese corruption of the Arabic term *al-funduq*.

amīr al-baḥr. The overseer of the port, an official who served under the city governor.

Baniyan, also **Banyan, Banian, Vanya.** A Hindu or Jain merchant from western India who operated in Indian Ocean, Persian Gulf, and Red Sea cities. In Mocha, the Baniyans served primarily as land-based brokers.

birka (pl. **birak**). A pool or a cistern used to collect rainwater.

funduq (pl. **fanādiq**). A wholesale trade structure with lodging and storage facilities; in the Mediterranean region sometimes used to specify a European trading establishment.

furḍa. The port, also used to refer to the customs house.

ghurāb, also **grab.** A two- or three-masted ship, literally "raven" or the "edge of a sword's blade."

ḥāra. A residential district within a city (in construction, *ḥārat*).

ḥarf. See *komassi*.

jalba (pl. **jilāb**). A small local ship of the Red Sea.

khān. A wholesale trade structure with lodging and storage facilities.

komassi. A local silver coin minted by the imam in the seventeenth and eighteenth centuries; the term was used primarily in the Tihāma and Ḥaḍramawt, probably derived from the Arabic *khumsiyya*; called *ḥarf* in the highlands.

Lotia, also **Lūtiyya** (pl. **Liwātiyya**). A Muslim merchant from western India who lived in the ports of Yemen and Oman as well as Sanaa.

maydān. City square.

miqhāya. A coffee house that also served as a modest rest house, often found on roads in the Tihāma.

Mocha dollar. A local currency fixed at a value under that of the Spanish riyal, in which values were calculated but never tendered; called *qirsh dhahab* locally.

nākhūdha, also **nakhūdha, nākhudhā, nākhudha, nachoda** (pl. **nawākhid**). The captain of a ship who does not fulfill the technical role of seafarer but rather serves as the main authority on the ship and the agent of the shipowner at the port.

Nayrūz (calendar). A solar calendar of 365 days beginning in October that was calculated according to the maritime seasons of travel and used to schedule the dates for reckoning accounts in Mocha.

tranke. A local vessel of the Persian Gulf.

qāḍī. A Muslim judge.

qayṣariyya. A freestanding retail structure used to sell specialized merchandise.

qubba. A dome, cupola, or tomb.

rawshan (pl. **rawāshin**). A projecting window found on the coasts of the Red Sea and Persian Gulf; referred to as *mashrabiyya* in Egypt and the Levant.

riyal, Spanish. The dominant silver coin used for international trade in Yemen, also known as the Spanish *real* of eight, the Spanish peso, and the Spanish dollar; called *qirsh ḥajar* in Mocha.

samsara. A *khān* or *qayṣariyya*.

ṣarrāf. A money exchanger.

sayyid (pl. **sāda**). A title for a male direct descendant of the Prophet.

sūq. A retail marketplace.

tājir (pl. **tujjār**). A wholesale merchant.

ʿushsha (pl. **ʿushshash**). Mud and thatch house found in the Tihāma region of Yemen and Saudi Arabia.

wakīl. A representative or proxy.

wazir, also **vizier.** An advisor or councilor to the imam.

wikāla. Generally, a wholesale trading establishment with lodging and storage facilities.

Zaydism. One of the subsects of Shīʿī Islam.

REFERENCES CITED

Sources and Studies in Arabic

ʿAbd al-Wahhāb, Muḥammad. "Iklīl al-Mukhāʾ." Unpublished manuscript, 1988. Personal library of Muḥammad ʿAbd al-Wahhāb, Mocha, Yemen.

Akwaʿ, Ismāʿīl b. ʿAlī al-. *Hijar al-ʿilm wa maʿāqila fī al-Yaman.* 5 vols. Beirut: Dār al-Fikr al-Muʿāṣir, 1995.

Anonymous. *Ḥawliyyāt Yamāniyya: Al-Yaman fī al-qarn al-tāsiʿ ʿashar al-mīlādī.* Ed. ʿAbd Allāh Muḥammad al-Ḥibshī. Sanaa: Dār al-Ḥikma al-Yamāniyya, 1991.

Burayhī, ʿAbd al-Wahhāb b. ʿAbd al-Raḥmān al-. *Ṭabaqāt ṣulaḥāʾ al-Yaman al-maʿrūf bi-tārīkh al-Burayhī.* Ed. ʿAbd Allāh M. al-Ḥibshī. Sanaa: Maktabat al-Irshād, 1983.

Ḥajrī, Muḥammad b. Aḥmad al-. *Majmūʿ buldān wa qabāʾil al-Yaman.* 2 vols. Ed. Ismāʿīl b. ʿAlī al-Akwaʿ. Sanaa: Dār al-Ḥikma al-Yamaniyya, 1996.

———. *Masājid Ṣanʿāʾ ʿāmiruha wa muwaffīha.* Sanaa: Maktabat al-Yaman al-Kubrā, 1361/1942–43, reprint 1398/1977–78.

Jurmūzī, al-Muṭahhar b. Muḥammad al-. *Tuḥfat al-asmāʿ wa al-abṣār bi-mā fī al-sīra al-mutawakkiliyya min gharāʾib al-akhbār: sīrat al-imām al-mutawakkil ʿalā allāh Ismāʿīl b. al-Qāsim, 1019–87.* 2 vols. Ed. ʿAbd al-Hakīm ʿAbd al-Majīd al-Hajrī. Amman: Muʾassasat al-Imām Zayd b. ʿAlī al-Thaqāfiyya, 2002.

Khurasān, Muḥammad Mahdī. "Introduction." In *Nuzhat al-jalīs wa munyat al-adīb al-anīs*, by ʿAbbās b. ʿAlī al-Mūsawī al-Makkī, vol. 1, edited by Muḥammad Mahdī Khurasān, 3–31. Al-Najaf, Iraq: Al-Maṭbaʿa al-Ḥaydāriyya, 1967.

Mawzaʿī, ʿAbd al-Ṣamad b. Ismāʿīl al-. *Al-iḥsān fī dukhūl mamlakat al-Yaman.* Ed. ʿAbd Allāh Muḥammad al-Ḥibshī. Sanaa: Manshūrat al-Madīna, 1986.

Muḥibbī, Muḥammad Amīn al-. *Khulāṣat al-athar fī aʿyān al-qarn al-ḥādī ʿashar.* 4 vols. Cairo: Maṭbaʿa al-Wahbiyya, 1284/1867–68.

———. *Nafḥāt rayḥāna wa rashḥat ṭilā' al-ḥāna*. 5 vols. Ed. ʿAbd al-Fattāḥ Muḥammad al-Ḥulw. Cairo: Dār Iḥyā' al-Kutub al-ʿArabiyya, 1388/1968.

Muḥsin b. al-Ḥasan (Abū Ṭālib). *Tārīkh al-Yaman fī ʿaṣr al-istiqlāl ʿan al-ḥukm al-ʿuthmānī al-awwal*. Ed. ʿAbd Allāh Muḥammad al-Ḥibshī. Sanaa: Al-Mufaddal Offset Printers, 1990.

Mūsawī al-Makkī, ʿAbbās b. ʿAlī al-. *Nuzhat al-jalīs wa munyat al-adīb al-anīs*. 2 vols. Ed. Muḥammad Mahdī Khurasān. Al-Najaf, Iraq: al-Maṭbaʿa al-Ḥaydāriyya, 1967.

Muṭayyir, Aḥmad ʿUthmān. *Al-durra al-farīda fī tārīkh madīnat al-Ḥudayda*. Al-Ḥudayda, Yemen: Dār al-Miṣbāḥ li al-Ṭibāʿa, 1984.

Nuʿmī, Aḥmad al-. *Ḥawliyyāt al-Nuʿmī al-tihāmiyya min tārīkh al-Yaman al-ḥadīth*. Ed. Ḥusayn b. ʿAbd Allāh al-ʿAmrī. Damascus: Dār al-Fikr, 1987.

Sharjī, Abī al-ʿAbbās Aḥmad al-. *Ṭabaqāt al-khawāṣṣ ahl al-ṣidq wa al-ikhlāṣ*. Ed. ʿAbd Allāh M. al-Ḥibshī. Sanaa: al-Dār al-Yamaniyya, 1986.

Shawkānī, Muḥammad b. ʿAlī al-. *Al-badr al-ṭāliʿ bi-maḥāsin man baʿd al-qarn al-sābiʿ*. 2 vols. Ed. Muḥammad Zabāra. Beirut: Dār al-Maʿrifa, n. d.

Sufyān, Muḥammad ʿAbduh. "Al-Mukhā māḍin muzdahir wa ḥāḍir mundathir." *Taʿizz*, March 1, 2000, 6.

Wazīr, ʿAbd Allāh b. ʿAlī al-. *Tārīkh al-Yaman khilāl al-qarn al-ḥādī ʿashar al-hijrī, al-sābiʿ ʿashar al-mīlādī*. Ed. Muḥammad ʿAbd al-Raḥīm Jāzim. Sanaa: Markaz al-dirāsāt wa al-buḥūth al-Yamanī, 1985.

Wushalī, Ismāʿīl b. Muḥammad al-. *Dhayl nashr al-thanā' al-ḥasan al-munabbi' bi-baʿḍ ḥawādith al-zaman min gharā'ib al-wāqiʿa fī al-Yaman*. Ed. Muḥammad b. Muḥammad al-Shuʿaybī. Sanaa: Maṭābiʿa al-Yaman al-ʿaṣriyya, 1982.

Yaḥyā b. al-Ḥusayn. *Ghāyat al-amānī fī akhbār al-quṭr al-yamānī*. Ed. Saʿīd ʿAbd al-Fattāḥ ʿĀshūr. Cairo, 1968.

Zabāra, Muḥammad. *Nashr al-ʿarf li-nubalā' al-Yaman baʿd al-alf*, vol. 1. Sanaa: Markaz al-Dirāsāt wa al-Buḥūth al-Yamanī, n.d.

———. *Nashr al-ʿarf li-nubalā' al-yaman baʿd al-alf*, vols. 2 and 3. Sanaa: Markaz al-Dirāsāt wa al-Buḥūth al-Yamanī, 1985.

———. *Nayl al-waṭar min tarājim rijāl al-yaman fī al-qarn al-thālith ʿashar*. 2 vols. Sanaa: Markaz al-Dirāsāt wa al-Abḥath, n.d.

Other Sources and Studies

Abdel-Daim, Dirar. "Mokha: The City of the Past and Future." In *Development and Urban Metamorphosis: Yemen at the Crossroads*, vol. 1: *Yemen at the Crossroads*, edited by Ahmet Evin, 81–90. Proceedings of seminar 8 in the series "Transformations in the Islamic World, Sanaʿa, May 25–30, 1983." Singapore, 1983.

Abdullah, Thabit. *Merchants, Mamluks, and Murder: The Political Economy of Trade in Eighteenth-Century Basra*. Albany, N.Y.: SUNY Press, 2001.

Abu-Lughod, Janet. "The Islamic City: Historic Myth, Islamic Essence, and Contemporary Relevance." *International Journal of Middle East Studies* 19 (1987): 155–76.

Allen, Calvin. "The Indian Merchant Community of Masqaṭ." *Bulletin of the School of Oriental and African Studies* 44 (1981): 39–53.

Alpers, Edward A. "The Somali Community at Aden in the Nineteenth Century." *Northeast African Studies* 8, nos. 2–3 (1986): 143–68.

Alsayyad, Nezar. *Cities and Caliphs: On the Genesis of Arab Muslim Urbanism*. Westport, Conn.: Greenwood Press, 1991.

ʿAmri, Husayn b. ʿAbdullah al-. *The Yemen in the 18th and 19th Centuries: A Political and Intellectual History*. London: Ithaca Press, 1985.

Amrousi, Mohamed El. "Beyond Muslim Space: Jeddah, Muscat, Aden and Port Said." Ph.D. diss., University of California, Los Angeles, 2001.

Aregay, Merid. "The Early History of Ethiopia's Coffee Trade and the Rise of Shawa." *Journal of African History* 29 (1988): 19–25.

Arendonk, C. van, and K. N. Chaudhuri. "Ḳahwa." In *The Encyclopedia of Islam*, vol. 4, 454. Leiden: E. J. Brill, 1978.

Asher, Catherine. "Mughal Sub-Imperial Patronage: The Architecture of Raja Man Singh." In *The Powers of Art: Patronage in Indian Culture*, edited by B. S. Miller, 183–201. Delhi: Oxford University Press, 1992.

Aponte, Salvatore. *La Vita Segreta dell'Arabia Felice*. Milan: A. Mondadori, 1936.

Au Yémen en 1856: Photographies et dessins d'Auguste Bartholdi. Colmar, France: Musée Bartholdi, 1994.

Bahkalī, ʿAbd al-Raḥmān b. Aḥmad al-, *Imams, notables et bédouins du Yémen au XVIIIe siècle, ou, Quintessence de l'or du règne de Chérif Muḥammad b. Aḥmad: Chronique de ʿAbd al-Raḥmān b. Ḥasan al-Bahkalī*. Edited and translated by Michel Tuchscherer. Cairo: Institut Français d'Archéologie Orientale du Caire, 1992.

Baldry, John. "The Early History of the Yemeni Port of al-Ḥudaydah." *Arabian Studies* 7 (1985): 37–52.

———. "The English East India Company's Settlement at al-Mukhā, 1719–1739." *The Arab Gulf* (University of Basra) 13, no. 2 (1981): 13–38.

———. "The Turkish-Italian War in the Yemen, 1911–12." *Arabian Studies* 3 (1976): 51–65.

Banga, Indu, ed. *Ports and Hinterlands in India, 1700–1950*. New Delhi: Manohar, 1992.

Barendse, R. J. *The Arabian Seas, 1640–1700*. Leiden: Research School of Asian, African, and Amerindian Studies, 1998.

Barnes, Ruth. "The Painted Decoration: An Influence from Indian Textiles?" In *The ʿAmiriya in Radaʿ: The History and Restoration of a Sixteenth-Century Madrasa in the Yemen*, by Selma Al-Radi, 39–48. Oxford: Oxford University Press, 1997.

Basu, Dilip, ed. *The Rise and Growth of the Colonial Port Cities in Asia*. Lanham, Md.: University Press of America, 1985.

Becker, Hans, Volker Höhfeld, and Horst Kopp, eds. *Kaffee Aus Arabien*. Wiesbaden: Franz Steiner Verlag, 1979.

Blier, Suzanne Preston. *The Anatomy of Architecture: Ontology and Metaphor in Batammaliba Architectural Expression*. Cambridge: Cambridge University Press, 1987.

Bonnenfant, Paul. "Les descendants des akhdâm à Zabid: Pauvreté, dépendance et exclusion." In *Dynamiques de la pauvreté en Afrique du Nord et au Moyen Orient*, edited by B. Destremau, A. Deboulet, and F. Ireton, 193–216. Paris: Karthala, 2004.

———. "La maison dans la péninsule Arabique." In *L'habitat traditionnel dans les pays musulmans autour de la Mediterranée*, vol. 3, edited by Jean-Claude Garçin, 715–97. Cairo, 1991.

———. "La marque de l'Inde à Zabid." *Chroniques Yéménites* 8 (2000) (http://cy.revues.org/document7.html).

———. *Zabid au Yémen: Archéologie du vivant*. Aix-en-Provence, France: Edisud, 2004.

Bonnenfant, Paul, and Jeanne-Marie Gentilleau. "Une maison de commerçant-armateur sur la mer Rouge: Bayt ʿAbd al-Udūd à al-Luḥayyah (Yémen)." In *Les villes dans l'empire ottoman: Activités et sociétés*, vol. 2, edited by Daniel Panzac, 125–88. Paris: CNRS Editions, 1994.

Bose, Sugata. *A Hundred Horizons: The Indian Ocean in the Age of Global Empire*. Cambridge, Mass.: Harvard University Press, 2006.

Boxhall, Peter. "The Diary of a Mocha Coffee Agent." *Arabian Studies* 1 (1974): 102–18.

Broecke, Pieter van den. *Korte historiael ende Journaelsche Aenteyckeninghe van al 't geen merckwaerdigh voorgevallen is, in de langdurighe Reysen, soo nae Cabo Verde, Angola, & c. als insodernheyd van Oost-Indien, beneffens de beschryving en afbeeldigh van verscheyden Steden op de Custe van Indien, Persien, Arabien, en aen 't Roode Meyr*. Amsterdam: Herman Jansz Brouwer, 1634.

Broeze, Frank, ed. *Brides of the Sea: Port Cities of Asia from the 16th–20th Centuries*. Honolulu: University of Hawaii Press, 1989.

———, ed. *Gateways of Asia: Port Cities of Asia in the 13th–20th Centuries*. London: Kegan Paul, 1997.

———. "Introduction." In *Brides of the Sea: Port Cities of Asia from the 16th–20th Centuries*, edited by F. Broeze, 1–28. Honolulu: University of Hawaii Press, 1989.

Brotton, Jerry. *Trading Territories: Mapping the Early Modern World*. London: Reaktion Books, 1997.

Brouwer, C. G. *Al-Mukhā: Profile of a Yemeni Seaport as Sketched by Servants of the Dutch East India Company (VOC), 1614–1640*. Amsterdam: D'Fluyte Rarob, 1997.

———. *Al-Mukhā: The Transoceanic Trade of a Yemeni Staple Town as Mapped by Merchants of the VOC, 1614–1640. Coffee, Spices and Textiles*. Amsterdam: D'Fluyte Rarob, 2006.

———. "Al-Mukhā as a Coffee Port in the Early Decades of the Seventeenth Century according to Dutch Sources." In *Le commerce du café avant l'ère des plantations coloniales: Espaces, réseaux, sociétés (XVe–XIXe siècle)*, edited by Michel Tuchscherer, 271–90. *Cahier des Annales Islamologiques* 20 (2001).

Brummett, Palmira. *Ottoman Seapower and Levantine Diplomacy in the Age of Discovery*. Albany, N.Y.: SUNY Press, 1994.

Bulbeck, D., A. Reid, L. C. Tan, and Y. Wu, compilers. *Southeast Asian Exports since the 14th Century: Cloves, Pepper, Coffee, and Sugar*. Singapore: Institute of Southeast Asian Studies, 1998.

Calabi, Donatella. "The Jews and the City in the Mediterranean Area." In *Mediterranean Urban Culture, 1400–1700*, edited by A. Cowan, 56–68. Exeter: University of Exeter Press, 2000.

———. *The Market and the City: Square, Street, and Architecture in Early Modern Europe*. Trans. Marlene Klein. Burlington, Vt.: Ashgate, 2004.

Casale, Giancarlo. "The Ottoman 'Discovery' of the Indian Ocean in the Sixteenth Century." In *Seascapes: Maritime Histories, Littoral Cultures, and Transoceanic Exchanges*, edited by J. H. Bentley, R. Bridenthal, and K. Wigen, 87–104. Honolulu: University of Hawaii Press, 2007.

Chaudhuri, K. N. *Asia before Europe: Economy and Civilisation of the Indian Ocean from the Rise of Islam to 1750*. Cambridge: Cambridge University Press, 1990.

———. *Trade and Civilisation in the Indian Ocean: An Economic History from the Rise of Islam to 1750*. Cambridge: Cambridge University Press, 1985.

Clarence-Smith, W. G., and S. Topik, eds. *The Global Coffee Economy in Africa, Asia, and Latin America, 1500–1989*. Cambridge: Cambridge University Press, 2003.

Combes, Edmond, and Maurice Tamisier. *Voyage en Abyssinie, dans les pays des Galla, de Choa et d'Ifat: Précédé d'une excursion dans l'Arabie-Heureuse, et accompagnés d'une carte des diverse contrées*. Paris: Louis Desessart, 1838.

Constable, Olivia Remie. *Housing the Stranger in the Mediterranean World: Lodging, Trade and Travel in Late Antiquity and the Middle Ages*. Cambridge: Cambridge University Press, 2003.

Curtin, Philip D. *Cross-Cultural Trade in World History*. Cambridge: Cambridge University Press, 1984.

Darley-Doran, Robert E. "Examples of Islamic Coinage from Yemen." In *Yemen: 3000 Years of Art and Civilisation in Arabia Felix*, edited by W. Daum, 182–203. Frankfurt: Umschau Verlag, 1988.

Das Gupta, Ashin. "Gujarati Merchants and the Red Sea Trade, 1700–1725." In *The Age of Partnership: Europeans in Asia before Dominion*, edited by B. B. King and M. N. Pearson, 125–58. Honolulu: University of Hawaii Press, 1979.

———. *Indian Merchants and the Decline of Surat, c. 1700–1750*. Wiesbaden, Germany: Franz Steiner Verlag, 1979; Delhi: Manohar, 1994.

———. "Indian Merchants and the Trade in the Indian Ocean, c. 1500–1750." In *The World of the Indian Ocean Merchant 1500–1800: Collected Essays of Ashin Das Gupta*, edited by Uma Das Gupta, 59–87. New Delhi: Oxford University Press, 2001.

———. "The Maritime Merchant and Indian History." In *The World of the Indian Ocean Merchant 1500–1800: Collected Essays of Ashin Das Gupta*, edited by Uma Das Gupta, 88–101. New Delhi: Oxford University Press, 2001.

———. "The Merchants of Surat, 1700–1750." In *Elites in South Asia*, edited by E. Leach and S. N. Mukherjee, 201–21. Cambridge: Cambridge University Press, 1970.

———. "A Note on Out-Station Factories: Mocha Factory." In *The World of the Indian Ocean Merchant 1500–1800: Collected Essays of Ashin Das Gupta*, edited by Uma Das Gupta, 457–61. New Delhi: Oxford University Press, 2001.

Das Gupta, Uma, ed. *The World of the Indian Ocean Merchant 1500–1800: Collected Essays of Ashin Das Gupta*. New Delhi: Oxford University Press, 2001.

DeGryse, K., and J. Parmentier. "Maritime Aspects of the Ostend Trade to Mocha, India and China (1715–1732)." In *Ships, Sailors and Spices: East India Companies and Their Shipping in the 16th, 17th and 18th Centuries*, edited by J. R. Bruijn and F. S. Gaastra. Amsterdam: NEHA, 1993.

Denoix, Sylvie, Jean-Charles Depaule, and Michel Tuchscherer, eds. *Le Khān al-Khalīlī et ses environs: Un centre commercial et artisanal au Caire du XIIIe au XXe siècle*. 2 vols. Cairo: Institut Français d'Archéologie Orientale du Caire, 1999.

Depaule, J. Ch., S. Noweir, J. F. Mounier, Ph. Panerai, and M. Zakariyya. *Actualité de l'habitat ancien au Caire: Le Rabᶜ Qizlar*. Cairo: Centre d'Études et de Documentation Économiques, Juridiques et Sociales, 1985.

Desfontaines, Pierre François Guyot. *Relation de l'expédition de Moka en l'année 1737 sous les ordres de M. de la Garde-Jazier, de Saint-Malo*. Paris, 1739.

Donzel, E. van. "Al-Mukhā." In *The Encyclopedia of Islam, New Edition*, vol. 7, 513–16. Leiden: E. J. Brill, 1960.

———. *A Yemenite Embassy to Ethiopia, 1647–1649*. Stuttgart: Franz Steiner Verlag, 1986.

Dresch, Paul. *A History of Modern Yemen*. Cambridge: Cambridge University Press, 2000.

Dufton, Henry. *Narrative of a Journey through Abyssinia*. Westport, Conn.: Negro Universities Press, 1970.

Facey, William. "The Red Sea: The Wind Regime and Location of Ports." In *Trade and Travel in the Red Sea Region: Proceedings of Red Sea Project I, Held in the British Museum, October 2002*, edited by P. Lunde and A. Porter, 7–18. London: BAR Series 1269, 2004.

Findly, Ellison B. "The Capture of Maryam-uz-Zamani's Ship: Mughal Women and European Traders." *Journal of the American Oriental Society* 108, no. 2 (1988): 227–38.

Finster, Barbara. "An Outline of the History of Islamic Religious Architecture in Yemen." *Muqarnas* 9 (1992): 124–47.

Floor, Willem. *The Persian Gulf: A Political and Economic History of Five Port Cities, 1500–1730*. Washington, D.C.: Mage Publishers, 2006.

Gavin, R. J. *Aden under British Rule*. London: Hurst, 1975.

Gensheimer, Thomas. "Cross-Cultural Currents: Swahili Urbanism in the Late Middle Ages." In *Hybrid Urbanism: On the Identity Discourse and the Built Environment*, edited by Nezar AlSayyad, 21–41. Westport, Conn.: Praeger, 2001.

Geoffroy, Éric. "La diffusion du café au Proche-Orient arabe par l'intermédiaire des soufis: Mythe et réalité." In *Le commerce du café avant l'ère des plantations coloniales: Espaces, réseaux, sociétés (XVe–XIXe siècle)*, edited by Michel Tuchscherer, 7–14. *Cahier des Annales Islamologiques* 20 (2001).

Glamann, Kristof. *Dutch Asiatic Trade, 1620–1740*. Copenhagen: Danish Science Press, 1958.

Goitein, S. D. "From the Mediterranean to India: Documents on the Trade to India, South Arabia, and East Africa from the Eleventh and Twelfth Centuries." *Speculum: A Journal of Mediaeval Studies* 29 (April 1954): 181–97.

———. *A Mediterranean Society: The Jewish Communities of the World as Portrayed in the Documents of the Cairo Geniza*. 4 vols. Berkeley: University of California Press, 1983.

Gokhale, Balkrishna. *Surat in the Seventeenth Century: A Study in Urban History of Pre-modern India*. London: Curzon Press, 1978.

Grabar, Oleg. "Review of *Venice's Mediterranean Colonies: Architecture and Urbanism*, by Maria Georgopoulou; *Venice and the East: The Impact of the Islamic World on Venetian Architecture*, by Deborah Howard; *Global Interests: Renaissance Art between East and West*, by Lisa Jardine and Jerry Brotton; and *Bazaar to Piazza: Islamic Trade and Italian Art*, by Rosamund Mack." *Art Bulletin* 85, no. 1 (2003): 189–92.

Grandpré, Louis de. *A Voyage in the Indian Ocean and to Bengal, 1789–90; An Account of the Sechelles Islands and Trincomale; A Voyage to the Red Sea, Mocha, Yemen*. 2 vols. Trans. from French. London, 1803; reprint, New Delhi, 1995. Originally published as *Voyage dans l'Inde et au Bengale* (Paris: Dentu, 1801).

Greenlaw, Jean-Pierre. *The Coral Buildings of Suakin*. Boston: published privately, 1976; London: Kegan Paul, 1995.

Greenshields, T. H. "'Quarters' and Ethnicity." In *The Changing Middle Eastern City*, edited by G. H. Blake and R. I. Lawless, 120–40. London: Croom Helm, 1980.

Grehan, James. *Everyday Life and Consumer Culture in Eighteenth-Century Damascus*. Seattle: University of Washington Press, 2007.

Guo, Li. *Commerce, Culture and Community in a Red Sea Port in the Thirteenth Century: The Arabic Documents from Quseir*. Leiden: E. J. Brill, 2004.

Habib, Irfan. "Merchant Communities in Pre-colonial India." In *The Rise of Merchant Empires: Long-Distance Trade in the Early Modern World, 1350–1750*, edited by James D. Tracy, 371–99. Cambridge: Cambridge University Press, 1990.

Haldane, Cheryl. "An Ottoman Period Shipwreck off Egypt's Red Sea Coast." In *Dirāsāt fī tārīkh Miṣr al-iqtiṣādī wa al-ijtimāʿī fī al-ʿaṣr al-ʿuthmānī*, edited by Daniel Crecelius, Ḥamza ʿAbd al-ʿAzīz Badr, and Muḥammad Ḥusām al-Dīn Ismāʿīl, 23–38. Cairo: Dār al-Āfāq al-ʿArabiyya, 1997.

Hamilton, Alexander. *A New Account of the East Indies*. London, 1930.

Haneda, Masashi, and Toru Miura, eds. *Islamic Urban Studies: Historical Review and Perspectives*. New York: Kegan Paul, 1994.

Hanna, Nelly. *Making Big Money in 1600: The Life and Times of Isma'il Abu Taqiyya, Egyptian Merchant*. Syracuse, N.Y: Syracuse University Press, 1998.

———. *An Urban History of Bulaq in the Mamluk and Ottoman Periods*. Supplement to *Annales Islamologiques* 3 (1983).

Hanssen, J., T. Philipp, and S. Weber, eds. *The Empire in the City: Arab Provincial Capitals in the Late Ottoman Empire*. Würzburg: Ergon Verlag, 2002.

Hardy-Guilbert, Claire, and Axelle Rougeulle. "Ports islamiques du Yémen: Prospections archéologiques sur les côtes yéménites (1993–1995)." *Archéologie Islamique* 7 (1997): 147–96.

Hattox, Ralph S. *Coffee and Coffeehouses: The Origins of a Social Beverage in the Medieval Near East*. Seattle: University of Washington Press, 1985.

Haykel, Bernard. *Revival and Reform in Islam: The Legacy of Muhammad al-Shawkānī*. Cambridge: Cambridge University Press, 2003.

———. "A Zaydi Revival?" *Yemen Update* 36 (1995): 20–21.

Ho, Engseng. *The Graves of Tarim: Genealogy and Mobility across the Indian Ocean*. Berkeley: University of California Press, 2006.

Höhfeld, Volker. "Die gegenwärtige Situation Mochas als Kleinstadt." In *Kaffee Aus Arabien*, edited by H. Becker, V. Höhfeld, and H. Kopp. Wiesbaden: Franz Steiner Verlag, 1979.

Horton, Mark. "Swahili Architecture, Space and Social Structure." In *Architecture and Order: Approaches to Social Space*, edited by M. P. Pearson and C. Richards, 147–69. London: Routledge, 1994.

Hourani, George F. *Arab Seafaring in the Indian Ocean in Ancient and Early Medieval Times*. Rev. by J. Carswell. Princeton, N.J.: Princeton University Press, 1951; reprint 1995.

Howard, Deborah. *Venice and the East: The Impact of the Islamic World on Venetian Architecture*. New Haven, Conn.: Yale University Press, 2000.

Jaffer, Amin, and Anna Jackson, eds. *Encounters: The Meeting of Asia and Europe, 1500–1800*. London: V & A Publications, 2004.

Jasdanwalla, Faaeza. "The Sidi Kingdom of Janjira." In *African Elites in India: Habshi Amarat*, edited by K. Robbins and J. McLeod, 176–217. Ahmedabad: Mapin Publishing, 2006.

Kawatoko, Mutsuo. "Coffee Trade in the al-Ṭūr Port, South Sinai." In *Le commerce du café avant l'ère des plantations coloniales: Espaces, réseaux, sociétés (XVe–XIXe siècle)*, edited by Michel Tuchscherer, 51–68. *Cahier des Annales Islamologiques* 20 (2001).

Khalidi, Omar. "Sayyids of Hadhramaut in Early Modern India." *Asian Journal of Social Science* 32, no. 3 (2004): 329–52.

King, Anthony D. *Urbanism, Colonialism, and the World-Economy: Cultural and Spatial Foundations of the World Urban System*. London: Routledge, 1990.

King, Geoffroy. *Traditional Architecture of Saudi Arabia.* London: I. B. Tauris, 1998.

Kopp, Horst, and Eugen Wirth. *Sanaa: Développement et organisation de l'espace d'une ville arabe.* Trans. B. Blukacz-Louisfert and F. Blukacz. Aix-en-Provence: Institut de Recherches et d'Études sur le Monde Arabe et Musulman, 1994.

Lachmann, Samuel. "The Ottoman Copper Coins struck at Mocha." *Spink Numismatic Circular* 51 (1993): 44.

———. "The Zaidī Imām al-Mahdī Aḥmad b. al-Ḥasan, 1087–1092H/1676–1681." *Numismatic Circular* (June 1988): 143–46.

Lambourn, Elizabeth. "Carving and Recarving: Three Rasulid Gravestones Revisited." *New Arabian Studies* 6 (2001): 10–30.

Laplace, Cyrille. *Campagne de circumnavigation de la frégate l'Artémise, pendant les années 1837, 1838, 1839, et 1840 sous le commandement de M. Laplace . . . pub. par ordre du roi, sous les auspices du ministre de la marine.* 6 vols. Paris: A. Bertrand, 1841–54.

Laulan, Robert. "Comment, en 1737, le drapeau français flotta sur Moka." *Terre, Air, Mer: Géographie* 57 (April 1932): 282–300.

Lewcock, Ronald. "Architectural Connections between Africa and Parts of the Indian Ocean Littoral." *Art and Archaeology Research Papers* (April 1976): 13–23.

———. "The Buildings of the Sūq/Market." In *Ṣanʿāʾ: An Arabian Islamic City,* edited by R. B. Serjeant and R. Lewcock, 276–302. London: World of Islam Trust, 1983.

Lewcock, Ronald, and R. B. Serjeant. "The Houses of Ṣanʿāʾ." In *Ṣanʿāʾ: An Arabian Islamic City,* edited by R. B. Serjeant and R. Lewcock, 436–500. London: World of Islam Trust, 1983.

Lézine, A., and A.-R. Abdul Tawab. "Introduction à l'étude des maisons anciennes de Rosette." *Annales Islamologiques* 10 (1972): 149–205.

Lowick, Nicholas. "The Mint of Ṣanʿāʾ: A Historical Outline." In *Ṣanʿāʾ: An Arabian Islamic City,* edited by R. B. Serjeant and R. Lewcock, 303–9. London: World of Islam Trust, 1983.

Macro, Eric. *Bibliography on Yemen and Notes on Mocha.* Coral Gables, Fla.: University of Miami Press, 1960.

———. "The First Americans at Mocha." *Geographical Journal* 130, no. 1 (1964): 183–84.

———. "Topography of Mocha." *Proceedings of the Seminar for Arabian Studies* 10 (1980): 55–66.

———. *Yemen and the Western World.* London: C. Hurst, 1968.

Marcus, Abraham. *The Middle East on the Eve of Modernity: Aleppo in the Eighteenth Century.* New York: Columbia University Press, 1989.

Margariti, Roxani Eleni. *Aden and the Indian Ocean Trade: 150 Years in the Life of a Medieval Arabian Port.* Chapel Hill: University of North Carolina Press, 2007.

———. "Like the Place of Congregation on Judgment Day: Maritime Trade and Urban Organization in Medieval Aden (ca. 1083–1229)." Ph.D. diss., Princeton University, 2002.

Matthee, Rudi. "Coffee in Safavid Iran: Commerce and Consumption." *Journal of the Economic and Social History of the Orient* 37 (1994): 1–32.

Matthews, Derek. "The Red Sea Style." *Kush* 1, no. 1 (1953): 60–86.

McChesney, R. D. "The Central Asian Hajj-Pilgrimage in the Time of the Early Modern Empires." In *Safavid Iran and Her Neighbors*, edited by Michael Mazzaoui, 129–56. Salt Lake City: University of Utah Press, 2003.

McPherson, Kenneth. *The Indian Ocean: A History of People and the Sea*. Oxford: Oxford University Press, 1993.

Meneley, Anne. *Tournaments of Value: Sociability and Hierarchy in a Yemeni Town*. Toronto: University of Toronto Press, 1996.

Mermier, Franck. *Le cheikh de la nuit, Sanaa: Organization des souks et société citadine*. Paris: Sindbad Actes Sud, 1997.

Miran, Jonathan. "Facing the Land, Facing the Sea: Commercial Transformation and Urban Dynamics in the Red Sea Port of Massawa, 1840s–1900s." Ph.D. diss., Michigan State University, 2004.

Mittwoch, Eugen, ed. *Aus dem Jemen: Hermann Burchardts Letzte Reise Durch Südarabien*. Leipzig: F. A. Brockhaus, 1926.

Muchawsky-Schnapper, Ester. *The Yemenites: Two Thousand Years of Jewish Culture*. Jerusalem: Israel Museum, 2000.

Murphey, Rhoads. "Traditionalism and Colonialism: Changing Urban Roles in Asia." *Journal of Asian Studies* 29, no. 1 (1969): 67–84.

———. "On the Evolution of the Port City." In *Brides of the Sea: Port Cities of Asia from the 16th–20th Centuries*, edited by F. Broeze, 223–46. Honolulu: University of Hawaii Press, 1989.

Nankivell, John. "Tihāmah Architecture: An Architectural Artist's View." In *Studies on the Tihāmah: The Report of the Tihāmah Expedition 1982 and Related Papers*, edited by Francine Stone, 57–59. Essex, UK: Longman, 1985.

Niebuhr, Carsten. *Description de l'Arabie: Faites sur des observations propres et des avis recueillis dans les lieux mêmes*. Trans. F. L. Mourier. Amsterdam: S. J. Baalde, 1774.

———. *Reisebeschreibung nach Arabien und den umliegenden Ländern*. 3 vols. Copenhagen: N. Möller, 1774. Reprint, Graz, Austria: Akademische Druck-u. Verlagsanstalt, 1968.

———. *Travels through Arabia and Other Countries in the East*. 2 vols. Trans. R. Heron. Edinburgh: R. Morison and Son, 1792. Reprint, Beirut: Librairie du Liban, 1968.

Osgood, Joseph B. *Notes of Travel or Recollections of Majunga, Zanzibar, Muscat, Aden, Mocha and Other Eastern Ports*. Freeport, N.Y.: Books for Libraries Press, 1972.

Özbaran, Salih. "The Ottomans in East Africa: A Tribute to Cengiz Orhonlu." In *The Ottoman Response to European Expansion: Studies on Ottoman-Portuguese Relations in the Indian Ocean and Ottoman Administration in the Arab Lands during the Sixteenth Century*. Istanbul: Isis Press, 1994.

———. "A Turkish Report on the Red Sea and the Portuguese in the Indian Ocean." In *The Ottoman Response to European Expansion: Studies on Ottoman-Portuguese Relations in the Indian Ocean and Ottoman Administration in the Arab Lands during the Sixteenth Century*. Istanbul: Isis Press, 1994.

Paluck, Bruce, and Rayya Saggar. *The al-Ḥasan bin al-Qāsim Mosque Complex: An Architectural and Historical Overview of a Seventeenth Century Mosque in Ḍūrān, Yemen*. Sanaa: American Institute for Yemeni Studies and Centre Français d'Archéologie et de Sciences Sociales de Sanaa, 2002.

Pearson, M. N. "Brokers in Western Indian Port Cities: Their Role in Servicing Foreign Merchants." *Modern Asian Studies* 22, no. 3 (1988): 455–72.

———. "Littoral Society: The Case for the Coast." *The Great Circle* 7 (1985): 1–8.

———. *Merchants and Rulers in Gujarat: The Response to the Portuguese in the Sixteenth Century*. Berkeley: University of California Press, 1976.

———. *Pilgrimage to Mecca: The Indian Experience, 1500–1800*. Princeton, N.J.: Markus Weiner, 1996.

Porter, Venetia. "The Ports of Yemen and the Indian Ocean Trade during the Tahirid Period (1454–1517)." In *Studies on Arabia in Honour of Professor G. Rex Smith*, edited by G. R. Smith, J. F. Healey, and V. Porter, 171–90. New York: Oxford University Press, 2002.

———. "The Rasulids in Dhofar in the VIIth–VIIIth/XIIIth–XIVth Centuries: Three Rasulid Tombstones from Ẓafār." *Journal of the Royal Asiatic Society* 1 (1988): 32–37.

Pramar, V. S. "Discovery of Architectural Links between Ancient Gujarat and Abyssinia." *Marg* 36, no. 1 (1984): 22–32.

———. *Haveli: Wooden Houses and Mansions of Gujarat*. Middletown, N.J.: Grantha Corp, 1989.

———. "A Study of Some Indo-Muslim Towns in Gujarat." *Environmental Design: Journal of the Islamic Environmental Design Research Centre* 0 (1984): 28–31.

Prutky's Travels in Other Countries. Translated and edited by J. H. Arrowsmith-Brown. London: Hakluyt Society, 1991.

Qāsim, ʿAlī b. ʿAbdullāh b. al-. *City of Divine and Earthly Joys: The Description of Ṣanʿāʾ*. Translated by Tim Mackintosh-Smith, edited by ʿAbdullāh b. Muḥammad al-Ḥibshī. Ardmore, Penn.: American Institute for Yemeni Studies, 2001.

Raben, Remco. "Batavia and Colombo: The Ethnic and Spatial Order of Two Colonial Cities, 1600–1800." Thesis, Rijksuniversiteit, Leiden, Netherlands, 1996.

Rathjens, Carl. *Jewish Domestic Architecture in San'a, Yemen*. Jerusalem: Israel Oriental Society, 1957.

Raymond, André. *Artisans et commerçants au Caire au XVIIIe siècle*. 2 vols. Damascus: Institut Français de Damas, 1973.

———. "A Divided Sea: The Cairo Coffee Trade in the Red Sea Area during the Seventeenth and the Eighteenth Centuries." In *Modernity and Culture: From the*

Mediterranean to the Indian Ocean, edited by L. T. Fawaz and C. A. Bayly, 45–57. New York: Columbia University Press, 2002.

———. "Une famille de grands negociants en café au Caire dans la première moitié du XVIIIe siècle: Les Sharāybī." In *Le commerce du café avant l'ère des plantations coloniales: Espaces, réseaux, sociétés (XVe–XIXe siècle)*, edited by Michel Tuchscherer, 111–24. *Cahier des Annales Islamologiques* 20 (2001).

———. *Grandes villes arabes à l'époque ottomane*. Paris: Sindbad, 1985.

———. "Islamic City, Arab City: Orientalist Myths and Recent Views." *British Journal of Middle Eastern Studies* 21, no. 1 (1994): 3–18.

———. "The *Rab*ʿ: A Type of Collective Housing in Cairo during the Ottoman Period." In *Architecture as Symbol and Self-identity*, 55–62. Philadelphia: Aga Khan Awards, 1980.

Reed, Howard A. "Yankees at the Sultan's Port: The First Americans and Early Trade with Smyrna and Mocha." *Contributions à l'histoire économique et sociale de l'Empire Ottoman: Collection Turcica* 3 (1983): 353–83.

Reichmuth, Stefan. "Murtaḍā az-Zabīdī (d. 1791) in Biographical and Autobiographical Accounts: Glimpses of Islamic Scholarship in the 18th Century." *Die Welt des Islams* 39, no. 1 (1999): 64–102.

Reid, Anthony. *Southeast Asia in the Age of Commerce, 1450–1650*. 2 vols. New Haven, Conn.: Yale University Press, 1993.

Revett, William. "Appendix B: William Revett's Narrative of Events at Aden, His Voyage to Mocha, etc." In *The Journal of John Jourdain, 1608–17, Describing his Experiences in Arabia, India, and the Malay Archipelago*, edited by William Foster, 350–56. Cambridge: Hakluyt Society, 1905.

Rezavi, Syed Ali Nadeem. "An Aristocratic Surgeon of Mughal India: Muqarrab Khan." In *Medieval India 1: Researches in the History of India, 1200–1750*, edited by Irfan Habib, 154–67. Delhi: Oxford University Press, 1992.

Risso, Patricia. *Merchants and Faith: Muslim Commerce and Culture in the Indian Ocean*. Boulder, Colo.: Westview Press, 1995.

———. *Oman and Muscat: An Early Modern History*. London: Croom Helm, 1986.

Roque, Jean de la. *Voyage to Arabia the Happy by Way of the Eastern Ocean, and the Streights of the Red-Sea: Perform'd by the French for the First Time, A.D. 1708, 1709, 1710*. Trans. from French. London: G. Straham, 1726. Originally published as *Voyage de l'Arabie heureuse par l'océan oriental et le détroit de la mer Rouge* (Paris: André Cailleau, 1716).

Ross, Robert, and Gerald J. Telkamp. "Introduction." In *Colonial Cities: Essays on Urbanism in a Colonial Context*, edited by R. Ross and G. Telkamp, 1–6. Boston: Martinus Nijhoff, 1985.

Salati, Marco. "A Shiite in Mecca: The Strange Case of Mecca-born Syrian and Persian Sayyid Muḥammad Ḥaydar (d. 1139/1727)." In *The Twelver Shia in Modern Times: Religious Culture and Political History*, edited by R. Brunner and W. Ende, 3–24. Leiden: E. J. Brill, 2001.

Salt, Henry. *A Voyage to Abyssinia*. London: Cass, 1814; reprint 1967.

Scerrato, Umberto, Giovanna Ventrone, and Paolo Cuneo. "Yemen: Archaeological Activities in the Yemen Arab Republic, 1985." *East and West* 35, no. 4 (1985): 337–95.

Schaefer, Charles G. H. "Coffee Unobserved: Consumption and Commoditization of Coffee in Ethiopia before the Eighteenth Century." In *Le commerce du café avant l'ère des plantations coloniales: Espaces, réseaux, sociétés (XVe–XIXe siècle)*, edited by Michel Tuchscherer, 23–34. *Cahier des Annales Islamologiques* 20 (2001).

Scharabi, Mohamed. *Der Bazar: Das traditionelle Stadtzentrum in Nahen Osten und seine Handelseinrightungen*. Tübingen, 1985.

Schroeter, Daniel. *Merchants of Essaouira: Urban Society and Imperialism in Southwestern Morocco, 1844–1886*. New York: Cambridge University Press, 1988.

Serjeant, R. B. "The Hindu, Bāniyān Merchants and Traders." In *Ṣanʿāʾ: An Arabian Islamic City*, edited by R. B. Serjeant and R. Lewcock, 532–35. London: World of Islam Trust, 1983.

———. "Omani Naval Activities off the Southern Arabian Coast in the Late 11th/17th Century, from Yemeni Chronicles." In *Customary and Shari'ah Law in Arabian Society*, 77–89. Hampshire, UK: Variorum, 1991.

———. *The Portuguese off the South Arabian Coast: Ḥaḍramī Chronicles*. Oxford: Clarendon Press, 1963.

———. "The Post Medieval and Modern History of Ṣanʿāʾ and the Yemen, ca. 953–1382/1515–1962." In *Ṣanʿāʾ: An Arabian Islamic City*, edited by R. B. Serjeant and R. Lewcock, 68–107. London: World of Islam Trust, 1983.

———. "The Yemeni Coast in 1005/1597: An Anonymous Note on the Flyleaf of Ibn al-Mujāwir's Tārīkh al-Mustabṣir." *Arabian Studies* 7 (1985): 187–91.

———. "Yemeni Merchants, 13th–16th Centuries." In *Marchands et hommes d'affaires asiatiques dans l'Océan Indien et la Mer de Chine, 13e–20e siècles*, edited by D. Lombard and J. Aubin, 61–82. Paris: Éditions de l'École des Hautes Études en Sciences Sociales, 1988.

Serjeant, R. B., and Ismāʿīl al-Akwaʿ. "The Statute of Ṣanʿāʾ (*Qānūn Ṣanʿāʾ*)." In *Ṣanʿāʾ: An Arabian Islamic City*, edited by R. B. Serjeant and R. Lewcock, 179–232. London: World of Islam Trust, 1983.

Serjeant, R. B., and R. Lewcock, eds. *Ṣanʿāʾ: An Arabian Islamic City*. London: World of Islam Trust, 1983.

Shivtiel, A., Wilfred Lockwood, and R. B. Serjeant. "The Jews of Ṣanʿāʾ." In *Ṣanʿāʾ: An Arabian Islamic City*, edited by R. B. Serjeant and R. Lewcock, 391–431. London: World of Islam Trust, 1983.

Stella, Alain. *The Book of Coffee*. Translated by Louise Guiney. Paris: Flammarion, 1996.

Stone, Francine, ed. *Studies on the Tihāmah: The Report of the Tihāmah Expedition 1982 and Related Papers*. Essex, UK: Longman, 1985.

Subramanian, Lakshmi. *Indigenous Capital and Imperial Expansion: Bombay, Surat and the West Coast*. Delhi: Oxford University Press, 1996.

Sutherland, Heather. "Eastern Emporium and Company Town: Trade and Society in Eighteenth-Century Makassar." In *Brides of the Sea: Port Cities of Asia from the 16th–20th Centuries*, edited by F. Broeze, 97–128. Honolulu: University of Hawaii Press, 1989.

Tabbaa, Yasser. *Constructions of Power and Piety in Medieval Aleppo*. University Park: Pennsylvania State University Press, 1997.

Taylor, Jeremy E. "The Bund: Littoral Space of Empire in the Treaty Ports of East Asia." *Social History* 27, no. 2 (2002): 125–42.

Thomas, P. *Festivals and Holidays of India*. Bombay: Taraporevala Sons, 1971.

Tibbetts, G. R. *Arab Navigation in the Indian Ocean before the Coming of the Portuguese, Being a Translation of* Kitāb al-Fawā'id fī uṣūl al-Baḥr wa'l qawā'id *of Aḥmad b. Mājid al-Najdī*. London: Royal Asiatic Society of Great Britain and Ireland, 1981.

Tobi, Yosef. *The Jews of Yemen: Studies in Their History and Culture*. Leiden: E. J. Brill, 1999.

Topik, Steven. "Integration of the World Coffee Market," In *The Global Coffee Economy in Africa, Asia, and Latin America, 1500–1989*, edited by W. G. Clarence-Smith and S. Topik, 21–49. Cambridge: Cambridge University Press, 2003.

Tuchscherer, Michel. "Coffee in the Red Sea Area from the Sixteenth to the Nineteenth Century." In *The Global Coffee Economy in Africa, Asia, and Latin America, 1500–1989*, edited by W. G. Clarence-Smith and S. Topik, 50–66. Cambridge: Cambridge University Press, 2003.

———, ed. *Le commerce du café avant l'ère des plantations coloniales: Espaces, réseaux, sociétés (XVe–XIXe siècle)*. *Cahier des Annales Islamologiques* 20 (2001).

———. "Le commerce en Mer Rouge aux alentours de 1700: Flux, espaces, et temps." In *Circulation des monnaies, des marchandises et des biens*, edited by Rika Gyselen and Michael Alram, 159–78. Bures-sur-Yvette: Groupe pour l'étude de la civilisation du Moyen-Orient, 1993.

———. "Commerce et production du café en Mer Rouge au XVIe siècle." In *Le commerce du café avant l'ère des plantations coloniales: Espaces, réseaux, sociétés (XVe–XIXe siècle)*, edited by Michel Tuchscherer, 69–90. *Cahier des Annales Islamologiques* 20 (2001).

———. "Trade and Port Cities in the Red Sea–Gulf of Aden Region in the Sixteenth and Seventeenth Century." In *Modernity and Culture: From the Mediterranean to the Indian Ocean*, edited by L. T. Fawaz and C. A. Bayly, 28–45. New York: Columbia University Press, 2002.

Um, Nancy. "A Red Sea Society in Yemen: Architecture, Urban Form, and Cultural Dynamics in the Eighteenth-Century Port City of al-Mukhā." Ph.D. diss., University of California, Los Angeles, 2001.

———. "Spatial Negotiations in a Commercial City: The Red Sea Port of Mocha, Yemen, during the First Half of the Eighteenth Century." *Journal of the Society of Architectural Historians* 62, no. 2 (2003): 178–93.

Valentia, George Viscount. *Voyages and Travels to India, Ceylon, the Red Sea, Abyssinia, and Egypt*. 2 vols. London, 1809.

Varisco, Daniel Martin. *Medieval Agriculture and Islamic Science: The Almanac of a Yemeni Sultan*. Seattle: University of Washington Press, 1994.

Vassallo, Giovanna Ventrone. "The al-Farāwī Mosque in Yemen." *Proceedings of the Seminar for Arabian Studies* 24 (1994): 210–19.

Voll, John O. "Linking Groups in the Networks of Eighteenth-Century Revivalist Scholars: The Mizjaji Family in Yemen." In *Eighteenth-Century Renewal and Reform in Islam*, edited by N. Levtzion and J. O. Voll, 69–92. Syracuse, N.Y.: Syracuse University Press, 1987.

Vom Bruck, Gabriele. "A House Turned Inside Out: Inhabiting Space in a Yemeni City." *Journal of Material Culture* 2, no. 2 (1997): 139–72.

———. *Islam, Memory, and Morality in Yemen: Ruling Families in Transition*. New York: Palgrave Macmillan, 2005.

Walls, Archibald. *Preservation of Monuments and Sites: Architectural Survey of Mocha*. Paris: UNESCO, 1981.

Warren, John, and Ihsan Fethi. *Traditional Houses in Baghdad*. Horsham, UK: Coach Pub. House, 1982.

Witkam, Jan Just. "Manuscripts and Manuscripts: Qur'ān Fragments from Ḍawrān (Yemen)." *Manuscripts of the Middle East* 4 (1989): 155–74.

Yule, Henry, and A. C. Burnell. *Hobson-Jobson: A Glossary of Colloquial Anglo-Indian Words and Phrases, and of Kindred Terms, Etymological, Historical, Geographical and Discursive*. London: Murray, 1903.

ILLUSTRATION CREDITS

Unless credited otherwise, photographs are by the author.

Maps 1.1, 1.2, 1.3, 5.1, and 5.3 were drawn by Barry Levely. Map 5.3 is adapted from Mermier, *Le cheikh de la nuit*. Map 5.2 is used courtesy of the Division of Rare and Manuscript Collections, Cornell University Library.

Figures 3.5, 6.9, 6.11, and 6.17–6.20 were drafted by Senem Zeybekoglu. Figure 3.5 is adapted from Paluck and Saggar, *The al-Ḥasan bin al-Qāsim Mosque Complex*. Figure 6.18 is adapted from Bonnenfant and Gentilleau, "Une maison de commerçant -armateur sur la mer Rouge." Figure 6.19 is adapted from Greenlaw, *The Coral Buildings of Suakin*. Figure 6.20 is adapted from Pramar, *Haveli*.

Figure 3.8 is used courtesy of Leiden University Library, Film A 1600. Figures 4.1, 5.4, and C.1 are used with permission of Bibliographisches Institut and F. A. Brockhaus AG, Mannheim, Germany. The following figures are used with permission of the Ethnologisches Museum, Staatliche Museen zu Berlin, Stiftung Preußischer Kulturbesitz: figure 5.1 is cataloged as K11; figure 5.6 is cataloged as K186; figure 5.8 is cataloged as K181; and figure 6.14 is cataloged as K86.

Figures 5.9 and 5.10 are used courtesy of the Peabody Essex Museum. Figure 5.9 is negative number 31,261, accession number M18855; figure 5.10 is negative number 31,262, accession number M18340.

Figure 5.12 is reproduced from Cyrille Laplace, *Campagne de circumnavigation de la frégate l'Artémise*, 1838, and used with permission of the Musée National de la Marine, Paris. Figures 6.3, 6.4, and 6.10 are used with permission of the Musée Bartholdi, Colmar, France, reprod. C. Kempf. Figure 7.1 is used with permission of the General Research Division, New York Public Library, Astor, Lenox and Tilden Foundations.

INDEX

Page numbers in italics denote figures or maps.

gate (Mocha): Bāb al-ʿAmūdī, 100, 117, 179–81; Bāb al-Ṣandal, 117, 226n78; Bāb al-Shādhilī, 103, 116–19, 122, 180–81, 223n25; Baniyan Gate (al-Bāb al-Ṣaghīr), 100, 103, 117, 164; Sea Gate (Bāb al-Baḥr, Bāb al-Furḍa, Bāb al-Sāḥil), 114, 117, 119, 180–81
gender relations, in domestic architecture, 142
Gensheimer, Thomas, 159
Gentilleau, Jeanne-Marie, 153
Geoffroy, Eric, 102, 207n6
Gogha (India), 82, 156–57
Goitein, S. D., 79, 129, 130
governor of Mocha (*ʿāmil* or *wālī*), 53–77, 211n27. *See also individual names of governors*
Grabar, Oleg, 11, 201n18
Grandpré, Louis de, 168, 170, 174
Greenlaw, Jean-Pierre, 155
Grehan, James, 8
Gujarat (India): Diu and Porbandar, 29, 166; Kathiawar Peninsula, 29, 97, 166; Tapi River, 82. *See also* Ahmedabad; Cambay; Gogha; Surat

Habib, Irfan, 163, 232n6
Ḥabūr, 52–53, 58; Great Mosque of, 58–64
al-Ḥabūrī, ʿAlī ʿAbd Allāh al-Tihāmī (*qāḍī* of Mocha), 52–53
Ḥadramawt: Baniyans in, 163; Qāsimī rule of, 5, 25–26; Sayʾūn, 48; Tarīm, 48; tower houses of, 152; Wādi Dawʿan, 178
Ḥajja, 19, 40
Ḥanafīs, 53
Hanna, Nelly, 8, 78–79, 204n8, 227n1
Hapsburg, 39
Ḥarāz, 32, 40
Ḥasan b. Imam al-Manṣūr Qāsim, 61; mosque of Ḥasan, 63
Ḥasan Pasha (Ottoman governor, r. 1580–1604), 19, 104, 107
Ḥāshid, 64
Ḥasūsā, Ḥasan (head *ṣarrāf* of Mocha), 52, 71, 175, 210n16, 236n60
Hattox, Ralph, 37, 222n15
haveli, 156, 157, 158
Ḥaydar Pasha (Ottoman governor, r. 1624–29), 19
Haykel, Bernard, 27–28, 76; on transformation of Zaydism during the Qāsimī period, 50, 53; on Yemeni Jews, 168–69, 234n37
al-Ḥaymī, Aḥmad (al-Mutawakkil Ismāʿīl's emissary), 23
Ḥays, 52, 89
Ḥijāz (Saudi Arabia), 29, 81, 208n22; consumption of *qishr* in, 38; al-Mūsawī, 73, 75; Ottoman control of, 36; Red Sea–style in, 152; al-Shādhilī's visit to, 101; slave trade of, 32. *See also* Jidda; Madīna; Mecca
hijrī calendar, 33
al-Hindī, Ibrāhīm b. Ṣāliḥ (Baniyan poet, d. 1101/1689–90), 164–65
Hindu: caste system, 156, 163; commercial buildings, 156; *dhimmī* status, 165, 233n17; festivals, 165, 183; merchants/communities, 23, 81, 97–98, 183, 222; residential quarters, 15, 175; scholarship on, 162; temple, 165, 233n20. *See also* Baniyans
Ho, Engseng, 48
Holy Cities, 56, 114
Horton, Mark, 160, 232n82
Howard, Deborah, 9, 11
al-Ḥubayshī, Muḥsin b. ʿAlī (wazir, d. 1737), 66–67, 71, 88, 214n75, 214n80

al-Ḥudayda: Baniyans in, 163; coffee trade of, 42–43, 45–47, 208n30, 209n41; houses of, 152; port of, 7, 21, 31, 40
al-Ḥuraybī, Ṣāliḥ b. ʿAlī (governor of Mocha, d. 1136/1723), 64–69, 71–72, 213n60, 214n69; appointment to wazir, 76, 213n58, 214n76; building of defensive structures, 116; relationship to highland court, 88; relationship to merchants, 87, 94, 214n80; as shipowner, 214n66

Ibb, 24, 40, 66–67; Baniyans in, 163, 175; Great Mosque of, 72
Ibn al-Amīr (Muḥammad b. Ismāʿīl al-Amīr), 90, 169
Ibn Battuta, 159
ʿĪd al-Aḍḥā, 33, 133, 178–81, 237n76
ʿĪd al-Fiṭr, 33, 66, 178–81, 237n76
Idāra building, 138, 148, 149, 150, 230n55; dating of, 147
"Iklīl al-Mukhāʾ." *See under* Muḥammad ʿAbd al-Wahhāb
Indian Ocean: sailing calendar, 33; scholarship on, 8, 14–16; vessels of, 29, 125, 204n11
Indian ports/port cities: Danda-Rajpuri, 86; Hugli (Bengal), 29; Janjira, 86; Kannur, 29; Karwar (Karnataka), 29, 44; Kochi, 29; Kozhikode, 29; Pondicherry (Coromandel Coast), 29. *See also under* Gujarat
Iran, 73, 75. *See also* Bandar ʿAbbās; Kung; Safavids
Iraq, 75, 86, 152; Najaf and Karbalāʾ, 73. *See also* Baghdad; Basra
Istanbul (Turkey), 8, 16, 35–39, 104

Jaʿfar Pasha (Ottoman governor, r. 1607–16), 19
Jaḥḥāf, Luṭf Allāh: on Aḥmad Khazindār 69–70; on al-Mahdī Muḥammad, 213n58; on Saʿd al-Dīn al-ʿUdaynī, 89–90; on Ṣāḥib al-Ḥuraybī, 213n60
Jaḥḥāf, Zayd b. ʿAlī (governor of Mocha, d. 1108/1696), 55–65, 212n38; appointment to wazir, 76; architectural patronage of, 55–65, 68; family of, 53, 186
Jains. *See* Baniyan
al-Jarādī, Aḥmad b. Muḥammad, 7, 98, 133
Java (Indonesia), 36, 40, 199n3
al-Jawhar (Sayyid Shakr Allāh), 178
Jews, Yemeni: cemetery of, 237n75; *dhimmī* status of, 165, 175, 177; expulsion of, 25–26, 168–71, 234n36; laws and taxation of, 168, 233n16; merchants/community, 25, 129–30, 162, 165, 167; Sabbatai Sevi, 25; Salīm al-ʿIrāqī, 34; synagogues of, 170, 235n52; vinters, 94; waning of mercantile power in Yemen, 176–77, 236n65. *See also* Mocha: Jewish quarter; Sanaa: Jewish quarter
Jidda, 4, 204n11, 222n16; coffee trade of, 31–32, 43–46, 101, 209n33; house, 155, 158, 231n73; merchants of, 23, 42, 87, 136, 153; pilgrims en route to Mecca via, 29, 83; port city of, 21; trade of, 35, 65, 86. *See also* Jidda gap
Jidda gap, 21–24, 79–80, 204n10; and urban *khān*, 155–56; maritime trade of, 28, 35; role in coffee shipping, 46
al-Jurmūzī, Ḥasan b. Muṭahhar (governor of Mocha, d. 1100/1688–89), 56, 76, 119
al-Jurmūzī, Ibrāhīm b. ʿAbd Allāh (governor of Mocha), 185–86, 217n122, 238n2

al-Manṣūr Qāsim b. ʿAlī al-ʿIyānī (Zaydī imam, d. 1003/1594–5), 55
al-Manṣūr Qāsim b. Muḥammad (Qāsimī imam, d. 1029/1620), 19, 25–26, 61, 64
Marcus, Abraham, 8, 171, 173
Margariti, Roxani: on Aden, 129, 199n2, 221n1, 228n24; on merchants' accommodations, 129–30; on *nākhūdhas*, 92; on Red Sea vessels, 205n27
market, 79; *dukkān*, 135; European, 120; *sūq*, 122, 126–27, 134, 164. *See also under* Sanaa; Mocha
Massawa (Eritrea): Baniyans in, 163; merchant houses of, 151, 159; port of, 20–21, 23; trade of, 32, 45, 65
Matthee, Rudi, 209n44
Matthews, Derek, 155, 231n71
Maṭraḥ (Oman), 31
al-Mawāhib, 26–27, 67
Mawzaʿ: exile of Yemeni Jews at, 25–26, 167–71, 176, 234n36, 235n52; houses of, 96; Mocha debate, 199n1, 222n16; route to, 117; trade of, 32
maydān, 113
McPherson, Kenneth, 14–15
Mecca: al-Mūsawī of, 68, 73, 75; orientation toward, 59, 179; pilgrimage to, 29, 33; pilgrims en route to, 132, 212n38; trade of, 6; travelers to or from, 65, 81, 214n69
medicinal products, 4, 47; aloe, 31, 44; coffee as medicine, 207n7
Mediterranean, 3, 234n45; coffee culture of, 38–39, 43; commercial architecture of, 126, 149, 155; comparative material from, 15; exchange of visual motifs around, 188–89; *funduq* as pan-Mediterranean institution, 130, 151–52, 228n13; merchants of, 176; port cities of, 8; relationship to Indian Ocean, 17, 21, 23, 35, 129; trade of, 31, 37, 168
Mehmed Pasha (Ottoman governor, r. 1616–21), 19, 114, 132
merchant houses: Bayt al-Akhḍarī, 109; Bayt Sīdī Nūnū, 109, 110; Bayt ʿUmar Effendi ʿUbayd (Sawākin), 153, 154, 155; commercial use of, 135–49; Mehta house (Gogha, India), 156–57; multiple-entry system in, 146–47, 153, 155, 158, 230n51; as signs of creditworthiness, 160–61; urban location of, 115–16. *See also* al-Mahfadī: house; Sawākin: merchant houses of
merchants: American, 8; Armenian, 97; Italian, 9, 11, 39, 147; Lotia, 97, 221. *See also* Baniyan; Dutch East India Company: merchants of; English merchants; European merchants; French Compagnie des Indes; Gujarat: merchants; Portuguese; *and names of individual merchants*
metal: bulk, 4, 31, 47, 79; copper, 31, 65, 209n42; precious, 37, 47; silver, 36, 164, 176; steel, 31, 65. *See also* coins/currency
Miran, Jonathan, 159, 231n81
al-Mizjājī, ʿAbd Allāh b. ʿAbd al-Bāqī, 53
al-Mizjājī, Ṣadīq b. ʿAlī, 53
Mocha: climate of, 96; coffee trade of, 37, 42, 44–47; commercial architecture of, 131–38; domestic architecture of, 138–49; foundation myth of, 101–2, 222n12; French attack on, 6, 53, 71–72, 75, 119; geographic position/location of, 4
—residential quarters of: al-ʿAmūdī quarter, 174; Baniyan quarters, 175–77, 181–84, 188, 235n56, 236n59;

Yemen (*continued*)
communities of, 167–69; scholarship on, 16–17, 28. *See also* Zaydism

Zabāra, Muḥammad: on Aḥmad Khazindār, 70, 215n90, 215n93; on Great Mosque (Ḥabūr) 59; on Mocha, 54; on Saʿd al-Dīn al-ʿUdaynī, 89; on Ṣāliḥ al-Ḥuraybī, 66, 213n60
Zabid: Baniyans in, 163; coffee house of, 133, 134; governor of, 95; Ḥārat al-Hunūd, 165; houses of, 152; market of, 103, 105; al-Mizjājī family of, 53; occupations of, 19, 24; Wādi Rimaʿ, 101
Ẓafār Dhī Bīn, 24, 51
Zaydism: connection to Safavids, 214n67; definition of, 24, 49–50; in Mocha, 97; Ottoman anti-Zaydī efforts, 104; rule in Yemen, 24–28, 61, 98, 115, 123; Sunnification of Zaydīs, 53; Tabaristan (Iran) community, 24; Zaydī families/elite, 5, 53, 64, 186, 188; Zaydī revolt, 17; Zaydī scholars, 13, 78, 91, 168, 203n2. *See also* Qāsimī imamate
Zaylaʿ (Somalia), 21, 26, 32, 123, 174. *See also under* prisons